THE
Natural Healing & Nutrition
ANNUAL
1995

Edited by Mark Bricklin, Editor,
PREVENTION Magazine,
and Matthew Hoffman,
PREVENTION Magazine Health Books

Rodale Press, Emmaus, Pennsylvania

Notice

This book is intended as a reference volume only, not as a medical manual. The information given here is designed to help you make informed decisions about your health. It is not intended as a substitute for any treatment that may have been prescribed by your doctor. If you suspect that you have a medical problem, we urge you to seek competent medical help.

ISBN 0–87596–249–1 hardcover
ISSN 1060–7846

Distributed in the book trade by St. Martin's Press

2 4 6 8 10 9 7 5 3 1   hardcover

The Natural Healing and Nutrition Annual 1995
Editorial and Design Staff

Book and Cover Designer: Charles Beasley

Studio Manager: Joe Golden

Layout Designer: Carl Nielsen/Bookhead Studio

Technical Artist: David Q. Pryor

Associate Research Chief, *Prevention* Magazine:
Pamela Boyer

Copy Editor: Durrae Johanek

Office Staff: Roberta Mulliner, Julie Kehs,
Bernadette Sauerwine, Mary Lou Stephen

Prevention Magazine Health Books

Editor-in-Chief, Rodale Books: Bill Gottlieb

Executive Editor: Debora A. Tkac

Art Director: Jane Colby Knutila

Research Manager: Ann Gossy Yermish

Copy Manager: Lisa D. Andruscavage

CONTENTS

Nutrition and Health Updates

Eating for Good Health

Pounds Away

You're in the Driver's Seat

For Women Only

Emotions and Your Health

Fit for Life

SUPPLEMENTS
AND COMMON SENSE

Some of the reports in this book give accounts of the professional use of nutritional supplements. While food supplements are in general quite safe, some can be harmful if taken in very large amounts. Be especially careful not to take more than these commonsense daily limits.

Vitamin A	2,000 IU
Vitamin B_6	50 mg.
Vitamin D	400 IU
Selenium	100 mcg.

INTRODUCTION

*You don't need miracles for good health—
just a good plan.*

Almost since the beginning of time, curious minds have sought the ultimate cure-all—a safe, surefire remedy for whatever ailed, from asthma and arthritis to digestive complaints.

Naturally, they've been disappointed.

Although some recent breakthroughs are nothing less than astonishing—for example, the discovery that aspirin may reduce heart attack risk by as much as 30 percent—there has never been a "magic bullet" that could relieve all ills.

What doctors have discovered, however—and what millions of people are putting into practice every day—is the next best thing. Not a cure, exactly, but an entire *system* of healing— a blueprint, if you will, of safe, proven techniques for beating disease and living a longer, healthier life.

Here's the system: *The Natural Healing and Nutrition Annual 1995.* You won't find any miracle cures here. What you will discover is a wealth of information to help you look great and feel better—not next month or next year, but today.

Many of us would like to lose weight, and here's one more reason that it makes good sense. In one study, women who successfully shed a few pounds were half as likely to develop the debilitating knee pain caused by osteoarthritis. And they didn't have to suffer doing it. All it took was losing an average of 11 pounds over *ten years.* Now that's encouraging!

Speaking of weight loss, the evidence is now overwhelming: To slim down you need to eat more, not less. The trick is to eat "high-octane" foods that are low in fat and high in carbohydrates and contain half the calories, per bite, as fatty foods.

Many of us know we should exercise, but who has the time? New research suggests you can get the benefits of regular workouts almost without breaking a sweat. And if you do add resistance training of some sort to your workout, you'll get more than strong muscles. Research shows that regular weight lifting can help lower blood pressure and stabilize blood sugar levels, as well.

So much for internal health. What about the outside? There's a plan for that, too. By following a careful skin-care regimen and adding certain enhancing, protective products to your grooming routine, you can maximize your youthful good looks, no matter what your calendar age.

Maybe someday doctors really will discover that elusive magic bullet. But until then, why wait? You're holding in your hands what may be the most powerful good-health system ever devised—one you can count on year after year.

—The Editors
Prevention Magazine

Nutrition

and

Health

Updates

POWER OFF YOUR POTBELLY

There's more than one way to lose a potbelly—but there's only one quick, surefire way. And that's exercise. In two studies of older men, those who dieted without exercising had to lose four times as much weight as exercisers in order to lose the same amount of abdominal fat!

Each study involved 20 volunteers. One group followed a strict 1,200-calorie-per-day limit for three months, while the other group continued their normal diet over the same period of time (in some cases increasing their food intake) while exercising regularly.

"Exercise may be smarter in the long run than just dieting, because it's a lot easier to keep off 5 pounds than it is to keep off 20," says Robert Schwartz, M.D., associate professor of internal medicine and gerontology at the University of Washington School of Medicine in Seattle.

Exercise doesn't just incinerate calories on the spot, it may also raise your metabolic rate, keeping it revving even after you stop exercising. The reward: You burn more calories at rest. You can still eat heartily (providing, of course, it's low-fat fare) because your body's metabolic motor is burning more fuel.

Beyond this metabolic mastery, why is exercise potentially better at targeting the midsection than plain old dieting? "There may be something unique to exercise that creates a preferential weight loss," says Dr. Schwartz.

Exercise may stimulate growth hormone secretion, which is known to decline in older people. "It's fairly clear that when you give growth hormone to growth hormone–deficient people, they gain lean mass and lose fat, especially abdominal fat," he says. "It's not clear right now, however, but activity may somehow prevent this age-related growth hormone loss. That means holding on to muscle and blocking an increase in central body fat that occurs with aging."

BEWARE THE FAT SEASON

If you notice your body's changing shape after winter and spring, don't get down on yourself. It's only as natural as the change in seasons.

In a study of 125 women, researchers from Tufts University in Medford, Massachusetts, found that seasonal changes in fat and lean mass occurred, even if the women kept the same weight and activity levels throughout the year. These postmenopausal women had increases in muscle and bone mass during the summer/fall period and a decrease during the winter/spring period. Their weights didn't change, though the women had a net loss of lean tissue in their legs and a net gain in fat tissue in their trunks.

But don't get bent out of shape: Even though these fluctuations had little to do with physical activity levels in this study, you can still use exercise to smooth them out, according to Bess Dawson-Hughes, M.D., from the U.S. Department of Agriculture Human Nutrition Research Center on Aging at Tufts in Boston. "Even though the overall changes are consistent with what we've seen in body-shape changes due to the aging process, stepping up the exercise could help prevent many of the changes."

The loss of valuable muscle tissue (needed to perform essential daily functions), for example, could be reversed with walking and a few strength-training moves—a leg press or a partial squat. Tacking on a few extra walking sprees might help burn off some of the fat.

Dr. Dawson-Hughes hasn't figured out the reasons behind these seasonal fluctuations, but she speculates it may have to do with the brain's hypothalamus-pituitary area, which regulates several major hormones. "These hormones are known to influence those soft and hard tissues of the body."

THE GLORIES OF GRAZING

If we were all smart, we'd eat like cows. That's because grazing may be a major key to a healthier life.

A recent study had 12 people with non-insulin-dependent diabetes eating either two large or six small meals over an eight-hour period on two different occasions. When they ate the two big meals, their insulin levels rose much higher than when they ate the six meals over the eight-hour period. The two large meals also induced a yo-yo effect, with an 84 percent difference between the lowest and highest levels of glucose.

"This attitude of 'Johnny, don't snack' is dead wrong for us today," says Aaron Vinik, M.D., Ph.D., director of the Diabetes Research Institute in Norfolk, Virginia. "Research suggests that you get much healthier blood-sugar and insulin levels from multiple feedings—having three small meals and three snacks throughout the day."

And never mind diabetes: When insulin levels are high, other equally bad things may happen. "Research suggests if you have elevated insulin levels due to insulin resistance, you're more likely to have a heart attack or develop heart disease than if you have normal levels," says Dr. Vinik. Even though this study involved people with diabetes, other studies have shown that the benefits of grazing apply to other people as well.

Another study looked at grazing's effect on cholesterol levels in a group of 19 women who ate either nine or three meals a day (with roughly 29 percent of calories coming from fat) over two weeks. The many-meal bunch saw their blood concentrations of total cholesterol fall 6.5 percent and LDL cholesterol 8.1 percent when compared with the three-mealers.

Of course, noshing nine small meals over one day may be a bit too much. That doesn't mean you can't try for something more realistic, however. Like six. Start with a small breakfast and add fruit or a nonfat yogurt snack in between that and lunch. Between your light lunch and light dinner, add another snack—a bowl of rice or some vegetable sticks. Then round out the evening with a postdinner snack—nonfat frozen yogurt or a small bowl of nonfat cereal with skim milk.

NIX MIDNIGHT NOSHING

Late-night snacking slows food metabolism? It may not be just what you eat, but when, as well.

A study finds that midnight snacking may slow down what's called diet-induced thermogenesis (DIT), the food's natural ability to boost metabolism and burn more energy. This means you'll burn off fewer calories after the meal, and you'll pack on more weight.

On three separate days over five weeks, nine men ate either a morning, afternoon or late-evening snack. Every other aspect of their diet was controlled. Researchers found a significant difference between the DIT of the morning and late-evening snack. The afternoon snack had no significant effect.

"Eating at night produces less heat and burns fewer calories than eating a snack in the morning," says Judith Stern, R.D., Sc.D., professor of nutrition and internal medicine at the University of California, Davis.

"Over a period of time it may mean trouble. By eating the bulk of your food late at night, even in one year there may be a substantial increase in body weight."

Why this effect occurs isn't known. "The thermic effect of a meal may be affected by the body's circadian rhythm, the inner clock that regulates certain hormones," says Dr. Stern. "Corticosterone and epinephrine, two such hormones affected by these rhythms, and perhaps insulin, could be impacted by the meal timing, though we don't know for sure."

The bottom line: Lay off the midnight snacks from the icebox. "It may not amount to a lot of calories, but every little bit helps," says Dr. Stern.

Sauce for the Goose Also Works for the Gander

If a woman wants her husband to leave his potbelly behind and get on a healthy track, it may be up to her to lead the way. A study shows a strong correlation between a wife's diet and her husband's eating habits.

"We were pleasantly surprised by the big difference in fat intake between husbands whose wives participated in low-fat dietary training and those who didn't," says Ann L. Shattuck, R.D., from the Fred Hutchinson Cancer Research Center in Seattle. The 188 husbands of low-fat-eating wives received 33 percent of their calories from fat, compared with 37 percent among the 180 spouses of the women not on a low-fat diet. Other studies have suggested similar effects, although they weren't of this magnitude.

The mechanism isn't rocket science, but more like nutritional tag. "If the person planning the meals can adopt healthier dietary habits, those habits may then be transferred to others. Thus, the husbands eat what the wives eat," says Shattuck. "We only looked at spouses, but we think this healthy transfer might also spread to the children."

The study lasted one year, and Shattuck thinks reductions in fat intake might have been even bigger if the study had continued. No research exists, however, suggesting that spousal influence would help in taking out the garbage.

FIT FOR LIFE

To put the brakes on aging, you must first put the wraps on fat.

Researchers looked at a measurement of oxygen uptake during exercise called VO_2 Max, which is a marker for functional capacity. Research suggests that after age 30, this declines at a steady pace. But most of the previous research has been done on men. A study with women shows that this decline, originally thought to be age-related and inevitable, can actually be slowed down.

"We found that the more body fat a person accumulates over the years, the more of a decline he or she will see in VO_2 Max," says Larry Wier, Ed.D., director of the health-related fitness program at the NASA Johnson Space Center in Houston. "Considering that VO_2 Max is the best overall measurement of fitness, as you grow older it pays to keep your body fat low and your exercise high." People tend to exercise less and less and get fatter and fatter as they age.

In his study of 300 women, Dr. Wier found that by simply maintaining the level of exercise and body fat over the years, a woman will reduce the age-related decline in VO_2 Max by 50 percent each year. The women had their body compositions tested while also having their exercise levels measured on a scale of 0 to 10 (0 being walking to your car as your only exercise, 10 being an equivalent of 26 miles of jogging over a week).

"VO_2 Max relates specifically to daily activities—going out and buying groceries, taking walks and enjoying yourself," says Dr. Wier. "Some folks over age 75 are more functional than others who are much younger, and that's due in part to their VO_2 Max."

Although aging is inevitable, not all of its consequences are. You can add VO_2 Max as yet another age factor you can control. "Start now with a daily brisk walk or some hard work in your garden," says Dr. Wier. "You don't have to be a marathon runner, just engage in consistent moderate exercise and you'll be doing yourself a favor."

SPREAD THE RISK

In matters of the heart, switching from butter to margarine makes sense. But a flurry of studies suggests that stick margarine may be sticking it to you, too—by harboring transfatty acids, a new heart-disease risk factor.

To make margarine, liquid vegetable oils are hydrogenated—turned into a semisolid state resembling butter. Some of the remaining unsaturated fats, called trans-fatty acids, take on the cholesterol-raising qualities of saturated fats. Results from dietary questionnaires of 85,095 women from Harvard's Nurses' Health Study suggest that high intakes of trans-fatty acids may up the risk for coronary death by 50 to 67 percent.

"Because it's not hydrogenated, switching to a liquid oil in food preparation may offer a significant benefit over solid margarine," says Alice H. Lichtenstein, D.Sc., from the U.S. Department of Agriculture Human Nutrition Research Center on Aging at Tufts University in Boston. She bolsters this advice with her study comparing three diets: one approximating the basic U.S. diet with 35 percent of calories from fat, another a corn-oil-margarine-enriched diet with 30 percent fat, and a diet using liquid corn oil also containing 30 percent fat. Both lower-fat diets cut cholesterol, but a bigger drop took place with the liquid corn oil, which is nonhydrogenated. In this study of 14 people, LDL (low-density lipoprotein) cholesterol, the bad kind, dropped by 17 percent, compared with just 10 percent in the margarine group.

"If you still feel you must use some margarine, then go with the softest you can find," says Dr. Lichtenstein. It can make a difference. In fact, another study put 38 healthy men on a diet containing a special soft, nonhydrogenated, trans-fat-free margarine and saw drops in total and LDL cholesterol when compared with a diet using hard margarine.

There's no easy way to determine the amount of trans-fatty acids in vegetable-oil products, so your best guide is appearance. The more solid means the more saturated and more trans-fatty acids. "If you're concerned about obesity, heart disease and cancer," says Dr. Lichtenstein, "avoid foods that contain saturated fat and trans-fatty acids."

MUSCLE DOWN CHOLESTEROL

When you pump iron, your muscles grow with gratitude. But it may be your heart that really owes you a special thanks. For the first time, research suggests it may be possible to put the muscle on LDL, the bad cholesterol, by strength training.

A group of 46 women ages 28 to 39 hit the weights for one hour, three times per week for five months. Another group of women acted as a comparison group, sticking to their normal exercise habits during the same time frame.

Cholesterol tests before and after the five-month period showed the lifters had significant drops in both total cholesterol and LDL (low-density lipoprotein) cholesterol. Total cholesterol decreased by 7 percent, while LDL cholesterol dropped 12 percent. The nonstrength trainers had much smaller declines. Both groups saw no changes in HDL (high-density lipoprotein), the beneficial cholesterol, however.

"We weren't expecting to find this encouraging result—in fact, we weren't even looking for it," says Thomas W. Boyden, M.D., chief of endocrinology at the Department of Veterans Affairs Medical Center in Tucson. "LDL cholesterol has been previously thought to be resistant to exercise."

In fact, this is the first study to show a beneficial effect on that harmful lipid using any form of exercise. Usually, exercise is thought to help by raising HDL cholesterol, the good stuff responsible for clearing arteries. "Because this is a first-time observation, the results have to be interpreted cautiously," says Dr. Boyden. "But it does suggest potential for reducing heart-disease risk through resistance training."

Even if these particular results may still be considered preliminary, other findings from this study echo strength-training benefits you already know about: The lifters lowered their body fat while boosting their fat-free muscle.

The next goal, he suggests, is to target more at-risk groups with a strength-training regimen and examine the effects for more confirming evidence.

Flex Your Circulation

Whether you hike to work, show the stair climber what you're worth or pump up in the gym, you already know that exercise can put heart disease on the skids: It can clean up your cholesterol profile and maybe trim your tummy. Research, however, hints that exercise may ward off that leading killer in yet another way.

A new theory holds that working out may actually exercise artery walls. That could put the brakes on the stiffening (or hardening) of the arteries that was once considered an inevitable part of aging. And more flexible arteries might squeeze down your risk of heart disease and high blood pressure.

Researchers found a link between an athletic lifestyle and limber arteries when they compared 14 male runners, ages 54 to 75, to 38 of their sedentary peers. Arterial stiffness in the athletes was about 30 percent lower than it was in the other men. Plus, these runners—serious types who compete and cover about 30 miles per week—had nearly the same aerobic capacity as inactive men who were half their age.

"Until now, we thought there was nothing you could do about arterial stiffening. Now, it seems that exercise might alter the degree to which it occurs," says Edward G. Lakatta, M.D., director of the Laboratory of Cardiovascular Science at the National Institute on Aging and author of the study.

If exercise does keep arteries agile, it might be because muscles in vessel walls (like muscles anywhere else) have a use-it-or-lose-it philosophy. Vessels expand to handle a workout's extra blood flow and spring back when you stop. The more they do it, the more limber they may stay.

When you exercise, your arteries may also be gaining from what you lose: Heavy perspiration takes with it sodium chloride. Loss of that artery-tensing mineral may somehow leave arteries more elastic in the long run.

PRODUCE WARDS OFF BLADDER CANCER

If you're looking for the most effective protection racket around—skip the Mob and hit the produce section. We know fruits and vegetables may protect you from a multitude of illnesses. Now, research suggests that these foods are linked to lower risk of yet another bad guy—bladder cancer.

In a study, the dietary histories of 351 men with bladder cancer were compared with 855 men without the illness. Researchers found that the highest consumers of fruits and vegetables had a 60 percent lower risk of developing this cancer.

"This is just one more potentially healthy benefit brought on by eating more fruits and vegetables," says John Vena, Ph.D., associate professor in the Department of Social and Preventive Medicine at the State University of New York, Buffalo.

"The antioxidant beta-carotene and other carotenoids found in fruits and vegetables seem to be the most likely disease fighters, though we need more research to back up that theory." Flavonoids, other potentially helpful substances in fruits and veggies, may be putting their preventive two cents in, too, he adds.

Plus, you may be lowering your intake of fats to make room for these healthier foods. "That will help cut down on the fat carcinogens from foods that are metabolized and end up in your bladder," says the researcher. Indeed, fat intake did show up as a prominent bad guy (a role it should be getting used to) in elevating risk for this disease in this study.

Higher total-caloric intake also increased risk as well as higher intakes of sodium (from foods—not the stuff sprinkled during cooking or at the dinner table).

The study also suggests that smokers—as usual—play with fire, tripling their risk of developing bladder cancer when compared with nonsmokers. Higher consumption of protein, however, appeared to lower risk. "Taken together, these findings suggest it's a combination of healthy habits that may protect you from this illness," says Dr. Vena. Almost 50,000 new cases of bladder cancer are reported each year.

PUNGENT PROTECTION

What vampires hate, we should embrace. For years, European doctors have studied garlic to see if it has potential in fighting heart disease. Now American researchers have finally picked up the scent—with a first, encouraging, stateside study.

After taking garlic tablets for 12 weeks, 42 adults with elevated cholesterol levels saw their total cholesterol drop 6 percent (compared with 1 percent in the placebo group). Low-density lipoprotein (LDL) cholesterol, the artery-clogging lipid, dropped 11 percent among the garlicky subjects, compared with just 3 percent in the placebo group. (Doctors estimate that heart attack risk drops by about 2 percent for every 1 percent decrease in total blood cholesterol.)

"The results need confirmation in a larger study, although it's clear we aren't dealing with your average vegetable," says F. Gilbert McMahon, M.D., clinical professor of medicine from Tulane University School of Medicine in New Orleans.

The preparation used in this unpublished study wasn't your average pungent garlic bulb, either, but a 300-milligram powder tablet containing a chemical precursor of allicin, the component believed to be the active ingredient in garlic. "From a pilot study of severely hypertensive patients, we found garlic, at large doses, also lowers blood pressure, probably via a vasodilating effect," says Dr. McMahon. Future research, with larger and longer studies, will be needed to confirm these two actions.

SUPPLEMENT YOUR IMMUNITY

Imagine one simple dietary change that could cut in half the amount of time you spend sick each year. If you're nutritionally deficient, a diet bolstered by nutritional supplementation may strikingly reduce the infections that occur as you grow older, a small preliminary study suggests.

"Small amounts of nutrient supplements not only corrected deficiencies commonly found in older adults, but for the first time we saw a reduction in infections as well," says Ranjit Kumar Chandra, M.D., university research professor at Memorial University of Newfoundland and director of the World Health Organization Center for Nutritional Immunology. In Dr. Chandra's study of 96 people 65 years and older, members of the group receiving a daily oral vitamin-and-trace-mineral supplement were sick with infection-related illnesses an average of only 23 days per year, compared with 48 days per year for those in a placebo group. Subjects in the supplemented group also had more immune cells and sharper immune responses (measured in natural-killer-cell responses and antibody responses to the influenza vaccine).

Roughly one-third of the study group began with a nutrient deficiency—not an unusual problem among older folks. "For most people you'd like to bolster the diet naturally with healthy foods like fruits and vegetables," says Dr. Chandra. "But many of these older people can't do that. So a supplement would be a simple and effective alternative."

The supplement used packed a wide array of vitamins and minerals, including zinc, vitamin B_6, beta-carotene, vitamin A and iron. Most amounts met the Recommended Dietary Allowance, with a few exceptions. "We were generous with beta-carotene and vitamin E because there may be an extra need for antioxidants as you get older," says Dr. Chandra. Antioxidants, as you probably know, may help prevent cell damage in the body caused by unstable molecules called free radicals. To be sure that this study is valid, larger studies need to be done.

CHICKEN SOUP
FOR STUFFY NOSES

From Beijing to Delhi, Moscow to Des Moines, grandmothers have used chicken soup for generations to soothe the sniffles. A new laboratory experiment offers cold, hard facts as to why grannies may have had the right idea: Chicken soup may have anti-inflammatory powers that help clear cold-clogged nasal passages.

When a cold hits, blood cells called neutrophils rush to the troubled area to fight the invading virus or bacteria. The extra traffic in that spot leads to inflammation and discomfort. One way to get relief is to slow down that neutrophil attack, an effect Stephen Rennard, M.D., chief of the pulmonary and critical medicine section at the University of Nebraska Medical Center in Omaha, suspected chicken soup might have.

So, in a laboratory setting, he pitted his wife's grandmother's recipe against oncoming neutrophils and found their onslaught to decrease significantly. Whether this would work in humans and how much less inflammation this might mean is yet to be determined.

"The vitamin-rich vegetables in the soup may be responsible for some of this inhibiting effect," says Dr. Rennard, but he suspects it's the whole concoction that helps you feel good. Across the globe, "it's chicken soup that's used. Nowhere do they simply use boiled vegetables."

As to whether there are ingredients in grandmother's recipe that enhance its medicinal properties, he said certain commercial soups had the same effect. "But we think hers tastes the best."

PUT THE SQUEEZE ON HEADACHE

Pressure can bring on a headache, but a little pressure might relieve it, too. One doctor suffering from migraines put that theory to work—with soothing results.

He designed an elastic band secured with Velcro to strap around an achy head. Firm rubber disks about the size of backgammon pieces were inserted at areas of maximum pain on the scalp, where they would apply extra pressure. He had 25 patients test the bands when their migraines hit. The bands were put on once the pain reached 5 on a subjective scale of 1 to 10, and were worn for 30 minutes. After two patients dropped out due to tender scalps, relief was reported in 60 of 69 headaches when the band was used. In 40 of the aches, the pain was reduced by over 80 percent. The pain returned, however, once the band was removed.

"Many people, including myself, have applied finger pressure or tight towels for temporary relief of migraine headaches. Here I just went a step further," says Nazhiyath Vijayan, M.D., director of the Sacramento Headache and Neurology Clinic and associate clinical professor of neurology at the University of California, Davis. "You could use the band along with your other headache medications or in temporary situations when you don't have drugs."

Dr. Vijayan offers two theories about why the band may offer temporary relief. It may help compress the blood vessels in the scalp, where some of the pain is coming from. It may also work as a counterirritant. "If you have pain in a location and you apply another painful stimulus, it will mask that other pain," he says.

The doctor's band isn't available at your nearby pharmacy, but you may be able to make do with a compress, ice pack or even the warm fingers of your spouse. Of course, for any serious headache, you should see a doctor first to get a diagnosis. Dr. Vijayan hopes to see the band making it to the marketplace within a year.

VITAMIN A FOR EYES

A dietary essential, vitamin A, may turn out to be a parachute for plummeting vision. That's if you have retinitis pigmentosa (RP), inherited eye disorders that cause night-vision deficiency, tunnel vision and eventual blindness.

When 601 RP patients (18 to 49 years of age) were given high doses of either vitamin A, vitamin E, both or nearly nothing (trace amounts of the vitamins), scientists found that those patients on vitamin A alone—15,000 international units (IU) per day—had on average a 20 percent per year slower rate of decline of remaining vision than those not on this dose. This is a significant finding for a disease in which hope used to be the only treatment. "The average patient in our study who started taking the vitamin at age 32 would be expected to retain some useful vision until age 70. Without it, useful vision might last only until age 63. That's an estimated seven-year benefit," says Eliot Berson, M.D., principal investigator in the study and professor of ophthalmology at Harvard Medical School. "What was surprising was the fact that the data suggest that vitamin E (in 400 IU doses) might make the condition worse."

So while vitamin A can't reverse the damage that RP does to the eye's rods and cones (the cells that receive light), it may put some drag on future degeneration. Researchers aren't yet sure exactly how it might do that. Since the treatment slows the rate of decline, the benefit begins in some sense when you start treatment.

Instead of the garden-variety A obtained through beta-carotene, this study used the less commonly available vitamin A palmitate. The large quantities required for treatment—three times the RDA and far beyond the 3,500 IU that you get from an average day's food—mean you'll need to work under a doctor's supervision. (Remember that this vitamin can be toxic in large doses. Women who are pregnant or planning to become pregnant should not take it because of the possibility of birth defects.)

For more information on this disease and its treatment, contact the RP Foundation Fighting Blindness at 1-800-683-5555.

WORK OUT, TURN IN

Working out may make it easier to log more pillow time, according to a recent study.

To gauge the effect of being physically fit on sleep, researchers looked at 24 men ages 60 to 72. Half of them, labeled "fit," had exercised vigorously at least three times a week for a year or more; their activities included aerobic walking, swimming, jogging, playing tennis and bicycling. The rest of the guys were sedentary, engaging in little, if any, aerobic activity. During the study, each group slept at night following either a 40-minute afternoon exercise session or no daytime exercise.

"The sedentary men had more periods of lighter sleep, less deep sleep and were awake more of the night than the fit subjects," says Jack D. Edinger, Ph.D., associate clinical professor of psychiatry at the Duke University Medical Center and staff psychologist at the Durham Veterans Administration Medical Center in North Carolina. "This occurred regardless of whether the fit men exercised that day or not, suggesting it's regular exercise that's doing the trick, not just a single workout."

On average, it took the inactive group twice as long (12 versus 27 minutes) to fall asleep at night. The inactive group also spent more time awake during the night.

"Light, fragmented sleep is much less satisfying and therefore could affect your daytime alertness and functioning," says Dr. Edinger. It could be that exercise, by making you a better sleeper, can help you function at your cognitive peak during the day.

Why being fit might make for a less fitful sleep isn't completely understood, however. It may be that your body has to compensate for the exercise, and deep sleep serves that restorative function. "If you have more tissue breakdown from exercise, sleeping may help rejuvenate bodily tissues," says Dr. Edinger. Exercise may also help by regulating your temperature. If you heat your body through exercise, you may stimulate a deeper sleep for a proper cooldown. "The key is not to exercise too close to bedtime, because it takes time to bring the temperature down so you can fall asleep," says Dr. Edinger.

Fill Up on "Mood" Foods

We know that low-fat and low-cholesterol foods can help keep your arteries clear and bolster your heart. According to research, a healthy diet may also give your mind and your mood an uplifting boost.

When people lowered their cholesterol over a five-year study period, they also experienced a reduction in depression and hostility. "Making positive changes in your diet may make you feel you have more control over your health—and that may improve your psychological well-being," says Gerdi Weidner, Ph.D., associate professor in the Department of Psychology at State University of New York at Stony Brook.

In this study of 149 men and 156 women, Dr. Weidner found that people who made dietary improvements and lowered their plasma cholesterol also showed significant improvements in hostility and depression. "This is an interesting finding, although we don't really know if good feelings lead to higher compliance with low-cholesterol diets or the other way around," says Dr. Weidner.

The study participants didn't take any cholesterol-lowering drugs, and the eating habits they adopted weren't monumental. Fat intake was cut to 20 percent of total calories. Limiting cholesterol intake was emphasized, while eating more complex carbohydrates (fruits, vegetables and grains) was encouraged. "If controlling your own health really has something to do with improved emotional states, then dietary changes may prove to be a better emotional uplifter than drug therapy," says Dr. Weidner. "You're in control of your diet, but you relinquish control to drugs."

MIND OVER PANIC

A rapid heartbeat. A feeling of confusion and helplessness. You start sweating. You swear it's the end of the world.

It's not a heart attack, but it can be every bit as frightening. It's what panic attacks are made of, and they can keep sufferers living in constant fear of their next one. A study suggests, however, that mindfulness meditation may be one way to help thwart these tidal waves of anxiety.

After 22 men and women with anxiety and panic disorders underwent an eight-week meditation course, significant reductions in anxiety and depression scores occurred in 20 of the subjects. Among patients with panic disorder, a significant drop in the number of attacks occurred. In a three-year follow-up, these improvements were maintained in 18 of the subjects. Patients were on medications during the study, although a few were able to discontinue their usage as their conditions improved.

"These people put their training to practical use in regulating their anxious feelings," says Jon Kabat-Zinn, Ph.D., director of the stress-reduction clinic in the Department of Medicine at the University of Massachusetts Medical Center in Worcester. "The meditation practice helps teach you to recognize and control the tension and agitation that may lead to panic, mastering those feelings instead of letting them master you."

In the stillness of formal meditation practice, patients are encouraged to cultivate moment-to-moment awareness, which leads to a mindful calmness that undermines the anxious feelings and gives more of a sense of control.

This study is a small, preliminary one, but Dr. Kabat-Zinn is encouraged by the findings. "Mindfulness may soon become an accepted approach for treating some patients with serious anxiety," he says. "It may also prove helpful for other types of disorders, including various phobias."

Of course, if you feel you're suffering from a panic disorder, you should see your doctor for a proper diagnosis first. Symptoms include difficulty breathing, a pounding heart, dizziness, tingling fingers and feet, chest pain or tightness and sweating, among others. Many of the symptoms occur suddenly and in bunches.

Eating

for

Good

Health

1

VEGETARIAN BASICS

Here's savory cooking that's great for the taste buds and fabulous for the heart.

Did you ever see a fat squirrel? Probably not. Squirrels, rabbits, chipmunks and many other animals usually eat a slimming vegetarian diet. Human animals would do well to follow their lead.

Some people are, of course, doing that already. It's been estimated that there are nearly 12.5 million vegetarians in this country. And some of the most highly respected doctors advocate a low-fat, meatless diet for both weight control and heart health. For example, Dean Ornish, M.D., has had great success treating heart patients with just such an eating plan. And he found that, as a bonus, his patients dropped considerable weight—without even trying.

Dr. Ornish, who is director of the Preventive Medicine Research Institute in Sausalito, California, is not alone in his advocacy of vegetarian cuisine. When asked what one bit of advice he would give people hoping to prevent coronary disease and increase their longevity, William Castelli, M.D., said, "Go on a vegetarian diet." Dr. Castelli, director of the long-running Framingham Heart Study, pointed out that Seventh-Day Adventists, who adhere faithfully to a vegetarian diet, experience less heart disease than those folks who regularly eat meat.

And the benefits could extend even further. "We might get a 60 percent reduction in our cancer rates," Dr. Castelli speculates. "You can't beat a vegetarian diet." He should know. He himself pretty much follows a meatless diet that he occasionally supplements with fish.

There's just one caveat these experts and others would dish up with the beans, grains and vegetables. People wanting to follow this dietary lifestyle must resist the temptation to replace meat with high-fat cheeses and other high-fat dairy products, says Johanna Dwyer, R.D., D.Sc., professor of medicine at Tufts University School of Medicine in Boston.

Dr. Dwyer has researched the health aspects of a meatless diet. She suggests that low-fat dietary patterns can have positive effects on weight control, blood pressure, heart-disease risk and some cancers. That's where some practical help from two of San Francisco's top chefs comes into play.

One of them is Annie Somerville, executive chef at Greens, a vegetarian restaurant that's been drawing rave reviews and a steady stream of satisfied diners since opening in 1979. And while some people come specifically for the vegetarian fare, others come because they know the food is just plain delicious.

The second chef is Joyce Goldstein, the creative force behind Square One. Although her restaurant is not exclusively vegetarian, meatless dishes do play a prominent role. And it was to Goldstein that Dr. Ornish turned to create the recipes for his latest book, *Eat More, Weigh Less.*

Here are a few of the creations these culinary wizards came up with to help us get off to a healthy, slimming start.

PRUNE CHUTNEY

This condiment is another recipe from the Caucasus region. You may serve the chutney warm, chilled or at room temperature. The mixture will thicken upon standing, so you may want to thin it with a little water until it's the consistency of a spoonable ketchup.

Per ⅓ cup: 140 calories, 0.3 g. fat (2% of calories), 3.5 g. dietary fiber, 1.4 g. protein, 37 g. carbohydrates, 0 mg. cholesterol, 3 mg. sodium.

MAKES 1⅓ CUPS.

- 1½ cups water
- 1¼ cups pitted prunes
- 2 tablespoons red wine vinegar
- 1 teaspoon grated lemon rind
- 2 tablespoons chopped fresh coriander
- 1 tablespoon chopped fresh basil
- 1 tablespoon honey
- 1 teaspoon minced garlic
- ½ teaspoon ground red pepper
- ½ teaspoon ground black pepper

In a 2-quart saucepan, combine the water, prunes and vinegar. Soak for 30 minutes. Bring to a simmer over medium heat. Cover, reduce the heat to low and cook for 30 minutes, or until the prunes are tender. Stir in the lemon rind and cook for 2 minutes.

Transfer to a blender or food processor and puree. Place in a medium bowl. Stir in the coriander, basil, honey, garlic, red pepper and black pepper.

SAVORY VEGETABLE CAKES

Annie Somerville attributes the subtle, delicious flavor of these pancakes to the sesame, ginger and coriander that accent the vegetables. For variety, you may add other vegetables, such as mung bean sprouts, sliced celery and water chestnuts. The key to success is keeping the batter very light; you need just enough to coat the vegetables. Serve with a dipping sauce made from diluted soy sauce flavored with ginger and a bit of dark sesame oil. And round out the meal with pickled shredded cabbage and steamed bok choy.

Per serving: 136 calories, 3.2 g. fat (21% of calories), 2.3 g. dietary fiber, 7 g. protein, 22.4 g. carbohydrate, 0 mg. cholesterol, 446 mg. sodium. Also a very good source of vitamin A and vitamin C.

SERVES 4.

    1 teaspoon dark sesame oil
    6 cups thinly sliced Chinese cabbage
    2 cups julienned carrots
    2 tablespoons grated fresh ginger
    2 tablespoons low-sodium soy sauce
    1 tablespoon mirin (sweet cooking wine)
    4 scallions, thinly sliced on a diagonal
    8 ounces shiitake mushrooms, sliced ¼ inch thick
    ¾ teaspoon hot pepper flakes
    2 tablespoons unbleached flour
    3 egg whites
    2 tablespoons chopped fresh coriander
    1 teaspoon canola oil
    1 teaspoon toasted sesame seeds (see note)

In a large frying pan over medium heat, warm the sesame oil. Add the cabbage and sauté for 3 to 5 minutes, or until the cabbage begins to wilt. Add the carrots, ginger, soy sauce and mirin. Sauté for 5 minutes, or until the vegetables are tender.

Add the scallions, mushrooms and pepper flakes. Cook for 2 to 3 minutes, or until the excess liquid evaporates. Transfer to a bowl and set aside to cool for at least 5 minutes.

In a small bowl, combine the flour and egg whites. Pour over the vegetables. Add the coriander and toss to mix well.

Wash and dry the frying pan. Place over medium-high heat. Add the canola oil and swirl the pan to coat the bottom. Spoon in the batter, using a scant ¼ cup for each cake (approximately 3-inch cakes). Cook for about 3 minutes. Turn and cook for another 2 to 3 minutes. Sprinkle with the sesame seeds. Serve hot.

Note: To toast sesame seeds, place them in a dry skillet, toast over very low heat, stirring or shaking the pan, until they're golden brown and fragrant, about 2 minutes.

BUCKWHEAT NOODLES
WITH MUSHROOMS AND BOK CHOY

This recipe from Greens, a vegetarian restaurant, was inspired by ingredients plentiful in San Francisco's Chinatown. Annie paired them with Japanese buckwheat noodles, or soba. These noodles are good served with wilted spinach and a salad featuring shredded carrots.

Per serving: 271 calories, 7 g. fat (23% of calories), 2.3 g. dietary fiber, 9.3 g. protein, 49.1 g. carbohydrate, 0 mg. cholesterol, 555 mg. sodium. Also a very good source of vitamin C. SERVES 4.

      4 ounces shiitake mushrooms
      2 small heads bok choy
      6 ounces thin dried buckwheat (soba) noodles
      2 teaspoons peanut oil
      3 cloves garlic, finely chopped
      1 tablespoon grated fresh ginger
    1–2 jalapeño chili peppers, cut in half lengthwise and
         thinly sliced (wear plastic gloves)
      1 scallion, thinly sliced on the diagonal
      2 tablespoons mirin (sweet cooking wine)
      1 tablespoon dark sesame oil
      1 tablespoon low-sodium soy sauce
      2 tablespoons coarsely chopped fresh coriander
      1 teaspoon toasted sesame seeds (see note)

Set a large pot of water on the stove to boil.

Remove the mushroom stems and cut the caps into ½-inch slices. (The stems can be saved for stock.) Cut the bok choy in half lengthwise, then slice the leaves into 2-inch-wide ribbons.

When the water boils, add the noodles and cook as directed, about 8 to 10 minutes. While the noodles are cooking, heat the peanut oil in a large frying pan over medium heat. Add the mushrooms and sauté for 3 to 4 minutes. Add the garlic, ginger, peppers and bok choy. Sauté for 2 minutes.

Drain the noodles. Reduce the heat and add the scallions, mirin, sesame oil and soy sauce to the pan. Quickly add the noodles. Remove from the heat and toss the noodles with the vegetables and coriander. Sprinkle with the sesame seeds.

Note: To toast sesame seeds, place them in a dry skillet and toast over very low heat, stirring or shaking the pan, until they are golden and fragrant, about 2 minutes.

SPINACH BORANI

Joyce Goldstein drew inspiration for this recipe from the region around the Caucasus mountains in eastern Europe. A hallmark of borani dishes is a topping of yogurt. Sometimes eggs are mixed in with the main ingredient and the whole dish is baked. But Goldstein left out that step to keep the recipe light. To turn the spinach into the centerpiece of a full meal, add some grilled slices of eggplant, a pilaf made from cracked wheat and the Prune Chutney on page 23 (or some commercial chutney).

Per serving: 185 calories, 4.8 g. fat (23% of calories), 5.6 g. dietary fiber, 11.4 g. protein, 27.7 g. carbohydrate, 7 mg. cholesterol, 175 mg. sodium. Also a very good source of vitamin A, vitamin C, calcium, folate, magnesium and potassium.

SERVES 4.

- 1 pound fresh spinach, tough stems trimmed
- 2 teaspoons olive oil
- 4 cups chopped onions
- 4 cloves garlic, finely minced
- 3 tablespoons chopped fresh basil
- 2 tablespoons chopped fresh coriander
- 1 tablespoon chopped fresh thyme (optional)
- ¼ teaspoon ground black pepper
- 2 cups nonfat yogurt
- ½ teaspoon ground cinnamon
- ½ teaspoon turmeric
  Pomegranate seeds (garnish)

Wash the spinach carefully in 2 or 3 changes of water; drain well. Tear any very large leaves into smaller pieces or cut into wide strips.

In a large frying pan over low heat, warm the oil. Add the onions and cook for 15 minutes, or until tender and translucent. Add the garlic and cook for 2 to 3 minutes.

Add the basil, coriander and thyme, if using; cook a few minutes longer. Add the spinach, a few handfuls at a time; cook, stirring, until wilted. Season with the pepper and transfer to a serving bowl.

In a medium bowl, stir together the yogurt, cinnamon and turmeric. Spoon over the spinach. Sprinkle with a few pomegranate seeds and serve hot.

Polenta with Mushroom Stroganoff

Polenta is very thick cooked cornmeal that makes an excellent change of pace from noodles, rice or bulgur. Here Joyce Goldstein tops the polenta with a low-fat version of stroganoff. She calls it the sizzle minus the steak—meaty mushrooms in a creamy yogurt sauce. If you have access to brown mushrooms, chanterelles or other wild mushrooms, Goldstein says, they add a greater depth of flavor to this dish. So do dried mushrooms that you've soaked in hot water. Serve the stroganoff with a mixed green salad and whole-grain bread.

Per serving: 174 calories, 1.8 g. fat (9% of calories), 7.1 g. dietary fiber, 6 g. protein, 36.4 g. carbohydrate, 0 mg. cholesterol, 40 mg. sodium.

Serves 4.

Polenta

About 4 cups water or vegetable stock
1   cup coarse cornmeal
½   teaspoon ground black pepper

Mushroom Stroganoff

2   cups sliced onions
1   cup defatted chicken or vegetable stock, divided
4   cups sliced mushrooms
1   tablespoon sweet paprika
Pinch of ground red pepper or hot paprika
1   teaspoon grated lemon rind
½   teaspoon ground black pepper
¼   cup nonfat yogurt cheese (see note)
2   tablespoons chopped fresh dill or parsley

To make the polenta: Place the water or stock in a heavy 2-quart saucepan. Whisk in the cornmeal. Cook over low heat, stirring often, for 30 minutes, or until thick. Taste a small amount and make sure it no longer feels grainy on your tongue. If necessary, add more water or stock and continue cooking until the graininess is gone. Stir in the pepper.

Line a jelly-roll pan with parchment paper or foil. Pour the polenta mixture into it and spread evenly. Refrigerate until firm, at least 30 minutes. Cut into triangles or other shapes.

To make the mushroom stroganoff: In a large frying pan, combine the onions and ½ cup of the stock. Cover and simmer over medium heat for 10 to 15 minutes, or until tender.

Stir in the mushrooms and simmer, uncovered, for 5 minutes. Stir in the sweet paprika, red pepper or hot paprika, lemon rind, black pepper and the remaining ½ cup stock. Simmer for 10 minutes, or until the liquid has reduced by half. Remove from the heat and let stand for 5 minutes. Swirl in the yogurt cheese and sprinkle with the dill or parsley.

Just before the stroganoff is ready, coat a baking sheet with no-stick spray. Add the polenta pieces in a single layer and broil about 5 inches from the heat until lightly browned on top. Turn slices and brown on other side. Serve topped with the stroganoff.

Note: To make the yogurt cheese, place about ½ cup of nonfat yogurt (use a brand with no gelatin) in a strainer lined with cheesecloth. Cover, set the strainer over a bowl and refrigerate. Let drain until thick, at least 2 hours.

NORTH AFRICAN-STYLE BEETS AND CARROTS

This pretty dish is Joyce Goldstein's variation on a Moroccan vegetable entrée. Serve it with soft flatbread and couscous. To make the couscous, follow the directions on the package and add a little ground cinnamon for an authentic flavor boost.

Per serving: 227 calories, 4 g. fat (16% of calories), 6.5 g. dietary fiber, 4.9 g. protein, 47.8 g. carbohydrate, 0 mg. cholesterol, 248 mg. sodium. Also a very good source of vitamin A, vitamin C, folate and potassium.

SERVES 4.

- 8   small beets
- ¾   cup hot water
- ½   cup raisins
- 8   carrots
- 1   tablespoon oil
- 1   tablespoon lemon rind
- 1   tablespoon lemon juice
- ½   teaspoon ground cinnamon
- 1   tablespoon honey
- 6   cups tightly packed beet greens, Swiss chard or escarole, cut into thin strips
- 3   tablespoons chopped fresh mint
- ¼   teaspoon ground black pepper

Trim the beets, leaving 1 to 2 inches of stem attached. Place in a saucepan with cold water to cover and bring to a boil. Reduce the heat and simmer until tender. (Start testing with a small knife after 40 minutes.) Drain, cover with warm water and let stand until cool enough to handle. Peel and cut into chunks or wedges; you should have 1½ to 2 cups.

Place the hot water and raisins in a small bowl. Let stand for about 15 minutes. Drain, reserving the liquid.

Cut the carrots into chunks about the same size as the beets. Cook in boiling water until tender, but not mushy, about 8 minutes. Drain and rinse under cold running water.

Heat the oil in a large frying pan over medium heat. Add the beets and carrots. Cook, stirring, 1 to 2 minutes. Add the raisins, lemon rind, lemon juice, cinnamon, honey and ½ cup of reserved raisin liquid. Simmer 1 to 2 minutes. Add the greens. Cook, stirring, until wilted. Stir in the mint and pepper.

LINGUINE WITH ONIONS, GOAT CHEESE AND WALNUTS

This dish from Annie Somerville delivers very rich flavor even though it contains only a small amount of oil and cheese. Long, slow cooking turns the onions sweet, so they complement the distinctive flavor of the goat cheese. Serve the linguine with steamed snap peas or green beans and crusty bread to round out the meal.

Per serving: 288 calories, 7.9 g. fat (25% of calories), 4 g. dietary fiber, 10.9 g. protein, 44.5 g. carbohydrate, 42 mg. cholesterol, 39 mg. sodium.

SERVES 4.

    1 tablespoon extra-virgin olive oil
    4 cups thinly sliced onions
    2 cloves garlic, finely chopped
    ½ cup defatted chicken or vegetable stock
    8 ounces fresh linguine
    ⅓ cup chopped fresh basil
    2 tablespoons chopped and toasted walnuts
    ¼ teaspoon ground black pepper
    1 ounce reduced-fat soft goat cheese, crumbled

In a large frying pan over medium heat, warm the oil. Add the onions and sauté for 10 minutes, or until the onions begin to soften and release their juices. Add the garlic and continue to cook; gently scrape the pan occasionally with a wooden spoon to keep the onions from sticking as they caramelize.

After 40 minutes, the onions should be a rich golden color and very sweet. At this point, add the stock. Simmer over low heat, scraping the pan with a wooden spoon to release the browned bits from the bottom.

Just before the onions are ready, bring a large pot of water to a boil. Add the linguine and cook for 1 minute, or until tender. Quickly scoop out ¼ cup of the cooking water and add to the onions. (This makes the sauce juicier without using more oil.)

Drain the pasta, then add it to the onions. Add the basil, walnuts and pepper. Toss well. Sprinkle with the goat cheese and serve immediately.

2

SOUTHERN COMFORT

Greens and beans pack a powerful one-two punch.

Traditionally, they are served together on New Year's Day to start the year off with a dose of health and wealth. "Health" because we all know that greens and beans, with their powerful healing potential, are an unbeatable combination. "Wealth" because, as any good Southerner knows, greens (dollar bills) and beans (small change) are guaranteed through the year if you eat the right foods on January 1.

Maybe you're a Northerner and don't know the old customs of the South. Maybe you have a different association with greens and beans from your past: the great Northern beans that always managed to spill from the package when your mother made bean soup—thick, rich, full of white beans, carrots, celery and tomatoes. There were saltine crackers to crumble into the soup and a huge wedge of iceberg lettuce topped with Thousand Island dressing rounding out a ritual Friday night meal you will always remember.

Today you might be a big-city dweller. Entranced with food and health, you have happily seen a wealth of greens—mustard and kale, broccoli rabe and collards, chard and beet greens—displayed in your favorite gourmet store. And you've stood amazed at the pretty beans packaged so handsomely in your corner convenience store. You've even eaten what fashionable chefs are preparing these days with greens and beans in combination. You've only to look at menus from trend-setting restaurants to know that thoughtful chefs realize they owe it to their customers to provide optimum nutrition along with delicious food.

With restaurants cutting costs and newspapers reporting daily about provocative scientific findings on the wisdom of eating less red meat and more vegetables, bright chefs and customers alike are realizing there is a world beyond pasta—and that we all need to look with renewed interest at the dynamic duo of greens and beans.

If you're ready to take all of this to heart, you're definitely headed in the right direction. For greens and beans both contain nutrients that are vital for heart health. Beans, in particular, are bursting with soluble fiber—the type that propelled oat bran into the limelight a few years ago as a potent cholesterol-lowering agent. (Remember that high blood cholesterol puts you at risk for heart disease.)

Studies done by famed cholesterol researcher James W. Anderson, M.D., professor of medicine and clinical nutrition at the University of Kentucky College of Medicine in Lexington, have shown just how good a job beans do in the fight against cholesterol. In one amazing instance, people with high cholesterol who ate 1½ cups of cooked beans every day for three weeks saw their levels plummet an average of 60 points.

Elsewhere, doctors at the University of Toronto found that soluble fiber can even multiply the effects of a diet that's already low in saturated fat and dietary cholesterol. And they got results from highly palatable foods, including beans, lentils, barley, oat bran and psyllium-containing breakfast cereal.

Keep in mind that ready-cooked canned beans are as good a source of fiber as dried beans you cook yourself. And the canned varieties are, of course, more convenient. Their only drawback is extra sodium used in the canning process. So dump them into a strainer and rinse well to remove a fair amount of it.

The recipes that follow all call for cooked beans. It's up to you whether you want to use canned ones or cook your own from scratch. (To do so, simply soak dried beans overnight, drain, add new water and simmer until tender, which will take 1½ hours or more, depending on the variety. Drain and proceed with the recipe.)

Greens, too, contain soluble fiber, although not in the impressive concentration that beans boast. Their contribution to the heart-disease-fighting equation may come from their stores of beta-carotene, that super antioxidant that's linked to a lower risk of heart disease. Fruits and vegetables are great sources of beta-carotene and other antioxidants.

Greens that qualify as decidedly heart-healthy include arugula, watercress, chard, mustard greens, chicory, beet greens, broccoli rabe, kale, radicchio, collards and dandelion greens.

All of this may explain why people in the Mediterranean—that region hailed for its heart-protective diet—instinctively turn to the combination of greens and beans for sustenance. They enjoy endless variations on bean soups— sometimes with

GREEN CUISINE

Choosing and using greens is easy:

• Pick up a bunch and feel it gently with your hands. The leaves should feel firm, erect and crisp, with no sense of limpness.

• Check the cut ends. They should be clean, unbrowned and neatly trimmed.

• Rub a leaf or two between your fingers. Fresh greens will "squeak" (as should fresh artichokes, snow peas and green beans).

• To store, rinse well with cold water and discard any less-than-perfect leaves. Shake off excess water. Trim a half-inch off the stem ends.

• Wrap the greens in paper towels and place in a plastic bag. Keep in the refrigerator, but use as soon as possible.

• When cooking chard or beet greens, allow more time for the stems than the more tender greens.

• Mustard greens, collards, kale and such have tougher leaves than, say, spinach and are best cut crosswise into thin strips (chiffonade) before cooking.

• Briefly steam greens or lightly sauté them to preserve their color and nutrients.

• If you must boil greens, be sure to drink the "pot likker" left after cooking. Any good Southerner will tell you it's pure tonic.

pasta added, sometimes with bread slices floating on top—that contain greens. A few other examples: beans and chard, dressed simply with olive oil and lemon juice, from Cyprus; Lebanon's mixture of lentils, chard, onions, garlic, coriander and olive oil; ribollita, a Tuscan soup of cannellini beans, shredded chard and cabbage to be eaten especially on meatless Fridays; mine-strone; Greek faki, full of lentils, herbs, onions, wild greens and a splash of cider vinegar. From region to region, dishes build on each other, using repetitive ingredients and providing the inexpensive protein that so much of the world survives on.

The real magic of greens and beans is that they are both keepers through the winter. The shelf life of dried beans is legendary. And hardy greens grow long into winter and seem to have some fresh leaves for the picking throughout the coldest season.

PILAF WITH LIMAS, MUSTARD GREENS AND MINT

This makes an excellent accompaniment to roast chicken or grilled fish.

Per serving: 377 calories, 4.9 g. fat (12% of calories), 5.3 g. dietary fiber, 11.2 g. protein, 61.5 g. carbohydrate, 0 mg. cholesterol, 104 mg. sodium. Also a very good source of folate, vitamin A, vitamin C and potassium.

SERVES 4.

2	cups lima beans
1	tablespoon olive oil
1	small onion, minced
1	cup basmati or long-grain white rice
2	cups defatted chicken stock
8	ounces mustard greens, stemmed and shredded
⅓	cup minced fresh mint
¼	cup minced fresh parsley

Steam the lima beans for 5 minutes, or until tender. Set aside.

In a 3-quart saucepan over medium heat, warm the oil. Stir in the onions and rice. Sauté 3 minutes. Add the stock and bring to a boil. Reduce heat to low, cover the pan and cook 15 minutes.

Meanwhile, steam the mustard greens for 5 to 7 minutes, or until very tender. Transfer to a food processor. Add the mint and parsley. Process with on/off turns until finely chopped.

Stir the greens mixture into the rice. Continue cooking over low heat until all the liquid has been absorbed and the rice is tender. Stir in the lima beans.

BLACK BEAN CAKES
WITH ARUGULA AND CORN

If you like, you can serve these as a first course instead of a main dish. In that case, allow one cake per person.

Per serving: 306 calories, 8.1 g. fat (24% of calories), 6.1 g. dietary fiber, 15 g. protein, 45.3 g. carbohydrate, 0 mg. cholesterol, 299 mg. sodium. Also a very good source of folate, vitamin A and vitamin C.

SERVES 4.

2	cups cooked black beans
1½	cups fresh bread crumbs
3	egg whites or ⅓ cup fat-free egg substitute
1	small onion, minced
1	small jalapeño pepper, seeded and minced (wear plastic gloves)
2	tablespoons tomato paste
1	clove garlic, minced
2	cups loosely packed torn arugula
1	cup cooked corn
1	small sweet red pepper, diced
2	tablespoons olive oil
¼	cup nonfat sour cream or yogurt
¼	cup salsa
2	tablespoons chopped fresh cilantro

In the bowl of a food processor, combine the beans, bread crumbs, egg whites or egg substitute, onions, jalapeño peppers, tomato paste and garlic. Process until very smooth.

Coat 8 muffin cups with no-stick spray. Divide the bean mixture among the cups. Coat a sheet of aluminum foil with no-stick spray and use to cover the muffin tin. Bake at 350° for 40 minutes, or until a toothpick inserted in the center of a cake comes out clean. Remove from the oven, let cool a few minutes, then unmold.

Divide the arugula among dinner plates. Top with 2 cakes per serving.

In a large no-stick frying pan over medium heat, sauté the corn and red peppers in the oil for 3 minutes. Sprinkle over the cakes.

In a small bowl, mix the sour cream or yogurt and salsa. Put a dollop on each cake. Sprinkle with the cilantro.

CHICK-PEAS WITH CHARD

You can serve this unusual dish hot as a main course or cold as a filling salad. Either way, accompany it with lemon wedges.

Per serving: 299 calories, 8.1 g. fat (24% of calories), 7.5 g. dietary fiber, 14.7 g. protein, 47.4 g. carbohydrate, 0 mg. cholesterol, 385 mg. sodium. Also a very good source of vitamin A, vitamin C, vitamin E, iron, magnesium and potassium.

SERVES 4.

- 1½ tablespoons olive oil, divided
- 1 large red onion, finely chopped
- ¼ cup tomato paste
- 1 teaspoon honey
- 4 cups cooked chick-peas
- 1 cup water
- 1½ pounds chard, trimmed and shredded
- ¼ teaspoon ground black pepper
- 1 small red onion, thinly sliced into rings

In a 3-quart saucepan over medium heat, warm 1 tablespoon of the oil. Add the chopped onions and sauté 10 to 12 minutes, or until onions just begin to turn golden. Stir in the tomato paste and honey. Cook 1 minute.

Stir in the chick-peas and water. Bring to a simmer. Add the chard. Cover and simmer for 20 minutes, or until the greens are wilted and tender. Stir in the pepper.

Ladle into soup bowls. Top with the onion slices and drizzle with the remaining ½ tablespoon oil.

THAI-STYLE BEAN SALAD WITH WILTED WATERCRESS

This tangy, filling favorite is almost a meal in itself.

Per serving: 274 calories, 7.5 g. fat (25% of calories), 7.3 g. dietary fiber, 13.4 g. protein, 40.8 g. carbohydrate, 0 mg. cholesterol, 175 mg. sodium. Also a very good source of folate. SERVES 4.

    1   cup frozen cut green beans
    3   cups cooked kidney or adzuki beans
    1   tablespoon olive oil
    2   cups chopped, loosely packed watercress
    1   tablespoon water
    ½   cup chopped fresh cilantro
    1   jalapeño pepper, seeded and minced (wear plastic
        gloves)
    1   scallion, chopped
    1   thick slice ginger, minced
    3   cloves garlic
    1   tablespoon toasted cashews or peanuts
    1   tablespoon mirin (sweet cooking wine)
    1   tablespoon low-sodium soy sauce
    1   tablespoon honey
    2   teaspoons sesame oil
    ½   teaspoon turmeric

Put the green beans in a strainer and rinse them with hot water to thaw. Let drain well, then place in a large bowl. Add the kidney or adzuki beans and set aside.

In a large no-stick frying pan over high heat, warm the olive oil. Add the watercress and water; stir-fry for 2 to 3 minutes, or until the watercress just begins to wilt and is still bright green. Drain, if necessary, and add to the bowl with the beans.

In a food processor, combine the cilantro, peppers, scallions, ginger, garlic, nuts, mirin, soy sauce, honey, sesame oil and turmeric. Process with on/off turns until finely chopped and well-blended. Spoon over the bean mixture and toss to mix well.

MÉLANGE OF FRESH BEANS AND GREENS

For variety, serve this dish with grilled polenta.

Per serving: 328 calories, 7.9 g. fat (22% of calories), 11 g. dietary fiber, 17.4 g. protein, 49.3 g. carbohydrate, 0 mg. cholesterol, 96 mg. sodium. Also a very good source of thiamin, folate, vitamin A, vitamin C, iron and potassium.

SERVES 4.

- 1½ cups peas
- 1½ cups frozen black-eyed peas
- 1½ cups lima beans
- 1 cup green beans, chopped to the size of peas
- 1 cup cooked kidney beans
- 1 clove garlic, minced
- 2 tablespoons olive oil
- 4 cups loosely packed torn arugula
- 1 tablespoon fresh tarragon or 2 teaspoons dried tarragon
  Chopped fresh parsley (garnish)
  Lemon wedges (garnish)

Place the peas, black-eyed peas, lima beans and green beans in a steamer basket. Steam until the largest items are just tender; do not overcook. Transfer to a large bowl. Stir in the kidney beans.

In a large no-stick frying pan over medium heat, sauté the garlic in the oil for 1 minute. Add the arugula and sauté for 3 minutes, or until wilted. Stir in the bean mixture and the tarragon. Heat through.

To serve, divide the mixture among plates. Garnish with the parsley and lemon wedges.

3

ITALIAN CLASSICS

*It's traditional fare that's delicious, healthful
and easy to prepare.*

Look at the sheer length of Italy, the long fashionable boot,
the toe of which seems to be kicking the islands of Sicily and
Sardinia out into the Mediterranean Sea, and it's easy to see
why this country, perhaps more so than any other, has long epit-
omized Mediterranean living.

Travel through Italy today, especially to its small villages
where local customs have withstood the changing times, and
you'll witness a lifestyle quite different from our own. Here
country ways still exist; time slows in the middle of the day to
ensure that everyone has a long lunch and a session of gossip to
keep abreast of village news. Meals still include coarse peasant
breads, a wealth of vegetables, pure olive oil, beans and rice and
polenta (a kind of cornmeal cake).

Even in the cosmopolitan centers, fashionable food shops
and a growing number of bakers make coarse-grained breads
and herb-studded focaccia, a bread made from pizza dough
drizzled with olive oil. Dishes like Tuscan beans in a flask, an
old-style method for cooking beans over a charcoal fire, and
simple fishermen's dishes like pasta with sardines appear on
menus.

The Sicilian-born cookbook writer and restaurateur Mim-
metta Lo Motta remembers growing up in the country. "We
lived in Palermo, then moved to my grandfather's farm. I remember the most wonderful, thick bread like I've never tasted
since, citrus fruits for which Sicily is famous, green vegetables
all year round. We had fresh peas and fava beans sautéed in
olive oil with a bit of onion. We ate artichokes on pasta, artichokes with parsley and garlic, lots of wild roots and greens like
wild asparagus, dandelion and borraggine, which was like kale.
We had soups made of dried beans and lentils, sometimes with
wild game; a stale-bread soup with onions and bay leaves for
frugality's sake. There were pigeons from our pigeon house and
mainly fruit for dessert.

"Our pattern of eating was to rise with the sun and eat a small breakfast of a cup of coffee and a slice of crusty whole-grain bread slathered with sweet preserves made in my grandfather's kitchen. The main meal was served around 2:00 P.M. Then at night, a light supper was served to adults after the children, who were fed earlier, went to bed. Frequently, there was a minestrone or salad, some cheese and olives. People believed strongly that eating too much at night wasn't healthy.

"The older people of our region were very vigorous. My grandfather cooked for himself until he was very old, in his nineties. He used to go to church at 6:00 A.M. every day, up and down five flights of stairs easily several times a day."

THREADS OF GOOD HEALTH

What Italy still has, when you search out the country by-ways and ancient city centers, is a wealth of regional cooking that doesn't travel out of its own district. But despite its regional exclusivity, the cooking of Italy does have some common threads. First and foremost is olive oil. Olive trees thrive in the poor, rocky soil of southern Italy and Sicily; most of the crop is used to produce olive oil. It permeates most of the region's cuisines.

With its volcanic soil, long growing season and temperate climes, Sicily also supplies Italy with an abundance of fruits and vegetables: all varieties of oranges—bitter, blood and sweet—and all manner of almonds, capers, lemons, fresh peas, tomatoes and asparagus.

Garlic is beloved in most of Italy, also. From the northern port of Genoa, where pesto with garlic and basil is the favorite sauce and every kitchen has its strand of woven garlic, every balcony its pot of basil growing, south to the area along the "toe" where fresh sardines are split, layered in a dish, and baked covered with oregano and olive oil—garlic is loved. The garlic and olive oil, the fresh produce, the game that is plentifully found, the fish from the surrounding waters (very little meat is consumed) and the bread of the region are important elements in the Italian diet.

HIGH-CARB TRILOGY

By far the mainstays, however, are carbohydrates—either pasta, polenta or risotto. These foods form the base upon which all other elements usually rest. Pasta shops and stores are common in large cities, selling a variety of fresh and dried pastas in every shape and length. But the making of pasta at home is still a time-honored tradition in smaller villages. Making pasta, with its easy turns and its slow formulation, is a job that tends to fall to the aunts and grandmothers of a household. Making pasta is easy but making superior pasta involves an instinctive touch and sense of timing.

Pasta is frequently composed in a large rustic bowl. A stream of pale, unbleached, cream-colored semolina flour, which is full of hard wheat protein, is poured into the center of a bowl. A well is made in the center of the flour, and then an egg yolk or two, a small slick of olive oil and salt are added, and the flour is slowly incorporated into the eggs. The dough must remain soft and pliable, as it will harden and firm in future handlings.

First the dough rests under a kitchen towel to allow the protein to relax. Thirty minutes later, it is kneaded through the blades of a hand-cranked machine. Folded over and over on itself, and growing progressively thinner as the blades are tightened, a long sheet of absolutely silken pasta soon emerges. It is then cut by the machine into thin strands or cut by hand into wide noodles.

A broom is then stretched over the backs of two chairs, and the pasta strands are hung to dry (briefly, if they are for supper; and there is nothing better than the melting tenderness of lovingly handmade pasta, which cooks in half the time of dried). Or it is totally dried and stored in a canister for future use.

Indeed, in most good classic Italian cooking, there are elements of time and ritual involved. A good polenta takes at least 30 minutes to make. First, cornmeal is added to simmering water in an almost painfully slow trickle. To prevent lumps from forming, the cook must be vigilant and possess a strong arm to keep stirring and turning the porridgelike mixture until it thickens and stands firm. The polenta is poured out onto an oiled slab. Then, when the mass has adequately solidified, its maker gets to twirl a taut string between the thumbs and gently use it to cut the polenta into wedges.

These are either grilled or heated and served as an accompaniment to vegetables, meat or fish.

A good risotto from an Italian home or restaurant kitchen takes time, too. Family and guests know when a risotto is in the making, and they gather around the table to wait for its execution, for there is a precise moment when the cook knows the dish is perfectly done. The grains of arborio rice have grown plump, exuded their milky starch, in a long, slow-cooking process wherein the cook stirs continuously for 30 minutes as the grains slowly absorb ladles of broth. Everyone waits on risotto at the table during the dish's final 5 minutes. The cheese melts into the rice and the additions of seafood or vegetables yield their last flavorings. Then the cover is removed under the diners' noses and cries of *"bella, bellissimo"* shower the cook.

SIMPLY PERFECT MEALS

A frugal cook can make a pasta dish fit for a king by simply drizzling virgin olive oil, a crush of garlic and chopped, seeded tomatoes over fresh tagliatelle (fettucine) in the summer. In the winter, even more frugal, just oil, garlic and a scraping of Parmesan dress one of the most widely consumed dishes of the Mediterranean. And in all the best Italian dishes, there is a simplicity, a dependence on excellent raw ingredients prepared with a minimum of complexity and few sauces.

One can imagine a perfect, simple meal in Genoa one night after a long day of travel. How wonderful it would be to sit by the moonlit harbor and have a first course of pasta dressed in an abundance of pesto, then a second course of tiny, impeccably prepared fish, served with lemon wedges on the side. For dessert, a cup of strawberries with a small pitcher of fresh lemon juice on the side to pour over the sweet, sun-kissed berries. (Other simple Italian desserts—sliced peaches sprinkled with slivered fresh almonds and a grate of nutmeg, figs drizzled with honey—would be tasty additions to your repertoire.)

Another night, you may enjoy a first course of a porcini mushroom that's been grilled, then dressed with olive oil and a simple fresh chop of garlic and parsley, followed by a perfectly roasted chicken. Or how about pasta primavera or fettucine with a thick, fresh tomato sauce and a bowl of grated Parmesan on the side?

Rituals of Eating

As in most Mediterranean countries, most people snack very little. There are street merchants with dried fruits and nuts, chestnuts in fall, slit and roasted pumpkin seeds, toasted favas and chick-peas, and you sometimes see small children with gray paper cornucopias, munching nuts on the streets.

One ritual that Italians all share and love, regardless of their region, is the taking of a coffee, a lemonade, a gelato in the central piazzas of all towns, large and small. There are more expensive items to be had—small ices frozen in the shapes of fruits or flowers, then hand-painted with natural food colorings. Melons and oranges are hollowed and filled with sherbets.

The "evening in the piazza" is a familial time. For single people, it's a time to mingle and be seen, for the young men to strut and preen. For families, going to the piazza is an evening's or Sunday afternoon's entertainment, an excuse to dress up, see friends, show off children. To spend the evening in such simplicity, out in the open air and surrounded by the reality of people, is one of the great pleasures of Italian life, a de-stressing ritual that is both convivial and communal.

Bruschetta

This is traditional Italian garlic bread, which is often made over coals. Serve it as an appetizer.

Per serving: 122 calories, 2.4 grams fat (1.7 g. monounsaturated fat), 1.7 g. dietary fiber, 3.6 g. protein, 20.9 g. carbohydrate, 0 mg. cholesterol, 157 mg. sodium.

Serves 6.

    6 thick slices homemade or Italian bread
    1 clove garlic, halved
    1 tablespoon olive oil
    2 tomatoes, seeded and minced
    1 small red onion, minced
    2 tablespoons minced fresh parsley
       Ground black pepper

Toast, broil or grill the bread on both sides. Generously rub one side of each slice with the garlic and brush with the oil.

In a small bowl, mix the tomatoes, onions, parsley and pepper. Spread the mixture on the bread slices, covering them completely. Let stand for 1 hour.

CAULIFLOWER AGROGOLCE

This sweet-and-sour cauliflower, despite its Chinese-sounding name, is an Italian dish. Serve it hot or cold.

Per serving: 192 calories, 14.3 g. fat (7.5 g. monounsaturated fat), 5.4 g. dietary fiber, 5.3 g. protein, 16.1 g. carbohydrate, 0 mg. cholesterol, 26 mg. sodium. Also a good source of vitamin C and folate.

SERVES 6.

> 1 clove garlic, minced
> 3 tablespoons olive oil
> 1 large head cauliflower, separated into florets
> 1 large tomato, seeded and diced
> 2½ tablespoons red wine vinegar
> 3 tablespoons toasted pine nuts
> 3 tablespoons golden raisins

In a large frying pan over medium heat, sauté the garlic in the oil for 1 minute, or until it just begins to turn brown but isn't burned. Add the cauliflower, tomatoes and vinegar. Cover and cook for 8 to 10 minutes.

Stir in the pine nuts and raisins. Cover and cook for 2 to 3 minutes, or until the cauliflower is just tender.

RED PEPPER PANZANELLA

Panzanella means bread salad, and it's one of the very best uses for red peppers and tomatoes. It tastes like summer even when made in winter. You can prepare the tomato-pepper mixture a day or two ahead, but once you add the croutons, serve the salad immediately.

Per serving: 185 calories, 14.4 g. fat, (10.1 g. monounsaturated fat), 2.4 g. dietary fiber, 2.3 g. protein, 13.5 g. carbohydrate, 0 mg. cholesterol, 62 mg. sodium. Also a good source of vitamin A and vitamin C.

SERVES 6.

SALAD

4   large fresh tomatoes (or 16 plum tomatoes)
3   large sweet red peppers
3   tablespoons olive oil, divided
2   large cloves garlic, sliced
1   medium red onion, sliced
1   tablespoon balsamic vinegar
    Ground black pepper
¼   cup fresh basil leaves, torn
¼   cup chopped fresh parsley

CROUTONS

3   tablespoons olive oil, divided
2   cups stale French or Italian bread cubes (¾ inch)
1   large clove garlic, halved

To make the salad: Core the tomatoes and cut into 8 pieces each (or cut the plum tomatoes in half). Cut the peppers into 1-inch squares.

In a large frying pan over medium heat, warm 2 tablespoons of the oil. Add the garlic and onions. Sauté until the onions are translucent; do not let the garlic burn. Add the tomatoes and peppers. Reduce the heat to medium-low. Cover and cook for 15 minutes. Remove the cover and cook, stirring frequently, for 5 minutes, or until most of the liquid has evaporated.

Remove from the heat and stir in the vinegar, pepper and the remaining 1 tablespoon oil. Cool to room temperature. If desired, refrigerate for up to 2 days.

To make the croutons: Place 2 tablespoons of the oil in a large frying pan. Heat over medium heat for 2 minutes. Add the bread and turn the pieces to coat with oil. Sauté, adding as much of the remaining oil as needed, until the cubes brown evenly and turn crisp.

Transfer the bread to paper towels and blot off the excess oil. When the pieces are cool enough to handle, rub one side of each with the garlic to flavor it.

Gently stir the croutons, basil and half of the parsley into the tomato mixture. Sprinkle with the remaining parsley and serve immediately.

ROASTED CECI

Ceci is Italian for chick-peas, here roasted in olive oil and garlic until brown and crispy.

Per ¼ cup: 113 calories, 2.6 g. fat (0.9 g. monounsaturated fat), 3.3 g. dietary fiber, 5.8 g. protein, 17.4 g. carbohydrate, 0 mg. cholesterol, 8 mg. sodium.

MAKES 4 CUPS.

    1   pound dried chick-peas
    3   tablespoons olive oil
    1   clove garlic, minced

Place the chick-peas in a 3-quart saucepan; cover with cold water. Bring to a boil and cook for 2 minutes. Turn off the heat, cover and let stand for 1 hour. Drain and add fresh water. Bring to a boil, cover and simmer over medium heat until just tender, about 1½ hours. Drain well. Transfer to a jelly-roll pan.

In a cup, mix the oil and garlic. Drizzle over the chick-peas, making sure they're all moistened. Spread them out evenly in the pan.

Bake for 40 minutes, or until browned, at 350°; shake the pan several times during baking to make sure the chick-peas color evenly.

Remove from the oven and place on paper towels to blot excess oil.

GRILLED POLENTA WITH CRISPED SAGE

*Polenta is a staple of northern Italy. Here it's served simply, with a
topping of fresh sage.*

Per serving: 253 calories, 11.8 g. fat (7 g. monounsaturated
fat), 5.8 g. dietary fiber, 4.3 g. protein, 34.2 g. carbohydrate,
0 mg. cholesterol, 94 mg. sodium.

SERVES 6.

6	cups defatted chicken stock
8	ounces coarse stone-ground yellow cornmeal
4	tablespoons olive oil
20–30	fresh sage leaves
	Ground black pepper

In a 3-quart saucepan over medium-high heat, bring the
stock to a boil. Reduce the heat to low.

Very slowly pour the cornmeal into the pan, whisking
with your other hand so no lumps form. Stir with a wooden
spoon for 25 to 30 minutes, or until the mixture is so stiff it
comes away from the side of the pot.

Oil a flat jelly-roll pan and pour the polenta out into it.
Spread evenly to about ¾ inch thick. Allow to cool.

Cut into 18 squares; cut each square in half to form 2 triangles. Broil or lightly grill the pieces for 2 minutes per side,
or until lightly toasted. Transfer to a serving platter.

In a large frying pan over medium heat, warm the oil. Add
the sage and cook just briefly until the leaves turn bright
green and translucent. Pour over the polenta. Season with the
pepper.

BEANS IN A FLASK

*This famous Tuscan dish is a quaint way to cook fresh white shelled
beans. To do it the traditional way, strip the straw covering from a
Chianti bottle. Fill the bottle with beans, olive oil and herbs. Bake it
for three hours in a bed of charcoal ashes. The flavor of the smoke
and oil perfumes the delicate beans, which you can then use as part
of an antipasto assortment.*

*If you don't have a convenient bottle, you may use a casserole
dish. And if you don't have fresh beans, use dried ones that you've
soaked.*

Per serving: 365 calories, 12.8 g. fat (8.8 g. monounsaturated fat), 3 g. dietary fiber, 15.9 g. protein, 48.9 g. carbohydrate, 0 mg. cholesterol, 14 mg. sodium. Also a good source of folate, thiamin, potassium and magnesium.

SERVES 6.

- 1 pound shelled fresh beans (try limas, favas, haricots, crowders)
- ⅓ cup olive oil
  Several sprigs fresh thyme
- 2 cloves garlic
- 1 large tomato, seeded and chopped
  Ground black pepper

In a 9″ × 13″ inch baking dish, mix the beans, oil, thyme and garlic. Sprinkle the tomatoes on top. Cover with foil and poke a few holes in the top. Bake at 300° for 2½ to 3 hours. Remove from the oven, sprinkle with the pepper and allow to cool to room temperature.

SICILIAN GRILLED SWORDFISH STEAKS

This recipe is adapted from Marcella Hazan's book Essentials of Classic Italian Cooking. *Although swordfish is the traditional fish of choice, you may use tuna, halibut, tilefish or mako shark.*

Per serving: 242 calories, 14.3 g. fat (8.7 g. monounsaturated fat), 0.1 g. dietary fiber, 26.2 g. protein, 0.7 g. carbohydrate, 51 mg. cholesterol, 119 mg. sodium. Also a good source of niacin and vitamin B_{12}.

SERVES 6.

- 2 tablespoons lemon juice
- 2 teaspoons chopped fresh oregano or 1 teaspoon dried
- ¼ cup olive oil
  Ground black pepper
- 2 pounds swordfish steaks

In a small bowl, combine the lemon juice and the oregano. Very slowly beat in the oil with a fork. Add a few pinches of black pepper.

Grill the swordfish for 2 minutes per side, or until cooked. Transfer to a serving platter. Prick each steak several times with a fork. Drizzle with the oil mixture.

4
FEEL-GOOD
FOOD

*These low-fat, high-comfort casseroles
allow you to eat lean
without giving up the taste.*

In feel if not in origin, casseroles are about as down-home as it gets. Irresistible feel-good foods like macaroni and cheese and hamburger casserole are linked for a vast generation of adults with polished memories of family dinners enjoyed at a close round table, Mom in an apron and Dad sporting a thin black tie.

If you grew up on traditional comfort foods, the word casserole conjures up nothing but warm fuzzies for you. Thanks to nutritionists, though, the association has changed quite a bit. Casseroles have gone from "fuzzy" to "fat" in one fell swoop.

Anita Hirsch, R.D., is a nutritionist with the Rodale Food Center in Emmaus, Pennsylvania. She analyzed three different casserole recipes, all family favorites. And in ferreting out the fat from the warm fuzzies, she found just as much of the former as the latter.

Miraculously, though, she had rolled up her sleeves, fired up the stove and transformed the recipes, cutting fat and calories in thick, oozing swaths. What's more, she did so without sacrificing the taste, feel and warm-fuzz factor of the casseroles.

In essence, Anita's culinary wizardry preserved the comfort and the casseroles, too. And the beauty of it is, you can do the same. Simply breeze through the following original recipes, then use Anita's modified recipes to make delicious low-fat, high-comfort meals for your family and friends—warm fuzzies guaranteed.

NEW MATH

If you've heard it once, you've heard it a thousand times: For optimal health, you should eat foods that derive no more than 25 percent of their total calories from fat. But shopping with a calculator is highly impractical, and number crunching might not be your strong suit. So forget percentages and think in quarters instead. With food labels in hand, simply follow this easy three-step formula.

1. Drop the last digit of the total calories listed for one serving. For instance, if an oatmeal cookie contains 163 calories, lop off the 3 to get 16.

2. Divide that number by 4. Using our oatmeal cookie as an example again, 16 divided by 4 is 4.

3. Compare. If the number you end up with is higher than the number of fat grams the label says is contained in one serving, the food is below the 25 percent ceiling, in which case you should add a fourth step: Eat and enjoy. Unfortunately, our oatmeal cookie contains six grams of fat per serving. And because four is smaller than six, we had to pass on this treat.

ORIGINAL MACARONI CASSEROLE

You probably have fond memories of a delicious macaroni-and-meat casserole, like this one, that your family feasted on at least once a week.

Per serving: 346 calories, 24 g. fat (62% of calories), 1 g. dietary fiber, 65 mg. cholesterol, 704 mg. sodium.

   1   cup elbow macaroni
   1   large onion, chopped
   1   large green pepper, chopped
   1   tablespoon margarine
   1   pound ground beef
  ½   cup whole milk
   1   can cream of mushroom soup
   1   cup grated Cheddar cheese
  ⅛   teaspoon ground black pepper
   1   teaspoon salt
       Dash of garlic powder

New and Improved Macaroni Casserole

Anita substituted a half-pound of ground turkey breast for the pound of ground beef and added a second cup of macaroni to substitute carbohydrates for the meat she removed. Since she omitted the salt, she added fresh sliced mushrooms, garlic and parsley for flavor. Rather than sautéing in margarine, she sautéed in 2 teaspoons of olive oil for added flavor (and for its heart-healthier monounsaturated fat).

Instead of using an entire cup of cheese, Anita sprinkled a strong-flavored cheese—extra-sharp Cheddar—on top, so she needed just 1 ounce. And she substituted skim milk for whole milk—all of which cut 135 calories and 19 grams of fat from each serving of the recipe.

Per serving: 211 calories, 5 g. fat (21% of calories), 1 g. dietary fiber, 29 mg. cholesterol, 209 mg. sodium.

Serves 8.

- 2 cups elbow macaroni
- 2 teaspoons olive oil
- 1 clove garlic, minced
- 1 large onion, chopped
- 1 large green or sweet red pepper, chopped
- 1 cup sliced mushrooms
- ½ pound ground turkey breast
- ½ cup skim milk
- 1 can Campbell's Healthy Request cream of mushroom soup
- ⅛ teaspoon ground black pepper
- 1 tablespoon chopped fresh parsley
- 1 ounce extra-sharp Cheddar cheese, shredded

Cook the macaroni for 12 minutes, drain and set aside. Heat the oil in a no-stick pan and sauté the garlic, onions, peppers and mushrooms until softened. Add the turkey and stir occasionally until the meat changes color.

Combine the macaroni, turkey mixture, milk, soup, black pepper and parsley in a 2-quart casserole dish coated with no-stick spray. Top with the cheese and bake, uncovered, at 375° for 20 minutes.

ORIGINAL SAUSAGE PILAU

Although sausage pilau (pronounced phi-LOW) isn't technically a casserole, it's what your mother might have referred to as a meal-in-one, meaning that the dish contains a meat, a starch and a green vegetable.

Per serving: 690 calories, 37 g. fat (48% of calories), 4 g. dietary fiber, 94 mg. cholesterol, 2,580 mg. sodium.

- 1   pound sausage
- 1   can onion soup
- 1   cup uncooked rice
  Salt, to taste
  Ground black pepper, to taste
  Accent seasoning, to taste
- 1   can (15 ounces) green peas

New and Improved Sausage Pilau

Anita chose a commercial precooked sausage that is lower in fat and sodium than most uncooked sausages available in the supermarket. She also opted to use a low-fat, low-salt canned chicken broth (to which she added fresh onions) instead of canned onion soup, which tends to be high in sodium. She used quick-cooking brown rice because it packs more fiber than white rice and requires less time to prepare. And she substituted frozen peas for the canned for fresher taste and lower sodium content. To add spice, Anita replaced the salt and Accent with cumin and she added red peppers for color and extra fiber.

The result? The new and improved version contains 253 fewer calories and 25 fewer grams of fat per serving than the original. Not bad for a few simple substitutions.

Per serving: 437 calories, 12 g. fat (25% of calories), 4 g. dietary fiber, 18 mg. cholesterol, 321 mg. sodium.

Serves 6.

7	ounces Swift Premium Brown and Serve fully cooked beef sausage, warmed and crumbled
1	large onion, thinly sliced
½	sweet red pepper, thinly sliced
½	teaspoon cumin
½	teaspoon ground black pepper
2	cans Campbell's Healthy Request chicken broth
2½	cups quick-cooking brown rice
1	package (10 ounces) frozen peas

Heat a 10- to 12-inch no-stick skillet. Add the sausage to the pan along with the onions and red peppers. Cook over medium heat for about 15 minutes, or until the onions are soft. Add the cumin, black pepper and broth. Bring to a boil over high heat, then add the rice and peas. Combine well. Lower the heat, cover and cook for 5 minutes. Remove from the heat and set aside for 5 minutes. Stir well before serving.

ORIGINAL BROCCOLI CASSEROLE

For broccoli lovers, this vegetable casserole is a dream come true.

Per serving: 488 calories, 44 g. fat (81% of calories), 4 g. dietary fiber, 113 mg. cholesterol, 986 mg. sodium.

- 2 packages (10 ounces each) frozen chopped broccoli
- 2 eggs, beaten
- 1 can cream of mushroom soup
- 1 cup mayonnaise
- 1 cup grated sharp Cheddar cheese
- 2 tablespoons minced onions
  Dash of ground black pepper
- ½–¾ cup crushed Ritz crackers

NEW AND IMPROVED BROCCOLI CASSEROLE

To reduce the fat content, Anita used an egg substitute instead of eggs and nonfat mayo instead of full-fat. She used a soup that is lower in fat and only six crackers for the topping. She also chose no-stick spray instead of butter to grease the dish. The result is a recipe with 335 fewer calories and 40 fewer grams of fat per serving.

Per serving: 153 calories, 4 g. fat (24% of calories), 6 g. dietary fiber, 7 mg. cholesterol, 866 mg. sodium.
SERVES 6 TO 8.

- 3 packages (10 ounces each) frozen chopped broccoli
- ½ cup fat-free egg substitute
- 1 can Campbell's Healthy Request cream of mushroom soup
- 1 cup fat-free mayonnaise
- ½ cup Kraft Healthy Favorites low-fat grated Cheddar cheese
- 2 tablespoons minced onions
  Dash of ground black pepper
- 6 Ritz crackers, crushed

Cook the broccoli according to package directions and drain. In a large bowl, combine the broccoli with the egg substitute, soup, mayonnaise, cheese, onions and pepper and mix well. Coat a 2-quart casserole with no-stick spray and pour in the mixture. Top with the crackers and bake at 350° for 30 minutes.

Pounds

Away

5

30 POUNDS DOWN— NOW AND FOREVER

The secret is adopting a new, leaner lifestyle.

Let's be brutally honest for a moment. Odds are you've attempted some form of weight loss in the past. It could even be that you were successful. But the fact that you're reading this chapter may mean that you weren't successful for very long. Like a pack of bloodhounds hot on your trail, those unwanted pounds picked up your scent and once again have you surrounded.

So how do you lose those dogs...er, pounds once and for all? You've got to change your scent. Become a new person. Become a person who no longer leads a 30-pounds-overweight lifestyle with its 30-pounds-overweight habits. And the trick is to do it without taxing your willpower, without subjecting yourself to undue deprivation and without adding additional rules and regulations that you can't wait to be rid of.

In other words, you have to create a new lifestyle that you can follow long enough to have it become second nature...an old friend that hangs around for the rest of your life, guarding you against ever gaining weight again.

UNDERSTAND THE BASICS

Does the phrase "Look before you leap" ring a bell? You can't make an honest commitment to do something unless you have some idea of what is required. So let's go through the weight-loss facts of life.

The first fact of life is that you're not going to become 30 pounds lighter by Valentine's Day...or by Memorial Day...or by the Fourth of July. Nor would you want to. After all, you want to not only lose the weight but also lose it permanently. And most experts agree that you have the best chances of doing just that if you take a gradual approach—no more than one pound a week.

The second fact of life is that through some combination of the right foods and the right exercise, you need to establish a daily deficit of 500 calories to lose that pound a week. Most weight-loss experts favor a program in which you cut 200 calories of fat (roughly 22 grams of fat) from your daily diet and burn off 300 calories through exercise to achieve the magic number. (When it comes to diet, it's actually better to count grams of fat instead of calories.)

And the third fact of life is that the first two facts are useless unless you follow them consistently and maintain them long after the 30 pounds are gone. That means being comfortable with the changes you make and not demanding more of yourself than you are prepared to give.

THE WORST FOE

Fat! Fat! Fat! We're not calling you names . . . we're talking about your diet. The average American's diet is approximately 40 percent fat. And because fat calories are more readily converted into body fat, those kinds of calories are the first ones you want to reduce. But the question is, by how much?

Diet experts advocate a fat intake of 25 percent of total calories. If you take a look at "Your Fat Budget" on page 60, you can see that for a woman to maintain a weight of 130 pounds, her caloric intake should be 1,600 with a fat allowance of 44 grams a day. If you are a 160-pound woman eating 2,000 calories a day (40 percent fat), you're currently consuming about 89 grams of fat. To reach a streamlined 130, you need to figure out how to be satisfied with 45 fewer grams of fat per day. But not all at once.

As mentioned, to jump onto the pound-a-week weight-loss wagon, you need to cut 500 calories a day: 200 from your daily intake and 300 through exercise. Since each gram of fat you eat is good for a whopping 9 calories, all that is really required to get the weight-loss wagon rolling is that you bid farewell to approximately 22 grams of fat per day.

After a certain amount of time, your 22-gram fat deficit, along with exercise, can slim your body to a point where it functions so efficiently that you stop losing weight. At this point, having become used to the dietary changes you've made, you can then go ahead and cut your fat intake far enough to reach

YOUR FAT BUDGET

Fat calories are more readily converted to body fat than carbohydrates and proteins are. And a high-fat diet is a risk factor for heart disease, diabetes and some cancers. Diet experts advocate a fat intake of 25 percent of total calories—that's substantially lower than the 38 to 40 percent most Americans consume.

The easy way to keep a handle on it is by using our "fat budget." Here's how it works: Find your goal weight. In the middle column is the number of calories you should eat each day to attain that weight. In the right-hand column is the number of grams of fat you should eat per day—your fat budget. Simply count the fat grams in each serving of the foods you eat to make sure you don't blow your budget. You can easily find that figure on most food products.

So, for example, if you're a woman weighing in at 140 and you'd like to get down to a lithe 130, your fat budget is 44 (25 percent calories from fat). That knocks a whopping 280 calories from your daily total, just from fat, assuming that you're eating about 1,700 calories a day, with 40 percent of those calories coming from fat. (Remember that each gram of fat equals 9 calories.)

the target fat budget on the chart that corresponds to your dream maintenance weight.

Warning: While sheer instinct may tell you to grit your teeth and cut all the fat in sight, hoping your willpower holds out, this is the last thing you should do. "Completely eliminating your problem foods may set you up for failure," says Judith S. Stern, R.D., Sc.D., professor of nutrition and internal medicine at the University of California, Davis. "You have to determine what those foods are and find ways to replace them if you can't control your appetite for them."

Diane Hanson, Ph.D., a lifestyle specialist at the Pritikin

Those figures don't take exercise into account—for every 100 calories you burn working out, you can add 3 grams of fat.

	Your Goal Weight (lb.)	Calorie Intake	Fat Budget (g.)
Women	110	1,300	36
	120	1,400	39
	130	1,600	44
	140	1,700	47
	150	1,800	50
	160	1,900	53
	170	2,000	56
	180	2,200	61
Men	130	1,800	50
	140	2,000	56
	150	2,100	58
	160	2,200	61
	170	2,400	67
	180	2,500	69
	190	2,700	75
	200	2,800	78

Longevity Center in Santa Monica, California, thinks of it as leveraging your food choices: "Doable changes make a big difference. For example, if that blue cheese dressing at lunch is dumping 16 or 24 grams of fat (equivalent to two or three tablespoons) onto your daily intake, a small packet of low-fat dressing brought from home can shave off the grams and still leave you satisfied."

The concept of food substitutes is nothing new. But what makes them so exciting now is the ever-growing selection of low-fat products that are on the market. The difference between a regular meat lasagna entrée and a low-fat one translates into a fat savings of seven grams. And the fastest-growing selection of products are the nonfat foods, which can really shave off the grams.

EXERCISE YOUR OPTIONS

Before you lull yourself to sleep with visions of breakfast-pastry weight loss, remember this: At some point you're going to have to sweat. A study conducted by Dr. Stern and her colleagues at the University of California, Davis, found that 90 percent of the participants who kept the weight off exercised regularly.

"To my mind, exercise has been undervalued with respect to weight loss," says Dr. Hanson. "As a matter of fact, when you look at what determines the continuation of a healthy lifestyle, exercise turns out to be the biggest behavioral driver."

It helps you look good and feel even better. It gives you a sense of accomplishment and mastery over your situation. "Current research is even showing that exercise may enhance your preference for fruits and vegetables," says Dr. Hanson.

Even if you already like veggies, exercise serves another important purpose. When you lower your caloric intake, your body, with an instinct for survival, slows down its metabolic rate and conserves energy. Exercise turns up the furnace so you become more efficient at burning fat. And, to drop a pound a week, you want that furnace stoked to the tune of 300 calories burned a day. How you accomplish that goal is a matter of what you like to do. But the good news is that even a brisk, 45-minute walk will do the trick. But the real trick is to do it every day.

MAKE THE COMMITMENT

The difference between losing weight and losing weight for good is commitment: a truly motivated desire not only to change but also to maintain that change. You can think of your commitment as a contract with yourself . . . a lifelong contract.

But as the old saying goes, "Contracts are made to be broken." And there isn't one of us who hasn't cheated on a deal with ourselves to become better, more effective or, more to the point, slimmer. In most cases, the problem is not our willpower but our initial commitment. It just wasn't strong enough.

Before starting your new, 30-pounds-lighter life, you need to make sure that you're revved and ready to do it. That the contract you make with yourself is so strong the Supreme Court couldn't break it, much less a tempting eclair with your name on it. Here's how to really, pardon the expression, commit yourself.

Choose the right moment. "It's not easy to begin a program during complicated periods in your life," says Kelly D. Brownell, Ph.D., a weight-loss expert and professor of psychology at Yale University. "Divorce, an illness in the family, problems at work—these are all things that can sap your energy and make your environment less supportive for the changes you want to make."

Of course, some people thrive on complications. A divorce, for example, may be just the motivating kick one person needs to make big changes as part of a whole new lifestyle. "The thing you need to consider," says Dr. Brownell, "is how you respond to complications. If stress, worry and a frantic pace erode your eating plan, making serious lifestyle changes in the midst of what's currently happening may be a mistake."

And you don't want to look just at the present. If you're due for stormy weather in the upcoming weeks and months, you may want to bide your time and embark on your new lifestyle once things calm down and the sun comes out again.

Choose the right commitment. Do you want to lose 30 pounds or do you want to lose the bad habits that made you overweight to begin with? While these two goals may seem to be heads and tails of the same coin, the side that lands up after the toss can make all the difference between 30 pounds down forever and 30 pounds down for an all-too-brief amount of time.

"If you find yourself fantasizing about the moment when you've lost 30 pounds and your diet is over, you're going to have problems," says Dr. Brownell. "At the point when you've finally reached that all-important number on the scale, there's a chance that your motivation to continue your healthy lifestyle may decrease, leaving you right back where you started."

So to make the commitment that will keep those pounds away forever, focus on the changes you plan to make, not on the 30 pounds. "Change your view of success," suggests Dr.

Hanson. "Rather than making weight loss your goal, make life-long health your goal. Rather than getting up each morning and heading for the scale, wake up and notice how much better you feel."

"I also find it helpful to think of overweight as a chronic condition," adds Dr. Brownell. "Just as diabetes requires constant maintenance lest it get serious, maintaining your ideal weight requires a lifetime of healthy eating and exercising practices."

Choose the right reason. "Some people lose weight because their husbands or wives want them to," says Jerome Brandon, Ph.D., exercise physiologist from Georgia State University in Atlanta and member of the American College of Sports Medicine. "The problem is that they make the effort to lose weight for someone else rather than because they themselves were personally motivated to do it. And eventually they will get tired of doing it."

So do it for yourself and not for someone else.

GET PREPARED

Every great journey begins with a great deal of preparation. How far would Christopher Columbus have gotten if he'd just awakened one morning, kissed his wife and headed out to discover the New World without the proper clothes, food, transportation or navigational equipment? To put it mildly, about as far as the Lisbon bus station.

Changing your life is not much different from making a journey. In both cases the most disappointing thing that can happen is that you have to give up because of difficulties you weren't prepared for. So no matter how charged up you are to start your new life, take some time to make the following preparations.

Educate yourself. If you're going to make lifestyle changes that you expect to practice for the rest of your life, you better darn well believe in them. And the best way to believe in something is to know beyond a shadow of a doubt how it works and, more important, why it works.

"First, when it comes to weight loss, there are scientific reasons for why it's best to eat and exercise a certain way," says Dr. Hanson. "If you understand how your body is designed to work, you'll believe in what you're doing and not be so inclined to give it up when the results are not happening as quickly as you want."

Second, by not understanding their body's own weight-loss mechanisms, people often select popular methods that doom them to failure. Then they blame themselves when they never really had a chance. "You may think that the more calories you deprive yourself of, the faster you'll lose weight, and that's initially true. But if you don't realize that the body slows down its fat-burning furnace when calories are suddenly reduced, you're ultimately in for a big disappointment," says Dr. Hanson. "The only thing that will happen over time is that you'll be hungrier, less inclined to continue your program and still not sure why you aren't maintaining the initial weight loss."

So start out right by getting the facts. Know without a doubt that what you are doing is right and will eventually provide you with the results you want regardless of how things appear to be going on a day-to-day basis.

Discover why you're really eating. "When talking to patients, I often ask them why they overeat, why are they doing something that they know is ultimately harmful," says Dean Ornish, M.D., author of *Eat More, Weigh Less* and director of the Preventive Medicine Research Institute in Sausalito, California. "And the answer often is, it helps to get them through the day. They may feel alienated or isolated, and eating helps them deal with the pain. One patient described how food temporarily fills the void and numbs the pain."

According to Dr. Ornish, change is not brought about solely by focusing on new behaviors such as changing your eating habits and exercising. You need to address the underlying reasons for your behaviors. Otherwise, the problem remains and will eventually sabotage all your good intentions and commitments.

If some form of mental stress is behind your eating problem, you'll need to find a nonfattening substitute. Relaxation techniques and spending more time with friends are both great alternatives that are far lower in calories than a banana split.

Remove roadblocks. Visualize the changes you want to make, then visualize all the things that could keep you from doing them. "It could be that you are unwilling to start exercising," says Dr. Brownell. "But if you dig a little deeper, you may find that the reason for this is that you are embarrassed to be seen exercising."

If this is the case, then starting your new lifestyle by taking out a membership at the trendy new health club that everyone is going to would probably be a mistake. Instead, acknowledge your fear and create an environment that guarantees privacy—maybe a stationary bike in your bedroom or an early-morning walk.

The same thing goes for food. If you know in your heart of hearts that you will never give up apple pie, then don't say you will and set yourself up for failure. Create a new recipe that makes apple pie less fattening.

Get support. "If you look at the factors that predict successful, permanent weight loss, social support ranks near the top of the list," says John Foreyt, Ph.D., coauthor of *Living without Dieting* and director of the Nutrition Research Clinic at Baylor College of Medicine in Waco, Texas. "I'd go so far as to say it is absolutely critical."

When starting your new lifestyle, Dr. Foreyt insists that you make a public commitment, but not for the normal reasons. "It's not that you want to force yourself into a situation you can't back down from because everyone knows about it. What you are actually doing is making an assertive appeal for people's help and understanding."

In his book, Dr. Foreyt outlines four levels of support, each with its own special purpose. "First there's your family. They're going to need to get used to your new lifestyle. It may be that certain foods have to be kept out of the house. Compromises on family time may need to be made when your exercise or other activities conflict with family plans."

The second level is composed of close friends. "Everyone should have someone they can call at 3:00 in the morning when temptation rears its ugly head," says Dr. Foreyt. "Even one really good friend can make the difference in a crisis."

The third and fourth levels involve support groups and your doctor. "Support groups are the perfect place to get advice and encouragement from people experiencing the same things you are," notes Dr. Foreyt. "And your doctor gives you information and knowledgeable feedback and helps you monitor your progress."

For some people, maintaining all four levels of support are not necessary. But Dr. Foreyt still maintains the need for some form of social support... even for loners. And more important, the kind of support you solicit needs to be specific.

"You don't want people giving you negative support," says Dr. Foreyt. "While someone pointing out your mistakes may work in the short run, it isn't motivating over the long haul. So you want to be very direct about asking people to say something positive about your accomplishments."

Find a monitoring system that works. "Your actual weight is the least important thing you can monitor," says Ronette Kolotkin, Ph.D., director of behavioral programs at Duke University's Diet and Fitness Center and coauthor of *The Duke University Medical Center Book of Diet and Fitness*. "Instead, I always encourage people to keep a diary not just of food and exercise but also of any important behavioral problems they encounter, such as rapid eating in certain situations or a tendency to binge at particular times."

At the end of each week, Dr. Kolotkin suggests that you study your diary as if you were a weight-loss professional studying someone else's case history. What advice would you give the patient? A one-year follow-up study conducted by Dr. Kolotkin found that people who monitored food intake, exercise and motivation were more successful than those who monitored weight only.

Paying daily homage to the bathroom scale is a dicey proposition for two reasons. First, your body weight is in constant flux. Up a pound today, down two tomorrow. A momentary gain in water weight may have you on the floor in despair despite the fact that the overall picture is improving.

Second, because your new lifestyle of healthy food and exercise is constantly trimming the fat while boosting the lean, a scale may show no change in weight even though you are getting slimmer and more toned by the minute. "That's why I always encourage people to wear form-fitting clothing," says Dr. Kolotkin. "As you lose weight, or even as your body composition changes, you'll get feedback every time you need to have your clothes taken in or even downsized a bit. You'll constantly be aware of what your body is doing by the way your clothes fit."

Plan for trouble. "I always tell people that they can expect to slip," says Dr. Kolotkin. "It will happen. And the difference between moving on and just plain giving up has to do with having some strategy to deal with momentary failure."

There are two ways you don't want to react to a temporary backslide. On one hand, you don't want to be cavalier: "Oh well, I ate that box of doughnuts, but I'll worry about it tomorrow." On the other hand, you don't want to overreact: "Oh no, this is the end! How can I go on after eating my weight in doughnuts? I'm no good."

"You've got to be rational," says Dr. Kolotkin. "The first thing to do is acknowledge exactly what happened. 'I was at a party, lost control and ate 5,000 calories.' Don't overemphasize or underemphasize what occurred. Next, put it into perspective. 'Over the past six months, I've made some great changes; I've exercised regularly, eaten right and made serious progress. Compared with what I've achieved, this one incident is hardly a catastrophe. I don't feel great about it, but it also isn't the end of the world.' "

Next comes action. A good general doesn't waste time dwelling on defeat. Instead, he immediately plots a course of action that will take him back on the road to victory. "This does not mean that you should exercise twice as long tomorrow to make up for today's mistake," says Dr. Kolotkin. "That's a lot like punishing yourself. Instead, you want to take steps to ensure that what happened does not happen again."

If you found yourself bingeing on a bag of chips lying wantonly open in the kitchen, you may want to purge your house of binge foods. If you stopped exercising for a week because of scheduling difficulties, spend some time arranging things so that it doesn't happen again. "Then get right back into your program," says Dr. Kolotkin. "Set two alarm clocks so that you can't avoid waking up and exercising. Meet a friend for lunch who will make sure you eat the right foods. Write out a meal plan."

In other words, make your lifestyle changes foolproof and inescapable for the next few days just to get yourself back on track. Dr. Kolotkin finds that for most people, it only takes three days for them to turn around a negative incident.

Learn from past mistakes. What went wrong the last time you tried to lose weight? "When I ask people that, I'll normally get an unproductive answer like 'I started eating again,' " says Dr. Kolotkin. "But you need to look at the underlying reasons. Was the diet you placed yourself on too restrictive? Did you find your meal plans were falling apart because you were often pressed for time and had to eat whatever was available?"

Take some time to dig deep and honestly analyze what went wrong.

Create an environment that makes change easy. Weight loss and lifestyle change are so often looked at as a matter of sheer willpower—that you can bulldoze your way through anything by the unyielding power of your mind. But why make things tough when you can make them easy? "I call it environmental engineering," says Dr. Hanson, "and it's really where you make changes in your environment that make it easier to succeed."

Environmental engineering is a powerful yet simple concept. If you find yourself getting hungry at 3:00 P.M. each day and the only thing available is a candy machine down the hall from your office, rather than fighting the urge to merge with a chocolate bar, why not reach into your desk and pull out the apple that you brought in for just such a moment?

As simple as the idea seems, it can be applied to all areas of your life. And more to the point, once you've determined why you've failed in the past, you can set up your new environment in order to help avoid past mistakes. "When I encounter people who have a problem with after-dinner eating, I often suggest that they get a small refrigerator for beverages and keep it in the den," says Dr. Kolotkin. "That way, even if they are thirsty, there's still no reason that they should enter the kitchen and be tempted by an open refrigerator."

What about exercise? The last time you tried a walking program it petered out after a week because you never seemed to have clean socks, batteries for your personal stereo or rain gear. This time, get equipped. Keep everything where you can get at it immediately. Keep an extra pair of walking shoes in your car for impromptu opportunities. Environmental engineering translates into "Make it so easy on yourself that you can't possibly fail!"

TAKE ACTION

You're ready to get started. But at what pace? Do you purge all the fat from your diet, change your eating habits and throw yourself into a daily exercise program in one fell swoop? Or should you ease into a lifestyle change like you ease into a hot tub: a few food substitutions . . . get comfortable . . . exercise a couple days a week . . . get comfortable?

When making your decision, you shouldn't be thinking about how fast you want to lose weight. The real question is, which technique makes it easier to assimilate changes that you can keep for life?

"If you're looking to make permanent lifestyle changes, my feeling is that incorporating them slowly makes them easier to get used to," says Dr. Kolotkin. "It's less overwhelming. The goals seem more attainable if you go step by step rather than full force."

Dr. Kolotkin experienced the power of small changes first-hand in working with a woman who, at 45, had never exercised and was so out of shape that a flight of stairs would leave her winded and grasping the banister for support. When she started her program, five minutes on a stationary bike was all she could do. "But rather than dwell on the thought that five minutes was not a very big or important change, she embraced the notion of small, gradual changes and took pride in the fact that she was actually exercising at all," says Dr. Kolotkin. "And gradually over the following months, as she got comfortable with one level of exercise, she increased it. She's now been in four walking marathons!"

Of course, Dr. Kolotkin is quick to admit that gradual change means gradual results, sometimes too gradual for some people. "It's not as exciting or motivating to make small changes, and so some people resist it, thinking that they'll never get where they want to be.

"But then I remind them that they tried cutting calories too quickly in the past and found the diet too restrictive to continue. Although they did lose some fast weight, in the end they went back to their old habits and gained it back."

But if you like big, exciting changes, you've got an ally in Dr. Ornish. According to him, comprehensive changes can make people feel so much better so quickly that rather than being overwhelmed by the changes, they are instead strongly motivated to continue.

So which is right for you? Part of the answer lies with your doctor and your current situation. Big dietary changes may be within your capability, but if you haven't been exercising regularly, too much activity too fast could be dangerous.

The second part of the answer has to do with your own mental makeup. Do big challenges bring out the best in you, or do you find them intimidating? What's worked for you in other situations? Remember, the only right answer here is the one that's right for you.

6
GENDER-FRIENDLY TACTICS TO TONE UP AND EAT SMART

When it comes to weight loss, you can turn sexual differences to your advantage.

Launching a weight-loss program with your spouse sounds so promising at the outset. But a few weeks later, you find yourself wondering why it isn't working for either of you. It could be because you're both going against your gender's built-in grain.

Research is beginning to show that what switches off her appetite might be a turn-on for his. Or that what sends her straight to the gym might leave him sitting on the couch. When it comes to food and fitness, each gender has its own preferences and behaviors. And the point is, if you wouldn't wear your spouse's Levi's, why try to fit into his or her weight loss plan?

Once you know where your own gender's best fat-fighting potential is, you can use it to tailor a weight-loss program that works for you. So here's a rundown of some of the most important (and surprising) his/her differences and how you can turn them to your advantage.

HE LIKES IT FLAMING.
SHE LIKES IT RELIABLE.

When it comes to food, men like it hot. In one study, spicy foods—hot peppers, in particular—rated high on the list of tastes men prefer. Researchers think this may be more about sensation seeking than it is about biology.

For women, it's healthy foods that score high. Among the favorites: yogurt, vegetables and fruits. Experts can't say for sure whether women love these tastes or just tend to love what's good for them. Either way, fostering this food preference puts you a step ahead when it comes to losing weight.

His strategy: Say *si* to salsa. This spicy convergence of tomatoes, hot peppers, cilantro, garlic, onion and other savory tastes adds zest to a meal without adding fat. Use it everywhere, advises Morton Shaevitz, Ph.D., author of *Lean and Mean*, especially where you used to load up on cheese, sour cream or other high-fat condiments.

Get creative about using salsa as an ingredient or topping. Put it on a baked potato and in omelets. Use it as a marinade for chicken or as a salad dressing. Just open a jar and pour it on—most packaged salsas contain little or no fat (although you'll want to check the label to be sure).

If salsa isn't your style, there are other hot and flavorful options, says Dr. Shaevitz. "Mushrooms, onions, green peppers, vinegar and mustards are good ways to give food excitement without calories."

Her strategy: Go wild with a good thing. While he's firing up his potato with hot peppers, rely on your more subtle favorites to spruce up yours. Try topping potatoes with nonfat or low-fat yogurt and vegetables. And take those veggies out of the ho-hum by cooking them in some chicken broth or by sautéing them with a little garlic and a bit of onion.

Capitalize on your taste for fruit by bringing it into the main course. American Dietetic Association spokesperson Evelyn Tribole, R.D., author of *Eating on the Run*, recommends a family favorite: fruit pizza. She creates hers on a homemade, low-fat, whole-wheat pastry crust, but any low-fat crust will do. It's only five steps to the finish from there: Mix fat-free cream cheese with nonfat or low-fat ricotta, and spread that over the baked crust. Add kiwi or other fruits—peaches, berries or other seasonal favorites—as if they were pepperoni. Zap some marmalade in the microwave and brush it on top with a pastry brush and eat.

HIS MIRROR SAYS ARNOLD SCHWARZENEGGER. HERS SAYS FAT LADY AT THE CIRCUS.

He looks into the mirror and sees burly and strong. She looks in and sees her hips stretched out to the size of Nebraska. What it's about is body image, and surveys show that high numbers of Americans are turning their reflections into funhouse mirror distortions. The problem is, basing a weight loss program on what you think you should look like or weigh undoes the efforts of both genders.

Many overweight men think they look fine. In fact, 40 percent of overweight men "felt at about the right weight," according to one *Prevention* magazine index, a survey of the nation's health. Others may weigh in on target according to the height and weight charts, but they have potbellies and no buns. Either way, what looks healthy from the outside might not be so on the inside—their heft may be heightening their risk for heart disease.

On the female side of the chart, the desire to be superslim may lead her to aim for a body weight far below what she's genetically programmed to be. Look at the facts: According to *Prevention*'s Healthy Women Survey, 73 percent of the women who responded felt they needed to lose pounds to achieve a healthy body weight. Yet only 44 percent of the surveyed women were actually overweight.

Both genders can avoid spinning the wheels of their diet plans by turning away from an ideal weight and setting their sights on a healthy one.

His and her strategy: Change your thinking. Don't let your weight determine your behavior. Let healthy habits determine your weight. That is, take your focus off what you believe your body should weigh and learn what's healthy for it to weigh.

"We don't think that everybody should be the same height. There's no biological reason why everybody should line up in a row and be the same weight. It's just not the way biology works," says diet expert C. Wayne Callaway, M.D., associate clinical professor of medicine at George Washington University Medical Center in Washington, D.C., and member of the U.S. dietary guidelines advisory committee. Some men can be perfectly healthy at 210 pounds, while others will be metabolically obese at 180 because their cholesterol levels will be way out of balance, with triglycerides climbing and high-density lipoprotein (HDL, or good, cholesterol) levels plummeting. It all depends on what your body's made to handle.

To determine what's healthy for you, set a new standard by looking inside. First, check your health statistics. According to the National Institutes of Health's National High Blood Pressure Education Program, you should make sure your cholesterol is under 200, your blood pressure is under 140/90 and your blood sugar levels are normal.

Next, look at fitness or performance. Can you do what you need to do and feel good? You don't have to be able to do everything your 22-year-old aerobics teacher does. But you should be able to walk briskly without being short of breath and be able to talk at the same time.

Finally, ask your doctor if your current weight will put you at risk for obesity-related diseases in the future.

If your inner health isn't where it should be, work with your doctor, registered dietitian or exercise physiologist to establish smart eating and exercise behaviors that will get you healthy and keep you there. When you do that, you might find yourself at a lower (or higher!) weight than you thought was ideal. If you feel good, you move well and your health is on target, why let the number on the scale determine what you do or how you feel about yourself?

HIS GUT WANTS TO GAIN IT. HER HIPS WANT TO HOLD IT.

Why is it that he can get a potbelly and lose it in no time, while her fat seems to settle on her hips and thighs for the duration, even though she's losing weight?

In a word, estrogen. Women have a greater number of fat cells on the hips and thighs than do men, and it's part of estrogen's job to take fat there and keep it there. In fact, the average female body wants 120,000 calories stored up as fat so it can deliver the next generation, even in a famine.

Guys, on the other hand, get fat in the belly first because, some experts believe, the fat cells there are more metabolically active. Bellies gain weight quickly but give it up quickly, too. As short-term energy stores, they were especially handy in hunter-gatherer days when quick access to body fuel got you safely out of the reach of what might have been hunting you.

If you're thinking that belly fat is the kind to have, think again. Big bellies can swell your risks for numerous diseases. "So far, nearly everything that's been studied that's associated with obesity—heart disease, strokes, diabetes and high blood pressure—has to do more with belly fat than hip and thigh fat," says Dr. Callaway.

Doctors determine risk with what they call the waist-to-hip ratio (WHR). The higher the ratio, the greater the risk. That puts men with "spare tires" at higher risk than so-called pear-shaped women. Women who are naturally apple-shaped, or postmenopausal women whose fat has redistributed farther north, fall in between.

Both genders can burn this excess fat with aerobic exercise. While you can't spot-reduce, you can choose exercises that tone your trouble spots, making them appear trimmer once the weight is gone.

His strategy: Smoothing your stomach is a threefold process. First, cut down on what's building it up. Research shows that the gut grabs fat when you drink alcohol, smoke or are under stress.

Second, reduce what's already there with aerobic exercise. You'll need at least 20 to 30 minutes of continuous aerobic exercise three times per week to get things moving. Remember that you not only have to exercise enough to release fat into the bloodstream, you also have to keep going long enough to burn it.

Third, put the crunch on it. Abdominal crunches, or sit-ups, won't do much to burn off fat. But they will tone the area so it looks tighter and firmer when the fat is gone.

Her strategy: Aerobic exercise is your best bet for fighting fat, too. Make your workout time do double duty by choosing fat-burning exercises that also tone your trouble spots. Walking, jogging and using stair-climbers and cross-country ski machines are good ways to get the large muscles in the legs and hips in shape so they'll look tighter and slimmer when the fat is gone. To give those areas even more tone, ask the gym fitness instructor to show you how to use the leg machine that works both the inside and outside muscles in your legs.

Finally, stay tuned to the subtle changes. While his gut seems to be just dropping off, keep in mind that you lose weight more uniformly, so your body gets smaller without changing shape dramatically.

HE LOSES 20 POUNDS. SHE LOSES 15.

Over the same amount of time and with the same amount of physical activity, he can actually lose more pounds than she can, says George L. Blackburn, M.D., Prevention advisor and chief of the Nutrition/Metabolism Laboratory at New England Deaconess Hospital in Boston. As he puts it, "The man would be a V8 engine and the woman a V6."

Men burn calories faster for two reasons. First, they're usually heavier to begin with and are burning more calories all the time. (It takes more energy to carry 200 pounds one step than it does to carry 150 pounds one step.) Second, guys have a greater proportion of fat-burning muscle, or fat-free mass, than women do. Healthy young men have about 12 to 19 percent body fat; older men have about 15 to 22 percent. Women, on the other hand, have between 19 and 26 percent when they're younger, which rises to 22 to 30 percent in older women.

His strategy: Don't get smug. When you compare percentages, not pounds, you'll see that you're making the same relative weight reduction as she is. If you weigh 200 pounds and lose 20, you're losing 10 percent of your body weight. If she weighs 150 pounds and loses 15, she's done the same thing. Don't let too much ride on the initial quick drop, says Dr. Callaway. Men tend to feel really great when the numbers are dropping, but when things level off, in comes boredom. Once the challenge is gone, you'll return to your old way of eating and put the pounds right back on. Here again, instead of focusing on the numbers, focus on how you feel.

Her strategy: Be patient. Not only do you burn calories more slowly because you're smaller, you may also have slowed down because you've tried to lose weight before—28 percent of you started doing it seriously at age 17 or younger.

"There's some evidence that the more you diet, the better you get at starvation," says Dr. Callaway. When frequent dieters cut their intake, their bodies prepare for starvation. Cells may clutch hard to the energy already in them and gobble up more when they get it. That makes it tougher to lose weight and easier to gain it back. You can break the cycle, however, with realistic weight-loss expectations of a half-pound to one pound per week.

To avoid feeling discouraged, don't compare the numbers on your scale with his. If you have to compare, use percent reductions.

HE CRAVES MEATS.
SHE CRAVES SWEETS.

Wouldn't it be great if when a craving hit, it was for apples or carrots? No such luck. Two studies, one on obese men and women, another on normal-weight people, suggest that men favor or crave meats and cheeses, and women prefer sweets and desserts—all fats, fats, fats.

Researchers can't yet pinpoint whether cravings are about texture, taste or emotions, says cravings expert Marcia Pelchat, Ph.D., research scientist at Monell Chemical Senses Center in Philadelphia. Studies do not show whether substituting low-fat or nonfat versions for your favorite high-fat foods will satisfy your cravings, but it's certainly worth a try. By knowing where your weaknesses are, you can plan substitutions that may put your fat intake at the right level. Letting it settle at about 25 percent of your total calorie intake will help you avoid eating fats your body can't use (and fats it sticks into storage). It can also put a hold on heart disease by reducing high serum cholesterol.

His strategy: First, switch to ground turkey or chicken breast instead of beef, and you'll find big fat savings. In a three-ounce serving, ground turkey has about 8 grams of fat. Ground beef has about 13.

Then, slice the portion size. "Most recipes say 'Use one

pound of meat.' There's nothing magic about one pound. You can usually cut that down without missing it," says Tribole. In any case, trim off the fat—one study shows that men are less likely than women to trim the visible fat from their meat, but it only takes a second to do.

Her strategy: Temper your chocolate cravings when premenstrual syndrome hits. Your best defense, advises Thomas A. Wadden, Ph.D., director of the weight and eating disorders program at the University of Pennsylvania in Philadelphia, is to decide ahead of time what to do about it.

You can decide to allow yourself a certain amount on the two or three days you're particularly craving it. Or if portions are difficult, remove chocolate from your house and just go out for a treat when you want it, he says.

By the way, the second biggest fat trap in the female diet is salad dressing. Although women haven't been shown to crave it, you definitely eat it. Studies show that women with the highest fat intakes ate regular salad dressing in larger portions and more frequently than did women with lowest fat intakes.

Try nonfat bottled dressings or make your own low-fat ones. Puree favorite ingredients, such as mustard, garlic, Worcestershire sauce and minced sun-dried tomatoes, into nonfat cottage cheese or plain, nonfat yogurt. Tracy Ritter, chef-owner of Stamina Cuisine in San Diego recommends a vegetable-based dressing made of steamed carrots. Simply puree them with defatted chicken stock and rice-wine vinegar. Some fresh ginger, lemon juice and a sprinkle of hot-pepper sauce finishes it off with zest.

HE GAINS WEIGHT WITH FRIENDS. SHE GAINS IT ALONE.

For both sexes, who's at the table may be just as important as what's on it. Dr. Shaevitz has observed that men do most of their overeating in social situations; women do it in private. Whether they're around other men or just Mom, men get encouraged to eat a lot—a "lumberjack appetite" can be a desirable male trait.

Women, in contrast, may eat less in public to appear more feminine, says Dr. Shaevitz. That works to their favor when they're out, but what they do at home is another story.

"Women are so busy taking care of other people that the one thing they do to 'care for themselves' is eat something that tastes good," says Dr. Wadden. In fact, women are nearly twice as likely as men to eat a special dessert to indulge themselves. When women are around food all day or are too busy to sit down and eat, it's easy to pick up too many calories. "The psychology there is that 'if you're not sitting down, it doesn't count,' " says Dr. Wadden. "Unfortunately, it does."

His strategy: Keep talking. "View the evening as a social event with food present, rather than an eating event with people present," says Dr. Shaevitz. Make your focus the people, not the food, and you'll find that you can keep both your weight loss plan and your social life intact. Chances are, people will remember how charming you were, not how much you ate.

If, however, you're in a situation where there's extreme pressure to eat a lot, fill your plate high. Just substitute less-calorie-dense foods for the standard fare. Beef up a meal, so to speak, with two baked potatoes, lots of vegetables or extra bread.

If lunches out lead healthy eating astray, find a standard meal that's 500 to 700 calories. Men have to avoid having a dinner meal at lunch and then again in the evening, says Dr. Wadden. Good lunch options include a good-size salad with turkey or chicken in it or a turkey sandwich that's easy on the mayo.

Her strategy: Give priority to yourself. Then make yourself dinner. When your schedule is tight, don't try to find time for yourself. Make it. Getting out of the kitchen will pick you up better than a hot-fudge sundae will. "If you can get 15 minutes to do something for yourself, whether that's going for a walk in the evening, reading a book for a few minutes or watching a show on television, that's more helpful than just eating," says Dr. Wadden. Plus, you won't feel bad about it later.

When you do need to be around food—if you're preparing it for the family—remember that a bite here and there can soon hit heavy below the belt. Stock the kitchen in your favor by keeping good foods in clear containers and fat-filled snacks in opaque, hard-to-reach ones.

Decrease your temptation to snack when the kids do by feeding them ready-made snacks or ones in single-serving packages. Contribute what's left to Mother Nature. You can't feel guilty about tossing leftovers when they help out the compost heap.

HE EXERCISES TO GET BIGGER. SHE EXERCISES TO GET SMALLER.

Both of you know that exercise is essential in any weight loss program. To get it, it's natural for him to head to the weight room and her to take up aerobics, says Dr. Shaevitz. That's a good start, but you're both missing weight loss opportunities unless you reach to the other's side of the gym.

His strategy: Add aerobics. This not only melts fat but also helps stave off cardiovascular disease in the process. According to the American Heart Association, being sedentary has as negative an effect on your heart's health as high blood cholesterol, high blood pressure or smoking.

Aerobics doesn't mean wearing a cute little outfit and going to class three times a week. It means getting out and moving. In a study of more than 18,000 people trying to lose weight, walking was the number-one favorite way to get physical activity. Walkers over the age of 40 also weighed less than the people trying to lose weight who reported no activity. For exercise, start with one-half mile and try to increase the distance by a half-mile each week.

Make walking a way of life, says Loretta DiPietro, Ph.D., epidemiologist and assistant fellow at the John B. Pierce Laboratory at Yale University School of Medicine. "If you're going to drive, park your car a little farther away and walk to your destination. If you take mass transportation, get off a little sooner and walk two or three stops. Take the stairs rather than the elevator. If you have to start by taking them down, then take them down and the elevator up. People wonder, what difference is that going to make? But think about the cumulative effect. If I deposit $5 a week in my checking account, over time, it adds up."

Her strategy: Borrow his barbells. When those 18,000 dieters were questioned about their exercise programs, weight training wasn't mentioned as a strategy for weight loss. If weights aren't part of your workout, you're missing an important way to boost your fat-burning ability. The more muscle you have, potentially the more fat you burn—even when you're not at the gym.

Three days a week is all it takes to bump up your metabolic rate, your strength and your percentage of muscle (called lean body mass). An added bonus is that weight-bearing exercise may help ward off osteoporosis, too.

"A woman can make phenomenal gains in strength with very little change in the overall size of her muscle," explains Sydney Bonnick, M.D., who has designed exercise programs especially for women at the Cooper Clinic in Dallas. "So if she's worrying about her appearance as a result of strength training, she should know that what you tend to see is a decrease in the size of her hips and thighs. The amount of fat goes down and cancels out the increase in the size of the muscle. So she really doesn't get bigger, but she does look better."

Women who have moved into the weight training arena tend to stick with it, says Dr. Bonnick. "When they realize how good they feel and how much better they look, you can't get them out of the gym."

He Likes a Solo Win. She Prefers Teamwork.

"Men approach weight loss almost like a competitive sport," says Dr. Wadden. "When you say that group A of dieters is going to compete against group B, you'll always find that the men in group A take on group B as fiercely as they can." Women, on the other hand, help pull each other toward the finish line. One woman can be another's personal cheerleader, support system and healthy-recipe file all in one. "Women enjoy discussing their feelings about food, about difficulties they're having controlling their eating, and they're more likely to share helpful comments," he says.

His strategy: Make a bet. Capitalize on your competitive nature by setting a weight loss goal with a friend. Then check in with each other every week.

Your best bet is one that encourages healthy eating habits. See who can stick to a challenge of the week, such as cutting down on fat intake or pruning the number of sugared sodas consumed in a day. That way, you're banking on healthy new habits, and you won't fall prey to lose-it-fast behaviors that can get you to your goal but can't keep you there.

"In order to lose a half-pound a week, it's best if you can do it by changing your behaviors over time," adds Dr. Callaway. There's some evidence that if you lose weight slowly, your metabolic rate doesn't decline in order to conserve energy. As a result, you don't set up the biological signals for bingeing that occur when you starve and refeed.

Her strategy: Find a buddy. Set aside time to trade strategies, recipes and food-preparation tips. Better yet, share what works while you're out for a walk. Capitalize on your cooperative nature by cooking together. Or use teamwork to find the lowest-fat food selections at the grocery store. Or trade shopping lists if impulse buys are your downfall.

7
FOODS FOR LIFE

Sink your teeth into this no-hunger weight-loss plan.

You probably already know all about why you should drop those extra pounds. Healthwise, you can cut your risk of heart attack by 35 to 55 percent and substantially lower your chances of developing other diseases, like diabetes and breast cancer. Your cholesterol, blood pressure and blood sugar levels will tumble, dramatically improving your health and sense of well-being. Not to mention that you'll again be able to wear that little black dress that's been gathering dust in your closet or appear in shorts on the tennis court without suffering embarrassment.

You know why you need to lose—the big question is how. If you've tried before, you may be haunted by memories of detailed food diaries, scales and measuring spoons to apportion your daily bread. You may recall choking down bowl after bowl of undressed salad and pining for foods you could really sink your teeth into.

FOODS YOU CAN COUNT ON

But here's some good news. Successful weight loss doesn't have to be that complicated—and you don't have to live on carrot sticks and lettuce.

In fact, while you may be able to lose some weight over the short term, if you drastically change your diet by cutting out substantial foods and relying too heavily on low-calorie foods, you may actually sabotage your chances of achieving weight loss that lasts.

Here's why. Food gives you energy. Your body needs a certain amount of it to get through the day. And the more active you are and the more muscle you have, the more fuel you need. When you're trying to lose weight, you're aiming to create a daily calorie "deficit"—to take in less fuel than you burn.

But if you don't fuel your body properly—if you restrict yourself to super low calorie, "low-octane" foods—it's like asking your Chevy to get you across town on "empty." You can end up weak, lethargic and starving. "That can stimulate your appetite and may cause you to binge," says George Blackburn, M.D., chief of the nutrition and metabolism laboratory at New England Deaconess Hospital in Boston. Desperate for energy and feeling deprived, you're likely to backslide—to gain back the weight you lost, and then some, by going back to your old eating habits.

The solution is simple. Focus on eating more—that's right, more—"high-octane" foods that are naturally low in fat, high in carbohydrates and high in fiber. These five kinds of foods, in particular, are:

• Potatoes and sweet potatoes

• Legumes: pinto beans, kidney beans and lentils

• Whole grains: whole-grain cereals, pastas, breads and brown rice

• Fruits: apples, bananas, berries and melon

• Skim milk and skim-milk products: cottage cheese and yogurt

These foods not only give you the energy you need to power through an active life, they also can help you lose weight the no-hunger way, Dr. Blackburn says. Here's how.

They help keep blood sugar levels stable. Dramatic swings in blood sugar from feasting and fasting can stimulate your appetite and cause you to overeat. They're hearty foods. They keep you feeling fuller longer.

They have half the calories, per bite, as fatty foods. That means you can eat twice as much and still take in fewer calories than you would if you were eating fatty foods. (But, because high-octane foods are so filling, you would probably be stuffed if you tried!)

They naturally drive down your fat intake. All you have to do is make sure they're not prepared with too much fat or doused with rich sauces that offset their weight-loss benefits.

Plus, if you focus on adding good-for-you foods to your diet instead of depriving yourself of the fatty foods you've always loved, you may have an easier time sticking with your new-found way of eating. "It's not what you shouldn't eat, it's what you should eat," Dr. Blackburn says.

Here's how this strategy can translate into a 15-pound weight loss in 12 weeks. To lose 1 to 2 pounds a week (the amount experts say is best to aim for if you want weight loss to last), you need to cut about 500 calories a day. You can do that by:

• Drinking one glass of skim milk (instead of whole milk)

• Eating one bowl of oatmeal (instead of a croissant)

• Snacking on fruit (instead of a granola bar)

• Having oven-fried potatoes, baked with a bit of vegetable-oil spray (instead of french fries)

• Having a bowl of bean-based vegetarian chili (instead of chili with ground beef)

That's your 500 calories, right there. And that doesn't take into account your exercise routine, which can burn off another 200 to 300 calories a day.

Most of the calories you cut when you fill up on these high-octane foods are from fat. That's important because fat calories are easily stored by our bodies as fat, while carbohydrates (found abundantly in the five kinds of high-octane foods) are more easily burned as fuel.

Don't worry so much about weighing and measuring how

much you're eating. Simply choose these heartier foods first when you're hungry and stop when you're full. You know when you need to eat and when you've had enough. And be a little creative with your meals and snacks. "For example, try low-sugar, whole-grain cereal in the evenings or for a serious snack," Dr. Blackburn says. That's also a way to sneak more skim milk into your diet—something that's crucial for women who need calcium to prevent bone loss as they age. If you're fighting the switch from whole milk to skim, first go to 2 percent, then from 2 percent to 1 percent, then to skim.

You're in the Driver's Seat

8
SMALL CHANGES, BIG BENEFITS

Fine-tune your healthy-living lifestyle.

We all know the benefits of getting more exercise, eating less fat and reducing the amount of stress and tension in our lives. Problem is, there's so much good health information out there, it's difficult to know where to begin.

It's important to remind yourself that you don't have to turn the entire world upside down in order to achieve a healthy lifestyle, experts say. For most of us, all that's required is a little fine-tuning. Best of all, the changes we need to make are, in most cases, fast, easy and, above all, fun.

MAKE THE MOST OF FITNESS

We all need to explore the pleasures of exercise. Despite the preachings of some fitness gurus, pain does not equal gain. In fact, as experts often remind us, the more we enjoy exercise, the more likely—and the more often—we'll do it. Here are some ideas that underscore the "pleasure principle."

Play to your preferences. Think about an activity that you really love. Any activity—it doesn't have to be fitness-oriented. Then get creative, combining fun with a physical challenge. Love to shop? Fitness walk along your favorite shopping district before the stores open and preview the window displays. Got the travel bug? Sign up for a fitness-oriented vacation. You'd rather be doing crafts? Take a nature walk and collect pinecones, twigs and other found objects for your next project.

Get active any way you choose. If you have an aversion to exercise, a fresh perspective may help, says weight-control specialist Susan Yanovski, M.D. "In our field, we're getting away from prescribing specific exercises. Instead we encourage our patients to develop an active lifestyle." Variety is the key. Try all kinds of activities—bird-watching, gardening, Ping-Pong, horseback riding, social dancing. The best workouts aren't necessarily the ones that deliver the greatest calorie burn; they're the activities you enjoy most because you're more likely to do them.

Socialize . . . actively! Instead of a sit-down dinner party, throw a backyard badminton party (with light finger foods and fresh fruit or vegetable cocktails between sets). Or invite a few friends to join you on a nature hike and share a picnic lunch. Don't miss a step at holidays, either; create active celebrations with family or friends.

Make the time. Exercise doesn't kill time, it creates time. After the first week or so of beginning a regular exercise program, many people say that their energy and stamina surge to the point where they feel like they've gained more productive hours in a day. Consider, too: By reducing your risk of heart disease, osteoporosis and other life-threatening diseases, regular aerobic exercise can add days, even years, to your life. Still wondering how to shoehorn an hour of exercise into a snug schedule? Try this:

• Borrow an hour of early-morning snooze time. Before your day begins, little can come between you and your workout. That may explain why morning exercisers tend to stick with their fitness programs better, says Dr. Yanovski. Cardiologist Debra Judelson, M.D., notes, "When patients come to me and say they're always tired, I say 'Get up early and take a brisk walk.' Inevitably, they come back and say 'I feel great and have much more energy.' "

• Walk and talk. Time spent chatting on the telephone, over lunch or across a desk may provide an opportunity for fitness. Whether it's an intimate conversation with a good friend or a brainstorming session for an annual fund-raiser, consider talking while you walk.

Join the resistance. Weight training may offer the most benefit to older (postmenopausal) women. In one study done with a group of people over age 90, a couple of them even ended up throwing away their canes! Resistance training can also help strengthen and maintain bone, to ward off crippling osteoporosis. So, get pumping!

Hop on your stationary bike. This is a resistance exercise that benefits the crucial hip area. "Just increase the resistance against which you're pedaling," says Sydney Bonnick, M.D., director of osteoporosis services at the Cooper Clinic in Dallas. "That strengthens the muscles of the upper hips and thighs, so they pull on the bone, which is a good stimulus to bone growth." You can get the same effect on a bicycle outdoors by going uphill. However, bicycling doesn't strengthen the spine; for that, the impact of brisk walking or jogging does wonders.

Power Up with Good Nutrition

We're doing a great job of trimming the fat. Now we need to tickle our taste buds.

"If healthy eating is always a kind of drudgery—a prison of rice cakes and water—you're not going to last and you'll go back to the full-fat stuff," says nutritionist Evelyn Tribole, R.D., author of *Eating on the Run*. To put flavor and fun on your plate:

Fresh is best. "Vegetables right out of the ground are incredible," says food consultant Aliza Green, a Philadelphia chef with 15 years experience. But that heavenly flavor vanishes when veggies sit around. To get the most intense flavor, look for vegetables in season. Go to farmers' markets or to roadside stands, or find the supermarket in your area known for the best produce.

Make new friends on the produce aisle. Have you had a plumcot—a sweet, tangy cross between plum and apricot? Or yellow fingers—rich, buttery-tasting potatoes the size of your fingers? New produce varieties can taste great—and they're fun to name-drop!

Try exotic herbs and spices, particularly fresh ones. The flavor success of many healthy recipes depends on them. Many wonderful seasonings, such as cilantro, coriander seed, cumin and chilies, are acquired tastes. You need repeated exposures—and then you love them! Green's gentle but firm advice for trying a new herb or spice? "Don't be afraid—give it a chance."

Bet on basil. Green calls it the "number-one, most important, don't-live-without-it herb!" She also says it's best when it's fresh: "It's practically worthless when it's dried." Look for fresh basil in farmers' markets or the produce section of your supermarket. To store it, cut the fresh stems and place the "bouquet" in a glass of water; cover with a plastic bag and refrigerate. If stored properly, it keeps about a week. Make sure your refrigerator isn't too cold, because basil freezes easily.

Break mealtime monotony with interesting breads. Round out summer meals of salad or chilled soup with luscious slices of multigrain, pumpernickel, herb, raisin or sourdough breads. Supermarket bakeries now offer them fresh. And hearty whole-grain breads don't need butter to taste fabulous.

Perk up bland meals with fat-free condiments. Try mango chutney with a plain baked chicken breast. Or coarsegrain mustard instead of mayo on a turkey breast sandwich.

BONE UP ON CALCIUM

Low calcium intake is almost certainly linked to osteoporosis, the notorious brittle-bone condition that can debilitate and kill. And few women are consuming enough calcium to prevent this. Some experts recommend 1,000 milligrams a day, with 1,500 milligrams for women under 25 (who are still building peak bone mass) and 1,500 milligrams for women after menopause (when bones lose calcium faster). To preserve strong bones:

Reach for the dairy. "Unfortunately, most women are running at least half a quart low on milk every day," says osteoporosis expert Doris Gorka Bartuska, M.D., director, Division of Endocrinology and Metabolism, Medical College of Pennsylvania in Philadelphia. And that's a source of concern. Nonfat milk and yogurt—along with calcium-fortified orange juice—are the top dietary sources of calcium. No other foods come close in terms of calcium availability and absorbability.

Other foods considered "good" calcium sources come up short by comparison. Regular cheese is higher in fat. Cottage cheese, kidney beans and cooked kale or broccoli deliver much less calcium. Nonfat frozen desserts, including frozen yogurt, contain less calcium and more calories. The calcium in spinach is much less absorbable. And sardines or salmon with bones is not a regular part of most diets. Consider these foods as extras only, not as mainstays, to boost calcium intake.

Reach for a calcium supplement. For many women, getting all the calcium they need from food is a tall order, says Dr. Bartuska. A daily multivitamin/mineral supplement usually supplies just 200 milligrams or less—not nearly enough to make up the difference. Most women need to supplement with 500 milligrams or more a day, Dr. Bartuska explains. She recommends chewable calcium carbonate. It provides the most calcium per tablet, and the chewing helps it dissolve for easier absorption. She suggests calcium citrate for women who find that calcium carbonate causes bloating or constipation. Note: If you take more than 500 milligrams of supplemental calcium, divide the dosage between morning and evening to maximize absorption.

There's no reason to exceed 1,500 milligrams total calcium intake (food plus supplement) per day, because there really is no proof that more than that is beneficial. If you've had kidney stones or you've been advised to avoid calcium, or if you are considering supplementation, discuss it with your doctor. To ensure optimum bone health, other factors—such as menopause (low estrogen), vitamin D status, lack of weight-bearing exercise, drugs that may drive calcium down, heredity and age—may need to be evaluated as well.

"In a perfect world, you'd have perfect eating habits. But in the real world, it's not a bad idea to take a multivitamin/mineral supplement," says Elaine Feldman, M.D., director emeritus of the Georgia Institute of Human Nutrition at the Medical College of Georgia School of Medicine in Augusta.

In particular, Dr. Feldman advises supplements for women who are dieting, past middle age or sedentary. These women are likely to be consuming too few calories to get all the essential nutrients—even with the best intentions, she says.

SLIMMING STRATEGIES

Many of us could benefit from fine-tuning our weight-loss programs. What do you do when a good exercise regimen and low-fat eating plan don't add up to your weight-loss goals?

Beware of hefty portions. Many nutritionists say they're now seeing "fat-free bingeing" in clients who treat reduced-fat foods as if they were calorie-free, which of course isn't true, says Tribole.

Forego the "fudge factor." This is the all-too-human tendency to underestimate how much we eat and overestimate how much we exercise. The fudge factor is extremely common, says Dr. Feldman. Recently, for example, researchers at St. Luke's–Roosevelt Hospital Center in New York City found that dieters who honestly believed they ate an average of 1,028 calories a day really were consuming an average of 2,081 calories a day—an extra 1,000 calories! Many also had a tendency to overestimate the amount of time they spent exercising.

The best way to keep a close watch on what you're consuming is to keep a food diary. Log in every morsel that passes your lips. Sometimes, just committing this information to paper is enough to heighten your awareness of how much you're really eating. For assistance in evaluating your fat or calorie intake, ask your doctor to recommend a dietitian.

As for keeping tabs on your exercise time: Wear a watch and log the actual activity time. Do not mistake activity time for gym time: Getting dressed, showering or chatting with friends doesn't count, unless, of course, you're working out at the same time.

Satisfy your sweet tooth. Experts say the craving for sweetness usually goes hand-in-hand with a craving for fat. How do you satisfy both without sabotaging your diet? Suck on a butterscotch drop. For all that buttery sweetness, you get only about 25 calories and about one-tenth of a gram of fat (from the tiny amount of butter it contains).

By delivering rich, sugary flavor in a measured morsel that takes about 15 minutes to dissolve in your mouth, butterscotch drops could help get you through your worst snack attacks feeling not so deprived. In the same 15 minutes, you could easily eat 1½ cups of nonfat frozen yogurt for 360 calories or 1½ cups of premium ice cream for up to 900 calories!

STRESS BUSTERS

Many of us could do well to seek a little support from our friends and community. Several studies have shown that social contacts improve quality of life, reduce anxiety and depression and increase life span.

"Both psychologically and physiologically, there's something about sharing problems that helps us put them in perspective, makes us blame ourselves less, enhances our coping skills," says David Spiegel, M.D., professor of psychiatry at Stanford University who's a leading researcher in this field. If you don't have a strong social network, here's how you can reach out and develop one.

Take "doing" classes. Listening to a lecture is not a great way to meet people. But a bridge class, a cooking class, a dancing class or a language class is. It's a perfect opportunity to interact with people who share interests with you and to expand your network of friends.

Find a support group in your flavor. Whatever your life situation or issue, there's probably a support group for you. Whether you've had your first baby after 35 or you're a home-based professional or you're looking for a new job, you can find a group of like-minded people. Check out the offerings in adult-education programs, hospitals and organizations of all kinds.

Volunteer. It's old advice, but good advice. Just make sure the volunteer work doesn't keep you at home—like making telephone calls. The most life-enhancing kind of volunteer work, research indicates, involves direct contact.

9
SUPPLEMENTAL PROTECTION

Why do some of America's top experts take dietary supplements?

Ask your doctor for advice concerning supplements, and the odds are he will tell you that your best bet is to get your vitamins from a balanced diet. But in light of all the news about vitamin research, this reply may leave you cold. You want more guidance than "Forget supplements and eat a balanced diet." You want help in making a very personal decision about whether to take supplements.

Certainly, knowing more about the relevant evidence can help. But wouldn't it also be interesting to know whether your doctor took supplements—and why? Better still, wouldn't you want to know whether prominent doctors who are up to date on the latest nutritional research use supplements—and, if so, what their reasons are?

There are few data on how many physicians take supplements. So we opted for the direct approach. We interviewed several of the nation's top physicians—all either prominent nutritional scientists themselves or highly regarded professionals knowledgeable about the latest research on supplements. We asked each one three questions: "Do you take supplements?" "If so, which ones?" and, most important, "Why?"

These doctors' responses aren't necessarily representative of most physicians'. But they do offer some compelling insights into their own thinking about supplement taking. What they have to say might surprise you.

WILLIAM CASTELLI, M.D.

DIRECTOR, FRAMINGHAM HEART STUDY, FRAMINGHAM, MASSACHUSETTS

Daily Supplemental Intake: 500 milligrams vitamin C, 400 international units (IU) vitamin E, 1 milligram folate, 1 multivitamin

Why do I take supplements? It's a compromise. I eat out all too often and seldom manage to work in the eight to nine cups of green vegetables a day that would provide me with the nutrients I need. It would be better if I could eat right, but since I can't, I take supplements. It's particularly important that I get these vitamins because I come from a very high coronary risk family. At age 60, I'm the first male member of my family to make it past age 45 without coronary disease. I'm trying for 70.

But what really persuaded me is the emerging medical literature. We have evidence from European studies showing that countries where people consume the most antioxidants have the lowest heart attack rates. And while those studies looked at antioxidants in the form of food sources, the Harvard Nurses' Health Study found a strong link between intake of the major dietary antioxidants in supplement form and reduced risk of stroke and heart attack. In that study, the nurses who took vitamin E supplements did much better than the ones who got vitamin E from foods alone. So that points in the direction of supplements.

WALTER WILLETT, M.D., DR.P.H.

PROFESSOR OF EPIDEMIOLOGY AND NUTRITION, HARVARD UNIVERSITY SCHOOL OF PUBLIC HEALTH, BOSTON

Daily Supplemental Intake: 400 IU vitamin E, 1 multivitamin

I take a multivitamin because of evidence that a sizable proportion of the U.S. population is not getting enough folate, vitamin B_6 or vitamin A in their diets. The dosage is safe, the cost is minimal, so why not cover the bases? Like most people, I'm busy, which makes it difficult to eat a balanced diet. But given the possible, but not yet proven, link between inadequate folate and both colon cancer and heart disease risk, it's important to make up for missed nutrients.

I chose to take 400 IU of vitamin E because of the two studies we published looking at the relationship between vitamin E and protection from heart disease, as well as other laboratory work supporting this relationship. (Note: Dr. Willett was a lead researcher on the Nurses' Health Study, referred to above, and in the Health Professionals Follow-Up Study of 51,529 male health professionals, which found a lower risk of coronary disease among men with higher intake of vitamin E from food or supplements.) We don't know for certain if the apparent protective effect of vitamin E we found is real, but even if it's only a quarter as strong as it looks in our studies, it would still be an advantage to take it. The amounts that seem to be protective in those studies are not achievable by diet. You need supplements.

James W. Anderson, M.D.

Professor of Medicine and Clinical Nutrition, University of Kentucky College of Medicine, Lexington

Daily Supplemental Intake: 15 milligrams beta-carotene, 1,000 milligrams vitamin C, 400 IU vitamin E

I started taking these antioxidants only in the past year after my professional research into diabetes and atherosclerosis made me recognize that oxidation in the cells is a major problem. The doses were based on my own research and a review of the literature. The evidence was so persuasive that I changed my thinking about supplements.

I do have high cholesterol, and the benefits of antioxidant vitamins for people at high risk of cardiovascular disease seem to far outweigh the risks, which are minimal even in large doses. I follow a high-carbohydrate, high-fiber, low-fat diet that includes at least seven servings of fruits and vegetables daily. I think it is difficult to achieve high levels of vitamin E intake unless one selects wheat germ or certain oils, so I think supplements are well-justified.

Dean Ornish, M.D.

Director, Preventive Medicine Research Institute, Sausalito, California; Author, *Dr. Dean Ornish's Program for Reversing Heart Disease* and *Eat More, Weigh Less*

Daily Supplemental Intake: 3,000 milligrams vitamin C, 1 multivitamin (includes 3 milligrams beta-carotene and 100 IU vitamin E)

The risks of vitamin supplementation are quite small when compared with the potential benefits. I've been particularly impressed by some of the studies indicating that antioxidants may play an important role in disease prevention by blocking free radical formation. This may prevent the oxidation of LDL cholesterol into a form that is more likely to clog blood vessels.

Sydney Bonnick, M.D.

Director, Osteoporosis Services, Cooper Clinic, Dallas

Daily Supplemental Intake: 200 IU vitamin E, 2 calcium citrate tablets (providing 400 milligrams elemental calcium), 1 multivitamin (without minerals)

I've been taking calcium supplements for about ten years, and since I have access to bone density testing, I know my density is excellent. In fact, it's above average for a 20-year-old woman . . . and I'm postmenopausal. I chose to use calcium citrate because it's one of the superior forms of calcium supplements. It is easily absorbed and tends not to cause gas or constipation. The foods I eat give me about 500 milligrams of calcium daily, so with the additional milligrams, my intake approaches 1,000 milligrams daily.

I take a multivitamin because, unfortunately, my diet is short on fresh fruits and vegetables. I travel a lot and eat on the run. I don't think vitamin supplements are preferable to a well-balanced diet, but at least they help somewhat to make up for what I miss. One reason my multiple contains only vitamins and not minerals is because the pill is smaller. Multivitamins with minerals are very large and leave me a little queasy. I've taken the multivitamin for about five years.

I started taking vitamin E in the past year because of the new information suggesting it may reduce risk of cardiovascular disease. We don't know the long-term effects yet. No one's done a study in which they deliberately put one group on vitamin E and prevented a second group from taking it, to see what happens after many years. What information we have suggests it is beneficial and not harmful.

KENNETH COOPER, M.D.

PRESIDENT AND FOUNDER, COOPER CLINIC

Daily Supplemental Intake: 1,000 milligrams vitamin C, 400 IU vitamin E, 15 milligrams beta-carotene

Special Additions: 300 milligrams magnesium (in the summer), 40 milligrams potassium (in the summer)

I take vitamin E because our research supports the theory that vitamin E prevents LDL cholesterol from oxidizing within artery walls and leading to development of cholesterol plaques. And vitamin C, beta-carotene and vitamin E all work together to enhance this possible protective effect. It's also possible that vitamin C may provide some protection against infectious disease, but this is very speculative. Nonetheless, it may have helped me, since I've been taking vitamin C for 30 years and haven't missed a day of work due to illness since an appendectomy in 1956.

Beta-carotene seems to work against lung cancer in smokers. For this reason it is also considered an important antioxidant. I take it to be on the safe side (though I don't smoke). I was impressed with the Chinese study that found that, among a population with high rates of gastrointestinal cancer, those given certain antioxidants wound up with lower cancer rates.

As for the other antioxidants, like selenium and chromium, I don't take them because I'm not convinced that there is enough scientific research to document their safety.

The reason I take magnesium and potassium in the summer is because of excessive sweating while I exercise. We did a study on Boston Marathon runners in the late 1960s and found a substantial reduction in their magnesium levels after completing the 26.2-mile run. More and more literature says magnesium can help prevent everything from muscle cramping and chronic fatigue to heart rhythm irregularities. Some results may be psychological, but I have patients who have seen an improvement with magnesium supplementation.

WHAT TOP DOCS TELL PATIENTS

Despite what doctors do themselves, there's little consensus when it comes to recommending supplementation. Most acknowledge that, especially in women, taking calcium can help prevent osteoporosis. And taking folic acid is advisable for women of childbearing age to prevent neural tube defects in infants. But, as far as recommending antioxidants, opinions are split.

James W. Anderson, M.D., professor of medicine and clinical nutrition at the University of Kentucky College of Medicine in Lexington, says he recommends antioxidant vitamin supplements to his patients over age 50 who have cardiovascular or cerebrovascular disease or who are at increased risk of cardiovascular disease, such as people with diabetes. Likewise, William Castelli, M.D., director of the Framingham Heart Study, suggests that his heart patients with very high cholesterol take vitamins E and C and beta-carotene, though he stops short of recommending them to the general public.

In fact, most of the doctors we interviewed say that, even though they themselves might take these supplements, they would not advise others to do so—at least not yet. At this point, they say, the research on antioxidants, while extremely promising, is not definitive.

Most of the evidence in favor of antioxidants comes from studies looking at the diets—and/or blood-nutrient levels—of large groups of people, then comparing these

MATTHEW LONGNECKER, M.D.

ASSISTANT PROFESSOR OF EPIDEMIOLOGY, UNIVERSITY OF CALIFORNIA, LOS ANGELES, SCHOOL OF PUBLIC HEALTH

Daily Supplemental Intake: 400 IU vitamin E, 15 milligrams beta-carotene

Special Additions: 1,000 milligrams vitamin C occasionally

findings with disease rates. They have established an association between high intake of antioxidants and low incidence of heart disease. But, we don't know if people who consume lots of vitamin E also eat less saturated fat and cholesterol or have other healthy habits that might be responsible for their reduced risk.

What remains to be proved is that taking antioxidants reduces the incidence of heart disease. The results of large-scale clinical trials that are designed to determine this have not yet been completed. And, until those results are in, many doctors say they just don't feel comfortable making blanket recommendations to the general public.

Besides, even though taking these vitamins in the levels noted previously appears to be perfectly safe, at least one doctor cautioned that there is a chance that side effects might surface after long-term intake of high doses of antioxidants.

The bottom line? You have to make your own informed decision, just as these doctors have for themselves. "Given the preliminary research, I think it's reasonable to take antioxidant supplements," says Meir Stampfer, M.D., Dr.P.H., associate professor of epidemiology at Harvard University School of Public Health. "But it's reasonable not to because the research is just that— preliminary."

I've taken beta-carotene for about a year, mainly because of the suggestion that it may reduce risk of coronary heart disease. I take my beta-carotene in an oil-based form because absorption is much better that way.

I actually started taking vitamin E about two years ago, right after writing a paper showing a relationship between high serum vitamin E levels and lower risk of colorectal cancer. In my study it looked like you needed a lot of vitamin E to get protection—maybe 800 IU daily.

Other studies, like the Nurses' Study, however, found that only 100 IU daily protected against heart disease. Both E and beta-carotene are safe and so inexpensive that I'd rather take the chance that I'm wasting the money than possibly losing the benefit.

I don't think taking supplements makes my diet any worse. I still try to eat five helpings of fruits and vegetables a day. I see supplements as a bonus. If you look at the research, a lot of times it's the supplement users who get the most benefit, like in the Nurses' Study.

MEIR STAMPFER, M.D., DR.P.H.

ASSOCIATE PROFESSOR OF EPIDEMIOLOGY, HARVARD UNIVERSITY SCHOOL OF PUBLIC HEALTH

Daily Supplemental Intake: 400 IU vitamin E

When I started researching vitamin E, I expected to find that vitamin E users had a lower risk of heart disease. (Note: Dr. Stampfer is a lead researcher in the Nurses' Health Study.) Indeed, that turned out to be true, but I thought I would be able to explain that finding in other ways—I thought we'd find that the women who took more vitamin E had other positive lifestyle practices that made them healthier. But after I adjusted for diet and exercise, the protective effect of vitamin E was unchanged. That's what made me start taking it.

In our studies, we found you had to have at least 100 IU of vitamin E in your daily diet to see a benefit. As far as we know, it's completely safe, so I figured why not go up a bit from that dose? Since I forget to take it sometimes, I take 400 IU pills—if I remembered every day, I'd probably take 200 IU pills.

I'm also considering a multivitamin because of evidence pointing toward the importance of getting adequate amounts of other vitamins, especially folate and B_6. I eat a good diet, and I've never had my blood levels of these nutrients measured, though I'm sure they're pretty high. But I do travel a lot and don't always eat the way I should.

JOANN MANSON, M.D.

ASSISTANT PROFESSOR OF MEDICINE, HARVARD MEDICAL SCHOOL, BOSTON, AND CO-PRINCIPAL INVESTIGATOR, NURSES' HEALTH STUDY, CARDIOVASCULAR COMPONENT

Daily Supplemental Intake: 1 multivitamin

I take a multivitamin that gives 100 percent of the Recommended Dietary Allowance. But that's all. I believe that it's important to have conclusive results from randomized clinical trials before taking individual supplements.

However, I've been trying very hard to increase fruit and vegetable consumption. I try to get at least five servings most days. I bring my own lunch whenever possible, eat fruit for dessert and include a salad during the day. I try to minimize eating out when I'm at home. I've eliminated red meat, and I eat more fish, pastas and grains than ever before.

We need evidence from randomized clinical trials that it is these supplements—and not some other component of the foods high in these micronutrients—that confer the benefit.

KRISTINE HARPER, M.D.

MEDICAL DIRECTOR, CENTER FOR BONE DISEASE, DUKE UNIVERSITY MEDICAL CENTER, DURHAM, NORTH CAROLINA

Daily Supplemental Intake: 500 milligrams vitamin C, 400 IU vitamin E, 3 milligrams beta-carotene, 1 multivitamin

Occasional Supplemental Intake: Selenium (very infrequently), Tums (for calcium)

Calcium is the only supplement whose long-term benefits—bone protection—I understood well when I first started taking it. But even as long as 16 years ago there was some suggestion that antioxidants might help prevent cancer. And more recent data suggest that antioxidants may be beneficial for cardiovascular protection. Of course this is all lab and test-tube work. There are no real data that prove it actually works with people.

I take the multivitamin/mineral because many people's diets (mine included) tend to be deficient. In particular, I avoid red meats—a great source of zinc. Zinc is necessary for cell integrity and wound healing. I think the more research that gets done, the more we're going to find that these minerals are important.

10

The Doctor Is "In"

These easy techniques can awaken your own "inner healer."

You've followed your physician's orders to the letter. But still, your symptoms persist: Your asthma's got you doubled over and wheezing, or that stubborn infection continues to overstay its welcome. What do you do? You already sought out a second opinion. Should you find yet another doctor?

Yes—but don't start flipping through the Yellow Pages. Take a look in the mirror instead. That's where you'll find your inner healer, a "doctor within" who can help you recover from, or cope better with, everything from the common cold to cancer. A growing amount of scientific evidence suggests that things like stress reduction, nutrition and support from friends and family may actually help your body fight disease and illness. And the best part is, these are all things you can control.

Here are some strategies, gleaned from the scientific literature and interviews with experts, for taking full advantage of your inner healing powers. Of course, listening to the inner healer doesn't mean you can turn a deaf ear to the physician-in-the-flesh. Rather, you should work together to ensure the best possible care and speediest recovery. First, before you make any decisions about adding to or changing your treatment, talk to your doctor.

EAT YOUR WAY TO A
SPEEDIER RECOVERY

Whether you're fighting a major head cold, you've got a wicked case of strep throat or you've just had major surgery, food seems to lose its allure when you're under the weather. But that's precisely when you should be extra careful to eat, says Susan Finn, R.D., Ph.D., president of the American Dietetic Association. "Food should be treated just like medicine," she says.

Here's why. When you're sick, your glands are pumping out hormones in response to the physical stress of infection and illness, and your immune system's frantically trying to put out fires. That speeds up your metabolism—meaning that you're burning calories and drawing on your body's reserves, including vitamins and minerals. If your nutrient intake is poor, your recovery can stall, and you set yourself up for infection and numerous other complications.

You're not in danger of totally tapping out those stores unless you're really sick—you have a major infection, for example, or severe burns that land you in the hospital for weeks at a time. But even a simple fever or minor surgery like a root canal can raise your metabolism slightly.

Keeping those reserves stocked with nutrient-dense fluids and foods gives your body's disease-fighting systems the energy they need to help you recover properly, Dr. Finn says. If you're in the hospital recovering from major surgery, you may receive intravenous or specially fortified feedings to keep you nourished. But if you're down with a less serious problem, try these tips.

Put fluids first. If you just can't stomach solid foods, go for nutrient-packed drinks like low-sodium vegetable juices or your favorite fruit juice diluted with water or broths and thin soups. Water—the standard eight glasses, or more, a day—is important. Fluids are crucial when you're sick, particularly if you're sweating from fever, you're vomiting or you have diarrhea, because you could end up becoming dehydrated.

GOOD SOURCES
OF "MEDICINAL NUTRIENTS"

NUTRIENT	GOOD SOURCES
Vitamin A (beta-carotene)	Cantaloupe, carrots, pumpkin, spinach, sweet potatoes, tuna
Vitamin B$_6$	Bananas, brown rice, chicken breast, halibut, navy beans, potatoes (baked with skin), swordfish, wheat germ
Folate	Broccoli, dried beans, orange juice, spinach, wheat germ
Vitamin B$_{12}$	Clams, mackerel, oysters, poultry and lean meat, salmon, tuna
Vitamin C	Broccoli, cantaloupe, citrus fruits and juices, strawberries, sweet red peppers
Vitamin E	Kale, spinach, sunflower seeds, wheat germ, whole grains
Iron	Fish, lean meat, poultry, and legumes like soybeans and navy beans
Zinc	Clams, crab, lean beef, oysters, plain yogurt, wheat germ, white chicken meat

Try a fruit smoothie. Throw bananas, some strawberries, orange juice, ice, plain yogurt and a sprinkle of wheat germ in a blender, and voilà! You've got a supernutritious, superpalatable minimeal. That combination's appealing for a number of reasons: First, cold, frosty foods are often attractive to people with a variety of illnesses. Second, smoothies are easy to swallow and digest. Plus, this combination is chock-full of many of the vitamins and minerals you need to help heal wounds and stimulate the immune system, like vitamins C, B$_6$, folate and zinc. (For a list of nutrients essential to healing and their best food sources, see "Good Sources of 'Medicinal Nutrients' " on page 106.)

Go with grazing. The mere act of eating can tire you out when you're sick, so cutting down on portions may help. It will also reduce your chances of developing tummy troubles like gas and bloating in response to a large meal. If you tend to fill up fast, save liquids for between-meal drinks—that way, you'll have more room for the main dish.

Fix your favorite fast foods. Figure out how to cut preparation time for your favorite foods—you want to save your strength for eating, not waste it on cooking. Use your microwave to fix low-fat frozen entrées, frozen, already-cut vegetables, baked potatoes and leftovers.

Steer clear of fat. For one thing, dietary fat's hard on the digestive system. Plus, research suggests that eating a low-fat diet may increase the activity of your immune system cells. That may mean a quicker recovery for you, experts say.

Take advantage of feel-good times. People who are sick usually feel better in the morning—starting off the day strong but fading as the afternoon approaches. So eat larger meals or eat more often when you feel best and your energy's running high.

GIVE YOURSELF A "MENTAL PHYSICAL"

It's a simple notion, but it's often neglected: The more aware you are of what's going on in your body, the more likely you are to pick up on subtle—yet possibly important—changes in your symptoms when you're sick. That, in turn, can help you take action—choosing the right home remedy or over-the-counter drug, for example, or giving your doctor crucial information that may affect your treatment or diagnosis.

How do you heighten your sense of body awareness? For one thing, you can avoid substances like caffeine and alcohol that may "mask" important symptoms like fatigue (and may also contribute to dehydration).

You can also increase body awareness by giving yourself a daily "body scan"—a technique popularized by Jon Kabat-Zinn, Ph.D., director of the Stress Reduction Clinic at the University of Massachusetts Medical Center and author of *Full Catastrophe Living*. It's kind of a "mental physical," in which you move your mind through the different regions of your body. Here's how to do it.

• Lie on your back, your eyes closed, in a comfortable place. Make sure you're warm enough.

• Become aware of your breathing. Feel the rise and fall of your stomach with each breath. Take a few moments to feel your body as a whole, from head to toe.

• Then bring your attention to the toes of your left foot. Direct your breathing to them, as if you're actually breathing into and out of your toes. (It may help you to imagine the breath traveling back and forth from your nose, through your torso and leg to your toes.)

• Allow yourself to feel any sensations from your toes. Don't avoid that area if you're in pain—experience the sensation in all its intensity.

• Next, take a deeper breath, and when you breathe out, remove your focus from your toes, allowing them to disappear from your mind. That's particularly important if you're experiencing pain in the area.

• Shift the focus of your breathing to the bottom of your foot, then to your heel, and repeat the process until you've covered the entire body.

ELIMINATE THE STRESS FACTOR

New laboratory evidence has uncovered what may be the biological framework supporting the notion that reducing stress may help you heal when you're sick—or keep you from getting sick in the first place.

George F. Murphy, M.D., professor of dermatology at the University of Pennsylvania School of Medicine in Philadelphia, and his colleague, Richard Granstein, M.D., associate professor of dermatology at Harvard Medical School, have seen an association between stress and skin problems like psoriasis, hives and eczema. In the upper layer of your skin (the epidermis), there are certain white blood cells that act like patrol cops, working for your immune system. They keep a lookout for foreign substances that penetrate your skin. When they spot an intruder, they capture it and deliver it to other immune cells, setting off a full-blown immune system attack.

Dr. Murphy, Dr. Granstein and their colleagues discovered that your wirelike nerve cells extend to just under the surface layer of your skin and appear to touch most of the patrol-cop immune cells. Those nerve cells contain a certain chemical that seems to inhibit the ability of the patrol-cop cells in the skin to initiate an immune system attack. Emotional states such as stress may act on the release of this chemical at the site of the patrol-cop cells and, so, influence immune function in the skin. This may be why stress seems to make some skin diseases worse.

"This doesn't mean we've proven that stress worsens diseases like psoriasis," Dr. Granstein says. "There are a number of factors involved—you can be genetically predisposed. But we think the mind-body connection is probably an important factor."

Though this evidence was discovered in the test tube, there is preliminary evidence hinting that this nervous system –immune system connection is at work in humans, Dr. Murphy says. He also notes that his research may have implications beyond skin conditions. Other parts of your body—your lungs and gastrointestinal tract—are also dense with nerves and contain immune cells similar to those you find in the skin. "Some of the same relationships we've seen in the skin, I predict, would be found in other organs where we know that there are linkages between stress and diseases, like peptic ulcer disease, ulcerative colitis and asthma," he says. In fact, connections between other types of immune cells and nerves have been shown to be present in the intestine.

"It may well be that stress management strategies that involve meditation, or simply acknowledging that stress may be a part of the problem, will be important parts of the treatment for these diseases," he says.

This biological evidence—added to the numerous other studies suggesting that people who are at high stress levels are more susceptible to ulcers, colds, heart problems, high blood pressure, chest pain and bowel disorders—is a compelling reason to make stress reduction part of your treatment regimen.

What's the best way to reduce stress? The answer is highly individual. It may be journal writing, taking a nature walk, spending time with a pet, watching your favorite movie, meditating or—for more serious and prolonged stress—counseling.

LEAN ON A FRIEND

"Having someone to talk to is very powerful medicine," says Redford Williams, M.D., professor of psychiatry and director of the Behavioral Medicine Research Center at Duke University Medical Center. He and his colleagues assessed the social support of 1,368 men and women admitted to the Duke Medical Center who had diagnosed coronary artery disease—severe blockage of at least one major artery. Five years after they were hospitalized, 50 percent of the people who were unmarried and said they had no one to confide in had died. That's compared with 18 percent of the people who had a spouse and/or a confidant.

Other studies have linked low levels of social support with a higher incidence of heart disease, stomach ulcers, headaches—even early death after a heart attack.

Researchers have also shown that a good support system may actually protect you from diseases like high blood pressure and give you better control over diabetes. In a landmark study, women with breast cancer who participated in a support group lived twice as long as women who didn't.

No one knows just how having social ties can change your health for the better. Some researchers theorize that having social support encourages people to take better care of themselves. But some studies also suggest that people who participate in support groups or have someone in whom they can trust and confide have increases in certain immune factors. In fact, one study suggests that as your social network expands, so does the number of certain disease-fighting cells, known as monocytes and lymphocytes.

Researchers at the University of Arizona and Canyon Ranch in Tucson measured the number of these killer cells in a group of 110 elderly people when they enrolled in an 11-day health promotion program. Researchers also assessed their levels of social support and perceived stress. After three months, patients who reported an increase in social support saw their monocytes increase. Those who reported a decrease in stress also showed a slight increase in lymphocytes. Scientists don't yet know, however, whether such immune increases can actually have a significant impact on someone's health.

"In any case, there's evidence that simply having a number of contacts without regard for the quality of those contacts is good for your health," Dr. Williams says. But he notes that a close, intimate relationship probably has the most powerful healing potential.

Those kinds of relationships don't just happen by chance, Dr. Williams says. Here are some strategies to help you turn mere acquaintances to true confidants, from *Anger Kills*, a book by Dr. Williams and his wife, Virginia Williams, Ph.D.

Find the right person. If you're married or are involved in an intimate relationship with someone, work on making that a "confidant" relationship. If you're not, join a club, volunteer or get involved in some community activity, and look for a like-minded potential friend there.

Spend time together. See each other—or talk on the telephone—every other day, at least. Even if you're busy, make time to do it.

Listen. Focus all your attention, both mental and physical, on your confidante when she is speaking. Let your confidante know you understand what she has said by repeating it back to her, before you go on to another subject. If you avoid the trap of concentrating on your own thoughts instead of really listening to your confidante, chances are she'll feel more comfortable sharing herself with you.

Make the first move. Once you're ready, take your conversations to a deeper level. What are you afraid of? What are your wishes for the future? Sharing these thoughts, feelings and ideas will let your confidante know you trust her—and may help strengthen her trust in you.

TAKE CONTROL OF YOUR TREATMENT

Acting like you have some control over your symptoms can be like a shot in the arm if you have a chronic illness like arthritis, heart disease, diabetes or asthma, experts say. "We have found that, for the most part, if you believe you can do something about your health, you probably can—and if you don't believe you can, you probably can't," says Kate Lorig, Dr.P.H., a senior research scientist at the Stanford Patient Education Research Center who has been working with the self-management program there for 15 years.

The program is designed to enhance that sense of self-confidence and control, Dr. Lorig says, and it has yielded impressive—and long-lasting—results. A group of arthritis sufferers who participated in the program reported 20 percent less pain and 40 percent fewer doctors' visits, four years after the seven-week program's end. Members of the group attended two-hour classes twice a week led by trained volunteers who had arthritis themselves.

A patient's participation in the program didn't stop the physical disease from progressing—disability increased by 9 percent over the four years (a typical increase for people with arthritis, Dr. Lorig says). But the effects on pain and the number of visits to the doctor made a big impact on their quality of life, she says.

Studies have suggested that being involved in your own treatment may have a similar effect on other diseases as well. Indeed, Stanford recently expanded the Chronic Disease Self-Management Program to include heart disease, chronic bronchitis, asthma, emphysema and stroke, as well as arthritis. "The physiologies of these diseases are very different, but the problems in managing them are very much the same," Dr. Lorig says.

Just how do you foster that healing sense of control? Here are some techniques used in the Stanford program. Most of them can apply to just about any condition.

Find a role model. If you have a chronic problem like asthma, look for someone with asthma who's coping with it successfully. You're likely to find a role model through self-help groups in your community, many of which are organized by hospitals. That can help you learn an if-he-can-do-it-I-can-do-it attitude, give you someone to talk to when you need support and provide a source for practical tips.

Hit the books. Read as much as you can about your condition—both hard-core health information and self-help books from a public or university library. Or look through your phone book for the local chapter of a national group like the American Heart Association or Arthritis Foundation—they may be able to send you easy-to-read information.

Set clear goals. Weekly, doable goals you're likely to succeed at are the best, Dr. Lorig says. If you're beginning a weight loss program, substitute a piece of fruit for your afternoon cookie snack (instead of thinking about the 30 pounds to go until you reach your goal). If exercise is new to you, try taking a ten-minute walk morning, noon and evening, instead of vowing to make it to a supertough exercise class every day. If isolation's bringing you down, commit to calling three friends this week—not to filling your social calendar to the brim.

Put it in writing. Create a contract that spells out your goals, and give a copy to a friend. Record your progress on a calendar. For example, log the time you spend exercising, the days you chose fruit instead of cookies, the friends you called.

Work with your doctor. Treating your doctor as a partner can multiply the effects of your treatment. "If you want to get the maximum relief from your treatment, you have to do both—use self-help techniques and let your doctor help, too," Dr. Lorig says. Here are her tips for building a solid doctor-patient partnership.

• List all your questions, but put a star by the two most important. Your doctor may not have time to answer all your questions. "And, give the whole list to the doctor because there might be something on that list that's very important, but you don't think it's important," Dr. Lorig says.

• Make the most of your time. Use the time he's examining you or performing a simple test on you to pose some of your questions or describe new symptoms.

• If you're really concerned about something, bring it up at the beginning of your appointment.

TAKE A WALK

Walking may just be nature's cure-all. Not only can a moderate walk help relieve the stress that may be aggravating your illness, it may actually stimulate your immune system, according to a number of studies. Indeed, one study found that taking a 45-minute walk (about three miles) increased the activity of certain immune cells by about 57 percent. The cells returned to normal levels three hours after the walk.

Researchers don't know for sure whether a walk will make you heal faster, but some studies suggest that consistent walkers suffer fewer illnesses than sedentary people. Experts believe that long bouts of intense exercise (like a heavy-breathing, hour-long run) actually can suppress immune function and make you more susceptible to infections and viruses. So it's probably a good idea to forgo prolonged, hard workouts when you're under the weather (unless you have your doctor's okay).

You should either opt for total rest or avoid hard workouts—even brisk walking—when you've got a fever, a sore throat or a cough, says Neil Gordon, M.D., director of exercise physiology at the Cooper Institute for Aerobics Research in Dallas. "Those symptoms could signal that you have an acute viral infection like the flu, and there's some evidence that strenuous exercise may make the virus replicate at a faster rate," he says. "A good rule of thumb is, if you have above-the-neck symptoms, like a runny nose, a headache or you're sneezing, you can go out and exercise if your temperature's normal. If you have a sore throat, a fever or you're coughing, it's probably better to rest."

For chronic problems like high blood pressure, back pain, diabetes, heart disease, arthritis or asthma, moderate exercise may actually reduce or eliminate your need for medication. If you have any of these problems, or any other condition you think may benefit from an exercise program, talk to your doctor before you start working out.

11
THE MOST POWERFUL HOME REMEDY

Aspirin is being used to treat heart attacks and help prevent heart disease.

If there's a magic potion for heart health, aspirin might just be it. That little white pill has proved to be beneficial for both treatment and prevention of heart attack and heart disease. Aspirin use reduced heart attack risk for people who have already had heart attacks by as much as 30 percent in one large, well-conducted scientific study. And it seems to work as well or better in preventing first-time heart attacks in low-risk groups, too. In a study of 22,000 healthy male doctors, the group who popped one adult aspirin (325 milligrams) every other day for five years had 44 percent fewer heart attacks than the group who didn't take aspirin.

Another study has suggested that you may be able to get similar benefits in treating those at high risk of heart attack with substantially lower doses of aspirin—as little as 30 milligrams a day. (A baby aspirin contains about 80 milligrams.) Aspirin thins your blood—much like adding extra skim milk to your pancake batter makes it more runny. That means your blood flows more easily and is less likely to clot. Clots lodged in the heart trigger about 98 percent of all heart attacks.

With the Benefits, Some Risks

Despite aspirin's reputation as a myocardial miracle worker, heart experts aren't quick to recommend it for everyone. Obviously, you should avoid using aspirin if you're allergic to it. And if you have a bleeding disorder or bleeding ulcer, aspirin could be dangerous because it keeps blood from clotting when it should.

In addition, aspirin can irritate the lining of your stomach, causing it to bleed. If that happens, you may feel a slight burning sensation, but it's usually not serious. In rare cases, aspirin use can trigger intense abdominal pain and even ulcers.

Of most concern, though, is the possibility that aspirin use might increase your risk of a stroke triggered by bleeding in the brain. Some studies have indicated a slightly increased risk, but the data are not clear yet, says Julie Buring, Sc.D., associate professor of ambulatory care and prevention at Harvard Medical School and director of the Women's Health Study. On the other hand, aspirin may decrease the risk of the most common stroke, that caused by clotting.

Do You Need Aspirin?

Before you decide to add aspirin to your heart disease prevention plan, get your doctor's go-ahead. That's the only way to be sure you need aspirin, and that it's safe for you to use. Right now, the guidelines for using aspirin as a treatment are clear. "If you've survived a prior heart attack or stroke, or you have transient ischemic attacks—ministrokes—or unstable angina, one 325-milligram adult aspirin every day is clearly indicated to prevent subsequent cardiac events," Dr. Buring says. If you're in one of those categories, your doctor will probably consider aspirin therapy.

Whether you should use aspirin as prevention if you don't have a history of serious heart problems is a bit more complicated. For one thing, aspirin's no substitute for making healthy lifestyle changes—eating a low-fat, high-fiber diet, exercising regularly, keeping your weight down and abstaining from smoking. And regular aspirin use may be associated with side effects in people who are otherwise relatively healthy. So it's even more crucial to discuss with your doctor the benefits and risks of regular aspirin use for preventing heart attacks and disease, Dr. Buring says.

"Right now, the best rule is that if you have one or more heart disease risk factors, you should talk with your doctor about taking aspirin as a preventive," she says.

AVOIDING GUT REACTIONS

You can avoid the unpleasant stomach upset that may come with aspirin therapy. Here's how.

Stick to a low dose. If your every-other-day dose of adult aspirin gives you trouble, try substituting a baby aspirin. At about 80 milligrams a tablet, it's only a fraction of the dose of an adult aspirin. But a number of studies have shown that it's just as effective. And lower doses should be easier on your stomach. You can also opt for the 165-milligram low-dose aspirin now available at most drugstores.

Use buffered or "enteric-coated" aspirin. Some regular-dose and low-dose aspirins have a special coating that causes them to bypass the stomach altogether. Because they're absorbed in the small intestine instead, there's little chance you'll have a gut reaction.

Take it with food or drink. Taking your aspirin with meals or swallowing it with a full eight-ounce glass of water may help you avoid irritation, too.

12

TAMING TUMMY TROUBLES

Experts answer some of the most common digestion questions.

There's no denying it—sometimes your plumbing just doesn't work right. Something you eat sets your chest afire, inflates your abdomen to twice its normal size or sends you sprinting to the john all morning long.

Problem is, most of us are pretty shy when it comes to talking about our gastrointestinal gurglings and glitches. Assembled here is a panel of topflight tummy experts to field questions you might be too red-faced to ask—and to offer advice for quelling your digestive disturbances.

Q. My healthy diet's giving me a chronic case of gas! What can I do?

A. A little gas is a common by-product of a diet high in carbohydrates and fiber, says Harris Clearfield, M.D., professor of medicine and director of the Division of Gastroenterology at Hahnemann University Hospital. But if you feel bloated more often than not, here are some simple tips.

• Substitute one healthy food for another. Some high-fiber foods are less likely to produce gas than others. It depends on the food and your system. So experiment. If you have a problem with bananas, for example, slice strawberries on your cereal instead.

• Graze instead of gorge. That is, eat smaller meals with healthy snacks in between. This is especially helpful if you eat a lot of foods like beans, broccoli or cabbage, which are notorious gas producers. Instead of downing a big bowl of chili at one sitting, for example, have a cup of lentil soup for lunch, then include a side order of baked beans with dinner.

• Give nature a helping hand. Beano, an over-the-counter product available nationwide at most supermarkets and pharmacies (check the antacid section), contains an enzyme that may help your body break down certain carbohydrates. Simply splash a few drops on your first forkful of beans or greens—and head off the gas production in the gut. (Note: People who are allergic to mold should check with their doctor before taking this product.) Activated charcoal and simethicone combinations may also help.

Q. My gut is extremely stress-sensitive. Whenever I'm feeling stressed out, my stomach cries out in pain; I get cramps, bloating and diarrhea. There's no way I can avoid stress all the time. But is there some way I can at least prevent these stress-related gut reactions?

A. Too often when we're feeling stressed out, our diets suffer, says Arvey I. Rogers, M.D., gastroenterologist and professor of medicine at the University of Miami School of Medicine. Paying closer attention to your eating habits during times of stress may help minimize your distress. Try eating more slowly and avoiding fatty foods, excess caffeine, carbonated beverages and alcohol.

Gulping down meals, snacking incessantly or even the nervous habit of swallowing excessively can provoke belching, bloating and intestinal pain. Sometimes, the symptoms can be mistaken for irritable bowel syndrome, says William E. Whitehead, Ph.D., professor of medical psychology, Division of Digestive Diseases, Johns Hopkins University School of Medicine. But people with aerophagia (as it's called) simply swallow air more than they should as a response to stress or bad eating habits. Awareness is your best protection, Dr. Whitehead adds. If you suspect that you swallow a lot, wear a collar or scarf around your throat for an hour each day to heighten your awareness. This should help reduce the frequency of swallowing enough to relieve your symptoms, he says.

Of course, your best gut protection against stress is to eliminate the cause if you can—and if you can't, to better manage your response. Some studies suggest that lack of a support network and emotions like anger and excitement may contribute to stress-related gut problems.

Q. I love spicy foods, but they don't love me. Every time I eat Mexican or Indian fare, I wind up with a royal case of heartburn. Any suggestions other than swearing off the hot stuff?

A. First, eat spicy foods in small portions—overeating exaggerates the heartburn effect. Avoid washing your meal down with alcohol or coffee (even decaf); both are known heartburn agitators. Request the no-smoking dining room; cigarette smoke increases the irritation to the esophagus.

It's important to understand that spicy foods don't cause heartburn, they make you aware of it, says William Ruderman, M.D., chairman of the Department of Gastroenterology at the Cleveland Clinic, Fort Lauderdale, Florida. Heartburn happens when the muscle that acts as a swinging door between the stomach and the esophagus inappropriately relaxes. This allows the contents of your stomach to back up and irritate the lining of the esophagus.

Heartburn sufferers who lie down after eating almost surely get burned. If you must take a siesta, lie on a bed on your left side with your head elevated. That way, your stomach is lower, so when stomach acid pools it's less likely to get to your esophagus, Dr. Ruderman says.

Q. I try to drink more milk to improve my calcium status. But unfortunately, dairy products don't seem to agree with me. Could I be lactose intolerant? How can I know for sure?

A. Take a breath test. Your doctor will ask you to sample some lactose (milk sugar). If there's an increase in the amount of hydrogen in your breath, you aren't fully digesting the lactose. People with lactose intolerance lack an enzyme that helps them digest the milk sugar in dairy products. (Undigested sugar migrates to the colon and may cause excessive gas, bloating, cramps and diarrhea.)

Once you know the source of your distress, you can modify your diet accordingly. Keep in mind that even if you are lactose intolerant, you can still include calcium-rich dairy products in your diet. Here's how.

• Use lactase supplements that contain the enzymes you need to digest the lactose in dairy products. You can add liquid lactase supplements directly to milk, or chew a lactase tablet along with or immediately after you consume a dose of dairy.

• Buy reduced-lactose milk, which has about 70 percent less lactose than regular milk.

• Eat yogurt with live, or active, cultures. These healthy bacteria cultures help break down the lactose.

• Make dairy part of a meal; lactose is easier to digest when it's combined with other foods.

Q. I've read that people who are lactose intolerant experience gassy, bloated, crampy symptoms when they eat dairy products. I frequently suffer from these symptoms after eating—whether or not I've eaten dairy products. Are there other forms of food intolerance?

A. You might have a fructose or sorbitol intolerance, says Pat Esposito, R.D., a dietitian at Hartford Hospital in Connecticut, working with researchers on carbohydrate malabsorption. Research suggests that some people have difficulty digesting common sweeteners like fructose and sorbitol.

Fructose is found in its natural state in dried and fresh fruit and fruit juices. It's also in soft drinks and other sweets, often listed on labels as high-fructose corn syrup. Sorbitol is also found in fruits and used as a sweetener in sugar-free gums and candies. Eating reasonable amounts of fruit is fine, but cut back on excess fruit juices and soft drinks.

By the way, the same type of breath test used to diagnose lactose intolerance can help your doctor determine if you have a problem with fructose or sorbitol, too.

Q. I've heard that you can mistake a heart attack for indigestion. How do I know if I should take an antacid or dial 911?

A. The early symptoms of a heart attack closely resemble heartburn. The trouble is, if you are having a heart attack, every minute you delay can cost you dearly. For the best possible outcome, treatment must begin within 60 minutes. Call 911 immediately if:

• You've never had heartburn before, and you experience chest pain and pressure.

• Antacids don't relieve the burning sensation in your chest within 10 to 15 minutes.

• Along with your heartburn symptoms, you experience short-ness of breath, sweating, nausea, dizziness, fainting, general weakness, or pain radiating from your chest to your back, jaw or arms.

If you're not sure, play it safe and call anyway, because any type of chest pain can signal heart troubles and should not be ignored. Then, while waiting for the ambulance to arrive, chew and swallow an aspirin (standard 325-milligram dose).

Q. I've heard of traveler's diarrhea. But, when I travel, I tend to get constipated. Why does this happen, and is there anything I can do about it?

A. Traveler's constipation may result simply from being away from your normal routine, Dr. Ruderman explains. "The functions of your body vary during times of night and day, and when you change that cycle, your body gets mixed up." With time, and a reinstatement of more normal eating patterns, your body will get back on track again. To help prevent the problem, eat fruit and other high-fiber foods, drink plenty of (bottled) water and avoid alcohol, which may interfere with your body's ability to get back on schedule.

Q. Now that I'm 50, my doctor says I should have a test called a sigmoidoscopy to examine my colon. I've heard it's a really embarrassing, uncomfortable exam. Since I'm feeling fine and have no symptoms that would suggest I've got a bowel or colon problem, I'm inclined to decline my doctor's invitation. That is, unless you convince me otherwise.

A. Sigmoidoscopy is the best way to detect precancerous polyps in the lower third of the colon so they can be removed before they erupt into colon cancer. And people over age 50 are at higher risk for the disease. It's no small risk, either; next to lung cancer, colon cancer kills more Americans than any other type of cancer, including cancers of the breast and prostate. That's why the American Cancer Society recommends that you have a sigmoidoscope exam every three to five years beginning at age 50.

The exam's not as bad as you've heard. Honest. A skilled and experienced doctor can do it in five minutes—ten, tops.

And with today's thin, flexible plastic-coated scopes, which have replaced yesterday's rigid stainless-steel probes, the procedure is at worst mildly uncomfortable.

Many people who've had it done say that the worst part is the anticipation—that and the preparation, which can involve taking a laxative and/or enemas. But the sigmoidoscopy itself is surprisingly quick and easy. You simply lie on your side, knees bent. The doctor inserts the well-lubricated flexible sigmoidoscope tube, which is about the diameter of your little finger, into your rectum. He or she may pump a little air through the tube to inflate the intestine for better viewing. This can produce a little gassiness and cramping—much like the minor gas you experience after a small bowl of beans—which can linger for about an hour afterward. That's usually as bad as it gets. "Many of my female patients say that, given the choice, they'd rather have a sigmoidoscopy than a pelvic exam and Pap test," says Benjamin Krevsky, M.D., associate professor of medicine at Temple University School of Medicine and Hospital in Philadelphia.

Q. I have an ulcer. I've tried all the standard remedies, but it keeps coming back. Is there anything else I can do?

A. Ask your doctor to perform a blood test to determine whether you're infected with a common bacteria called *Helicobacter pylori*. Research suggests that more than 85 percent of people who have ulcers are infected.

In one study, the recurrence rate for duodenal ulcers dropped from 96 percent to none when the bacteria were eliminated. "If you eradicate the infection, you've cured the disease, in most cases," says David Graham, M.D., chief of gastroenterology at the Veterans Affairs Medical Center in Houston.

The most effective therapy so far is the combination of three relatively inexpensive, common drugs—the antibiotic tetracycline, metronidazole and bismuth subsalicylate (Pepto-Bismol). There is a chance, though, that the bacteria will be resistant to that treatment. For that reason, researchers are continuing to test other drug combinations, Dr. Graham says.

Q. Occasionally, after I go to the bathroom, I find bright red blood in the toilet. I'm sure it's just hemorrhoids. But do I need to see a doctor anyway?

A. Certainly, the most common cause of bright red blood in the stool is hemorrhoids. But it's a good idea to see your doctor anyway, says Henry D. Janowitz, M.D., former head of the Henry D. Janowitz Division of Gastroenterology at Mount Sinai Medical Center in New York City. Even though it's usually not serious, bright red blood could be an early sign of inflammatory bowel disease or colon cancer. Make sure you see your doctor at the first sign of blood, especially if you're over age 50 (because you're at increased risk of colon cancer), or if your bleeding is accompanied by weakness, dizziness, shortness of breath, fatigue, cramps or diarrhea.

Even if the suspected cause is hemorrhoids, your doctor will probably do a sigmoidoscopy or a more comprehensive exam to find out for sure and rule out the more serious problems.

Q. Almost every time I eat, my stomach burns, I get bloated and I have sharp abdominal pains. I thought for sure I had an ulcer. But, after doing an endoscopic exam of my stomach, my doctor told me that everything looks normal. What else could it be?

A. You may suffer from nonulcer dyspepsia, a condition that continues to mystify the gut experts. While its symptoms may mimic ulcer disease, endoscopic examinations and even biopsies of the lining of the stomach may show mild inflammation without evidence of ulcer disease, or they can even be normal. "Nonulcer dyspepsia is characterized by pain just above the belly button that may become worse when you eat or better when you eat," Dr. Ruderman says.

Although the condition isn't serious—it's not a warning that you're going to get an ulcer—it's uncomfortable and frustrating for both sufferers and their doctors. The best advice for now is to avoid irritants like alcohol, aspirin, nonsteroidal anti-inflammatory drugs, caffeine and acidic foods. There's no evidence that people with nonulcer dyspepsia produce too much stomach acid. But you may find some relief with over-the-counter antacids, prescription acid-blockers or ulcer medications, Dr. Ruderman says.

13

PRUNE HYPERTENSION FROM THE FAMILY TREE

Lower the numbers and reduce your risks.

Do you have high blood pressure in your family tree? That puts you at increased risk of developing hypertension yourself, which could mean going on blood pressure–lowering drugs to control it. And high blood pressure, in turn, ups your risk of heart disease and is the prime risk factor in cases of stroke.

You can't rewrite your family history. "But even if both your parents have hypertension, that doesn't necessarily mean you're going to develop it," says Marvin Moser, M.D., clinical professor of medicine at Yale University School of Medicine and senior adviser to the National High Blood Pressure Education Program. That's because there may be simple strategies you can use to protect yourself from high blood pressure and its dangerous fallout.

Experts aren't quite sure how high blood pressure is linked to heart disease. They think, though, that the force of the blood moving through your blood vessels and arteries somehow damages them, making them more likely to develop hardening of the arteries.

Even slightly elevated blood pressure—a systolic (top) number of 130 to 140 or a diastolic (bottom) number of 85 to 89—can increase your risk, especially if that's combined with other risk factors, such as being overweight or sedentary, eating too much salt or too little potassium or possibly experiencing high levels of stress.

Fortunately, there are many things you can do to beat the odds if you're at increased risk.

Shed ten pounds (if you're overweight). Those extra pounds you're sporting on your hips aren't just unattractive. Experts say excess weight can cause a two- to six-fold increase in your risk of developing high blood pressure. In fact, it's estimated that 20 to 30 percent of all cases of hypertension are caused by being overweight.

"Research indicates that losing weight is probably the most effective nondrug method of lowering blood pressure," says Dr. Moser, author of *Week by Week to a Strong Heart.* "In some cases, weight loss of 10 to 15 pounds may be enough to lower slightly elevated blood pressures to normal and help you avoid medication."

Toss a teaspoon of salt over your shoulder. Instead of on your food, that is. One to 1½ teaspoons of salt represents about half of most people's intake of salt each day. "Reducing salt intake by half will probably lower blood pressure an average of three to five points systolic and three to four points diastolic in some people," Dr. Moser says. You cut it in half by swapping the salt shaker in your kitchen and on your dinner table for spicy, no-salt herb blends. Then, opt for no-salt or low-salt versions of processed foods, such as sauces, low-fat lunch meats and dairy items such as cottage cheese and low-fat cheeses, whenever they're available. How much that affects your risk of developing high blood pressure depends on how "sodium-sensitive" you are. (Certain people are genetically more likely to have blood pressure responses to sodium, a key component in salt, than others.) There's no good test for sodium sensitivity, yet—so it's a good idea for everyone to try to cut back, and it can't hurt, Dr. Moser says.

Go easy on the hard stuff. It's well established that if you're a heavy drinker—three or more alcoholic beverages each day— you're more likely to develop high blood pressure than people who drink less. Experts suggest that you should limit yourself to an absolute maximum of two drinks a day. But you may reap even more blood pressure benefits by drinking even less.

Get a morning or midday workout. That may help ward off the effects of daytime stress on your blood pressure, according to a published study.

Researchers at Wake Forest University in Winston-Salem, North Carolina, exposed a group of 48 women to two stress-producing tasks as they monitored the women's blood pressure. One day, the women simply rested before the stresses; on the other day, those same women rode stationary bicycles for 40 minutes at 70 percent of their heart-rate reserve (moderate work intensity). Then, after 30 minutes of rest, they were exposed to the stressful situations a second time.

The women's blood pressures during the stressful experiences were significantly lower after they exercised than on the day they didn't exercise. Data from another study suggest that these effects may last up to four or five hours after exercise.

"Our study suggests that exercise may actually buffer responses to stressors that occur after exercise," says Jack Rejeski, Ph.D., professor in the Department of Health and Sport Science at Wake Forest University. That could have wide-ranging implications, he says. "One theory argues that the spikes in blood pressure from repeated stress are a cause of hypertension." Brisk walking, stationary cycling, running or any other aerobic exercise lasting 30 minutes or more may yield similar results.

Go bananas. They're packed with potassium—a mineral some studies suggest may help prevent high blood pressure. Some people with hypertension have low potassium intakes. And some unconfirmed pilot studies have suggested that increasing potassium intake lowers blood pressure slightly in both those with hypertension and people with normal blood pressure levels. Potassium may dilate your blood vessels, allowing your blood to flow more freely through them. Potassium isn't as powerful a tool against high blood pressure as losing weight and salt restriction. And studies of potassium supplements are too small and short-term to justify taking potassium pills to lower or prevent high blood pressure. But there is enough evidence right now that you should make sure you're eating potassium-rich foods, especially bananas, potatoes with skins, apricots, prunes, tomatoes and broccoli.

Learn to relax. Researchers say that job stress, public speaking, even the stress of arguing and lying can cause temporary spikes in blood pressure that may, if experienced long-term, result in high blood pressure. Exercise is only one way to ward off the effects of stress. Small, preliminary studies have hinted that relaxation methods—like meditation, progressive relaxation (where you tense and then relax the muscles in your body in succession) and biofeedback—may help lower blood pressure in people with hypertension. While larger and better-controlled long-term studies are needed to confirm that evidence, there's a reasonable chance that coping with stress may help you control high blood pressure.

"Relaxation can help break the adrenaline cycle—the release of hormones during stress that makes your blood vessels constrict or narrow. This increases blood pressure," Dr. Moser says.

14
AWAY WITH ALLERGIES

*Keep nuisance-makers at bay
with this step-by-step approach.*

Allergies are merely a seasonal annoyance for some of the 50 million people who have them. But for others, they're a year-round struggle with watery eyes, a nose that won't stop running and a horrible stuffy feeling. And for still others, allergies can trigger asthma attacks so severe that emergency care is needed.

If you have allergies, your doctor should prescribe a treatment program that may include antihistamine or decongestant medications or injections for severe cases. But the first line of defense is separating yourself from the allergen that causes the problem. And that starts at home.

"The more people can do to control their exposure to allergens where they live, the better the medications are likely to work," says Stanley J. Szefler, M.D., director of clinical pharmacology at the National Jewish Center for Immunology and Respiratory Medicine and professor of pediatrics and pharmacology at the University of Colorado Health Sciences Center in Denver. "A careful review of the environment is important to identify critical sites of exposure. If I suspect that environment is a problem, I sometimes ask a person to bring some pictures of the home to help identify sources of allergens," he says.

Removing allergens may be especially important for young children: Studies show that early exposure to allergens may be linked to later development of respiratory problems, such as asthma. Scientists theorize that one of the possible reasons for the steady rise in childhood asthma since the 1970s may be the increasing energy efficiency of our homes. This increased efficiency allows little exchange of outside air and hence more contact with allergens.

Your doctor can determine what you're allergic to by taking a medical history and doing skin tests. But before you can begin avoiding allergens, you need to know what these allergens are and where they lurk. Here's what you're up against.

Dust mites. These critters (so tiny you can't see them) dine on little particles of skin that fall from your body. They like to live wherever you spend the most time—notably your bed, sofa and carpeting. (Nearly 100,000 of them can live on a square yard of carpet.) A mite produces about 20 minuscule waste pellets a day, containing a protein many of us are allergic to. The mites thrive in humidity and die off when the humidity drops below 50 percent.

Dander. It's not pet fur that people are allergic to—it's the protein in tiny flakes of pet skin and saliva that's the culprit. Cat allergies are the most common, but you can also be allergic to dogs, rabbits, guinea pigs, birds or other animals. Animal dander is light, easily remains in the air (especially cat dander) and is prevalent wherever pets live.

Cockroaches. As many as 60 percent of people with allergies are allergic to cockroach body parts and droppings. Roaches tend to hang out near kitchens, although you can find them anywhere.

Mold. It thrives in moist areas, such as bathrooms and basements; it reproduces via spores carried in the air, and this is what causes allergic reactions.

Pollen. This seasonal problem can invade your home through an open window or plague you in your yard.

HOME IMPROVEMENTS

So, does the idea of allergy-proofing your home sound exhausting? It doesn't have to be, says Lanny J. Rosenwasser, M.D., head of allergy and clinical immunology at the National Jewish Center and professor of medicine and co-head in the Division of Allergy and Immunology at the University of Colorado Health Sciences Center. "You want to do what's necessary without eroding the quality of your life," he says.

Some people advocate stripping rooms of all possible allergens, but others think this is overkill. "I have trouble getting hung up over the pennant hanging on the bedroom wall," says Harold Nelson, M.D., senior staff physician at the National Jewish Center and 1 of 11 members of a panel of experts that developed national guidelines for diagnosing and treating asthma.

Instead, he advises, concentrate on the bed, where you spend about a third of your life with your face nestled up near pillow and mattress that are likely teeming with dust mites and their waste, or animal dander if a pet has been there. "Your bed is critical," says Dr. Nelson. "If you don't do anything else, treat the bed and you've done the major thing."

And don't assume that being allergic means you have to get rid of your beloved pet, which can be traumatic for adults and children alike. Although that's the easiest way to banish the allergen, in many cases there are ways to coexist with animals, says Thomas A. E. Platts-Mills, M.D., professor of medicine and head of the Division of Allergy and Clinical Immunology at the University of Virginia School of Medicine in Charlottesville.

So unless your doctor advises otherwise, start small with changing your life to accommodate your allergies. If one step doesn't work, take the next.

THE INS AND OUTS
OF CARPET CARE

Dealing with carpeting can be a major challenge when you have an allergy-prone person in your household. But deal with it you must: A study at the University of Virginia in Charlottesville found that carpeting accumulates allergens at 100 times the rate of a bare, polished floor.

If you have thick or shag carpeting, your best bet is to remove it, particularly in the bedroom and family room and especially in the basement, says Dr. Rosenwasser. If that's not practical, your next step is to try to keep the carpet as allergen-free as possible. Here's how.

Keep Fido and Fluffy away. If the problem is animal dander and you have pets that can't live outdoors, keep them away from the carpet (and furniture) in living areas, says Dr. Rosenwasser, whose family coexists comfortably with a dog despite their allergy problems. "My wife has trained our dog to never come upstairs, to never get on the furniture. The dog has learned she can come to the edge of the family room and lie down on the wooden floor, but not on the carpeted areas."

Realize that if your pets—or the pets of previous tenants—have been on the carpeting or furniture, you may have to treat the areas to deactivate the dander. Pet allergens can persist long after a pet is gone.

Time your vacuuming right. Vacuums swirl dust-mite debris and animal dander into the air, where they're more likely to be breathed in than when sitting quietly on the carpet. Dust-mite particles settle down in about 45 minutes, so you can avoid many problems by having the person with allergies stay away until the dust has settled, says Dr. Nelson. With animal dander, however, this is seldom practical. "Animal dander stays in the air for a long time," he says.

Choose the right vacuum. A central vacuum system avoids many problems by venting particles outdoors. The problem with conventional vacuums and regular vacuum bags is that allergen particles pass right through and into the air, says Dr. Nelson. Some filters, however, can trap animal dander and mite debris. HEPA (High-Efficiency Particulate Air) filters are made of tightly woven fibers pleated to increase surface area. You can buy a special HEPA vacuum cleaner, HEPA filters to fit your vacuum or new vacuum cleaner bags (non-HEPA) designed to be more impermeable than traditional bags.

"If money is no object, the best choice is a HEPA vacuum cleaner," says Dr. Nelson. "If money is an object, then buy HEPA filters for your existing vacuum cleaner or try the new bags." (If the allergic person does the vacuuming, a mask should be worn.)

Avoid water vacs. Vacuums that filter dust into a canister of water aren't recommended for either dander or mite debris: These vacuums can spew out a fine mist loaded with allergens, says Dr. Nelson. No vacuum removes many mites because they cling so tightly to the carpet.

Avoid shampooing. Soap residue from shampooing can produce an irritating dust, and the wetness can encourage mite growth and mold. Steam cleaning is preferable since the carpet doesn't get as wet, says Dr. Rosenwasser. "The key thing is to make sure you steam-clean at a temperature greater than 130°F to kill mites," he says.

Another possibility is a product called HOST, a dry extraction carpet-cleaning system. It's supposed to reduce mites without adding moisture. As a last resort, your doctor may advise you to treat your carpets with chemical products. Benzyl benzoate, marketed under the name Acarosan Moist Powder, kills mites. "It has to be used correctly," cautions Dr. Nelson. "It must be left in a carpet overnight." Because mites tend to die off anyway when the temperatures drop in the fall, the best time to treat carpets is early in the summer, he says. And while this product kills mites, it doesn't remove allergy-causing dust-mite debris.

Another product, Allergy Control Solution, can be sprayed on both carpets and upholstered furniture. It's made with tannic acid, which doesn't kill mites, but neutralizes the allergy-causing proteins in mite droppings and animal dander.

"This is most often appropriate for the person who moves into a place where there has been a pet to which she is allergic, or someone who gets rid of her pet and needs to rid her home of allergens," says Dr. Nelson. Disadvantages include cost and time required, and the fact that tannic acid may darken light areas of the carpet or upholstery.

HOUSEHOLD HOT SPOTS

When it comes to allergies, every room in your house is a potential battlefield. To come out victorious, you need a room-by-room action plan. What follows are dozens of tips that will help keep your home allergen-free.

Kitchen and Laundry Room

1. Keep the inside of your refrigerator mold-free by cleaning regularly. If there's a drip tray, empty and clean it regularly.

2. To battle cockroaches and cockroach allergy, set baited traps (physical traps, not poisonous ones). To discourage cockroaches from setting up housekeeping, keep foods in tightly closed containers, rinse all cans and bottles before tossing them in your recycling bin, and keep surfaces and floor clean.

3. If you have an asthma-prone family member with severe allergies, consider choosing an electric range over a gas one. One Canadian study suggests that gas ranges contribute to children's asthma problems, and breathing combustion by-products may cause eye, nose and throat irritations. Hint: Spray air freshener can be an irritant; instead, some people set out an open box of baking soda to freshen the air.

4. Water temperatures should be set above 130°F for washing to kill dust mites.

5. Your dryer should be vented outdoors to avoid humidity buildup that could contribute to mold or dust-mite growth. Hint: Fabric softener sheets can be an irritant, as can highly scented cleansers.

6. Washing pets once a week can dramatically decrease the amount of allergens in your home. Washing cats will likely be difficult, however, unless you start the practice when your pet is a kitten. Hint: If you have a pet that needs regular grooming, have it brushed outdoors by a nonallergic member of the family.

The Bedroom

1. Your bed is most likely home to thousands of dust mites. These critters can't get through vinyl or plastic, so use zippered covers to encase the mattresses and box springs of allergic people. You can find plastic ones at department stores; however, allergy supply companies offer more comfortable fabric-textured ones. Cover your pillows, too, or buy new polyester ones that you can pop in the washing machine.

Choose bedding you can wash regularly in temperatures over 130°F. (Note: Water temperature should be below 120° to prevent scalding, but it needs to be at least 130° to kill dust mites.) Probably the best way to make your wash water hotter without danger of scalding at tub or shower faucets is with a point-of-use, instantaneous water heater. This device, which supplements the water heater, attaches to the plumbing that serves your washer and can be set at a higher temperature for that appliance alone. Local codes regulate water-heater temperatures in most localities.

Avoid feather pillows or down comforters. (Dust mites

love nesting in feathers.) Also avoid bunk beds or canopies, which collect dust.

2. Carpets collect both dust mites and animal dander; your best bet is a washable floor, such as hardwood, tile or vinyl, with washable scatter rugs if desired. If you're stuck with carpeting, follow the tips in "The Ins and Outs of Carpet Care" on page 129.

3. If mite-allergy symptoms occur even after you've allergy-proofed the bed, move on to the windows. Curtains and even venetian blinds can harbor dust mites, so washable curtains and roller shades that can be wiped clean are better. If you're dealing with pollen allergies, keep windows closed. (Air-conditioning has the added benefit of reducing humidity levels, which discourages the growth of both mites and mold.)

4. If you have a pet and are allergic to pet dander, keep the bedroom door shut or put a gate across to keep the animal out.

5. If there is or has been an animal in your home, your heating system may be circulating animal dander throughout the household. For severe allergies, you may want to close the heating vent to the allergic person's bedroom and seal it with a piece of plastic behind the grill and provide an electric radiator to heat the room instead.

6. Persistent problems with dander allergies or mold allergies may warrant the use of an air cleaner. Look for a HEPA filter and ask your doctor for advice before buying. The important thing is to have an air cleaner with a suction fan that's powerful enough to circulate room air through the system. Systems without a suction fan may deposit particles outside the unit.

7. For severe dust-mite allergies, keep knickknacks and papers put away where they can't collect dust.

8. Small amounts of cat dander can cling to walls, and wallpaper may harbor dust and dust mites. If you need to rid the room of all allergens, replace wallpaper with paint and then regularly wipe walls before mopping or vacuuming. Remember to dust crevices and overhangs.

9. Keep clothing stored in closets with the door closed, and clean the closet at the same time as the rest of the room.

10. Stuffed animals and dolls collect dust and mites, too. If your child is heartbroken at the idea of being separated from her favorite Teddy, wash it in hot water. (If it's not washable, carefully open one seam, remove stuffing, and replace it with old nylon stockings or washable stuffing, preferably synthetic.)

Family and Living Room

1. If your sofa has been around for several years, it's likely full of dust mites, and if Fido and Fluffy have been taking turns sleeping on it, it's filled with animal dander as well. If a new sofa is in the budget, replace the old one. A leather sofa is best, but regardless, keep animals off. If you can't replace your sofa, your doctor may recommend treating it to neutralize the dust-mite debris or animal dander.

2. Avoid upholstered chairs whenever possible.

3. As in the bedroom, your best bet is no carpet or washable throw rugs. If you do have carpets, follow the tips in "The Ins and Outs of Carpet Care" on page 129.

4. An air conditioner is useful because it helps lower humidity, which contributes to the growth of dust mites and mold. But, a central air system that doesn't drain properly can grow molds inside, so if you're allergic to molds, have your air system checked out. Filters should also be cleaned regularly.

5. Severe cases of pet-dander allergies may warrant the use of an air cleaner. HEPA filters trap dander particles. Run filters on high an hour or two immediately after vacuuming to trap the particles stirred up by the vacuum. Hint: If your physician diagnoses you as dust-mite sensitive, you can determine if mites are a problem in your home with a home test kit.

6. Fires and smoke from fireplaces or wood-burning stoves can trigger allergic reactions. If you're affected by this, forgo the charms of a crackling fire, unless you have a snug-fitting glass fireplace cover. Smoke from cigarettes and cigars can also be an irritant.

Basement

1. Use a dehumidifier to keep humidity levels below 50 percent (30 to 40 percent is ideal) to discourage growth of mold and dust mites.

2. A gauge can help you monitor humidity levels.

3. To discourage mold growth, keep boxes stored on shelves, rather than on the floor, if you have any water seepage in your basement.

4. Central heating or cooling systems may disseminate animal dander throughout the house. Installing HEPA filters may trap the dander.

Bathroom

1. The bathroom is a prime site for mold to take hold. Clean the tub, shower, curtain and liner with bleach solution and scrub grout and tiles with a mold-killing cleaning solution.

2. Replace wallpaper that shows traces of mold with mold-proof paint.

3. An exhaust system can help keep your bathroom dry. The drier your home, the less comfortable a haven it is for dust mites and mold.

4. To avoid mold problems on the floor, choose tile or vinyl flooring rather than carpeting.

For more information, call the American College of Allergy and Immunology information line, 1-800-842-7777. Or call Lung Line, 1-800-222-LUNG or (303) 355-LUNG. Registered nurses answer questions about lung and immunologic diseases and provide free booklets. You can also call or write: Allergy and Asthma Network/Mothers of Asthmatics, 3554 Chain Bridge Road, Suite 200, Fairfax, VA 22030; 1-800-878-4403. (For information, send a self-addressed business envelope stamped with 52 cents postage.)

15
STEP AWAY FROM BACK PAIN

Walking strengthens the muscles
and promotes relaxation.

Walking helps keep your back healthy by conditioning and toning your whole body. It's an essential part of the healing programs of most back clinics. Walking works the large muscle groups, which can help to release endorphins that subdue pain and encourage relaxation. It strengthens postural muscles of the buttocks, legs, back and abdomen.

"People who have already developed a consistent walking program will probably have an easier time recuperating from a strained back," says Augustus White III, M.D., professor of orthopedic surgery at Harvard Medical School, specialist in spine surgery at Beth Israel Hospital in Boston and author of *Your Aching Back*. "Walking strengthens the abdominal muscles and the erector spinae muscles that protect the spine and make it less vulnerable to injury and irritation. And people who are already walkers have the self-discipline and the enthusiasm that is sometimes missing in sedentary patients."

Also, as a walker you may be several steps ahead in keeping your weight under control, a top priority for healthy backs.

But being a fitness walker isn't a guarantee against straining your lower back. Undue stress from improper lifting, straining to reach something, an extra-hard game of tennis or golf or an emotional crisis are common culprits that send backs into painful muscle spasms. Back pain can reduce a hale and hearty walker to a howling basket case in minutes. But don't despair. With proper care, you can feel like a walker again in no time. Here's your strategy for getting back on the walking trail.

LYING LOW

When you find yourself in pain, your first decision is whether you need to see a doctor. Check the box "Warning Signs to Watch Out For" for the special symptoms that should

WARNING SIGNS
TO WATCH OUT FOR

Although back pain often gets better with self-care, there are some symptoms that should always send you seeking help. You should see your doctor if:

• Your pain is so intense you can't move around at all.

• You lose control over bladder or bowels.

• Pain is accompanied by fever, nausea or vomiting, abdominal pain, urinary discomfort, weakness or sweating.

• Your pain is the result of some trauma, such as a car accident.

• Your leg or foot feels numb or tingly.

• You have pain radiating to your buttock, thigh or leg.

send you seeking help. If none apply, you're a good candidate for self-care.

You may feel pain immediately following an injury, or it may take a few days to show up. Lifting the air conditioner on Saturday may have gone off without a hitch, but Monday morning your back muscles are so tight you can't even roll over in bed. That's a sign you may need to stay in bed for a day or two. Taking a day or two off at first is the fastest way to get you back on your feet. If there's a pooch begging to go for an outing, you're going to need help. Martyrs don't get better as fast as people who know when to ask for favors.

Take aspirin or ibuprofen for pain and to reduce any swelling. But don't go out for a hike as soon as the ache quiets down. You can afford to skip a day or two of your walking regimen. "Walkers shouldn't be too concerned about losing their conditioning if they've injured their backs," says Dr. White. "It would take several days to lose muscle tone and aerobic conditioning. Walkers can probably regain what they lose more easily than sedentary people."

The hardest part of your recovery will be taking it lying down. As a walker, you're probably an active person. If you stay home from work, you'll think of all kinds of projects you can get into at home. Control yourself. You can extend a bad-back episode for months if you don't take care of the initial acute problem properly. Lie on your back with your knees bent and your back flat, or put a pillow or towel under your knees to take any strain off your back. Read, watch TV, listen to music, talk on the phone. And avoid chairs. Sitting puts the greatest strain on back muscles, so you may want to eat standing up.

Applying ice to your back may be helpful in reducing pain. Most doctors recommend ice during the first 48 hours and heat after that. Place an ice pack wrapped in a towel on the painful area for 20 minutes, remove for 40 minutes and try again. Dr. White thinks moist or dry heat is okay, depending on personal preference. The temperature should feel comfortably warm, not burning hot. Hot or warm showers are good, too.

An Action Plan

Research has shown that there is no reason to prolong bed rest. Two to three days seems to confer as many benefits as a week or more.

After resting for a day or two, spend a few days getting comfortable on your feet. When you can sit or stand comfortably for 20 minutes, consider taking a short stroll. Walk around the house, or perhaps in the driveway to get some fresh air. Don't go too far.

Don't be concerned if you can't stand up completely straight at first. Often you'll find that as you walk, your back straightens. "It's a matter of relaxation and an increased sense of confidence you get as you walk," says Dr. White. "Plus it gives a boost to your circulation, which may help relax your back muscles."

Still, your injured muscles are in a vulnerable state. Keep your walk short and easy, on even ground. Avoid hills completely; they force you to lean forward, straining your already weak back. Wear your most comfortable and supportive walking shoes. You may wish to wear a lumbar support to take some stress off your lower back. Don't worry about your muscles wasting away. Leave your hand weights in the closet. Avoid backpacks, fanny packs or heavy personal radios. You may be able to take several short walks throughout the day, with long rest periods. That may keep you from feeling that your past walking efforts are slipping away, and at the same time keep your back limber without stressing it.

Increase the duration of your walks, day by day. If you begin to feel pain as you tire, it's time to stop. Create walking routes that continually take you past your door, so you never have to walk too far to lie down.

DECIPHERING YOUR PAIN CODE

When you begin walking, you will probably be feeling some pain. The question, of course, is how much pain do you tolerate before you decide you're doing more harm than good?

Dr. White suggests that pain that increases 30 to 50 percent is okay and may be unavoidable at first. That's 30 to 50 percent more pain walking than you felt lying flat on your back. "It's a judgment call—very individual. You may feel a lot of pain for 15 minutes, then limber up and feel great. But if you walk for 15 minutes and then continue to have pain for the rest of the day, you've done too much. It's a matter of trial and error."

If you find walking uncomfortable, consider swimming, stationary biking or any combination of the three. "For whatever reason," says Dr. White, "you may find walking doesn't work for you when you're hurting. Try riding a stationary bike (sit in whatever is the most comfortable position) or swimming, and you can go back to walking when you're stronger."

Be sure you get out of bed by first rolling on your side and pushing yourself up with your arms. Make an effort not to lift anything heavy or put any extra strain on your back while you're recuperating. If you feel you have reinjured yourself through some activity, start from day one again.

PAY ATTENTION TO POSTURE

Your daily walks can aggravate your back and neck if you're hunched over, hanging your head, leaning forward or in any other way pushing your body out of alignment. People with lordosis, commonly known as swayback, as well as people with a flat lumbar curve may be vulnerable to chronic lower-back pain. They may feel more pain after a long walk, rather than less, due to the pressure their posture creates. So if you've injured your back muscles, do everything you can to take unnecessary pressure off them while you walk. Take a moment to check your posture before you begin to walk, then tune in regularly as you move along. Mary Pullig Schatz, M.D., of Centennial Medical Center, Nashville, Tennessee, a yoga expert and author of *Back Care Basics*, gives the following guidelines for good-for-your-back posture while walking.

To improve alignment, don't stiffen your spine and throw your shoulders back, military-style. Just think tall. The old image of a wire attached to the top of your head, pulling it upward, works well. You can practice by having a bag of rice or dried beans (wrapped in a towel so it won't slide) on your head, which automatically improves your posture as you work to keep the bag from falling.

Relax your shoulders and imagine that your pubic bone is moving up toward your navel. This image creates just enough muscle tension to create a slight pelvic tilt without interfering with your walking gait. Don't try to hold your lower back flat as you walk. The spine should undulate back and forth as you move from one leg to the other. Land on your heel and roll forward on your foot. Your stride should be natural. Don't try to increase your stride length. The farther you reach out with your foot, the more impact you send up your spine as your heel meets the ground. And an abnormally long stride could strain lower back muscles.

Stretch Yourself

The best time to stretch is after a walk, when your muscles and ligaments are warmed up and in a stretching mood. "I think stretching both before and after a walk is important," says Dr. Schatz, "especially if you have back, hip, buttock or leg pain.

"When muscles are tight from yesterday's walk or other daily activities, the muscles actually tighten around the blood vessels and impede circulation. With gentle stretching beforehand, the muscles are loosened and the blood flows more freely, which in turn helps the muscles adapt to exercise. Without circulation, there is more likelihood of injury or spasm."

Dr. Schatz recommends gentle stretching of the calves, hamstrings, quadriceps (front of thigh), buttocks and psoas (the set of muscles that run from the front of the spine to the hips). She suggests holding each stretch for at least 20 to 30 seconds to be effective.

For

Women

Only

16

BONE UP
ON GOOD HEALTH

These proven strategies can maximize skeletal strength.

What's the worst disease afflicting women today? It may, in fact, be osteoporosis—if you add up the disabilities, pain, deformities and expenses from bone fractures that about half of all American women over 50 will suffer. The millions of individual lives blighted by this crippler make it a top health issue for women.

Until recently, women (and doctors) viewed brittle bones as a built-in hardship of old age. Today experts agree it doesn't have to be that way—if only we take the right action. Trouble is, most advice about stopping osteoporosis (a chronic thinning of bones) seems aimed at only two groups: young women in the peak bone-building years under age 35, when the focus is lots of calcium and exercise to build up the bone bank, and older women at menopause, when the focus becomes medication to stem the rapid bone loss triggered by declining estrogen levels.

That leaves a huge forgotten chunk of women between 35 and 50 wondering what they need to do to protect their bones. As it turns out, however, there's a lot you can do—starting today—to put your bones in the best shape possible to withstand menopause.

BONE BASICS

Osteoporosis—the silent crippler, it's called—creeps very softly into victims' lives. Day by day, year by year, bones slowly (or not so slowly) lose density. Yet you don't have a clue—you feel fine! Until one day—usually after menopause—you grab your purse and snap a wrist. Or sneeze and crack a rib. Or step off a curb and break a hip.

Or, microfracture by microfracture, the vertebrae of your spine crush under the weight of your own body (which is why so many "little old ladies" are little). You may lose up to eight inches in height, and back pain may become chronic. Drastic changes in appearance often bring emotional pain as well.

Who does this happen to? The answer is shocking: Half of all American women over 50 will have an osteoporosis-related fracture. (Though men are afflicted less, they're not immune; one of five osteoporosis victims is male.) Each year, Americans suffer over 1.5 million broken bones (usually hip, wrist or vertebrae) linked to osteoporosis. Of those who break hips, one year later less than one in four can walk without assistance, one in four is in a nursing home and nearly one in four has died from complications of surgery or hospitalization.

Though we think of bones as a lifeless scaffolding, they're very much alive—a busy network of soft collagen fibers hardened by deposits of calcium and phosphorus crystals. Throughout life, bone tissue undergoes constant turnover—a process of breaking down old bone and building up new that's called remodeling.

In both sexes, until about age 35, bone buildup exceeds breakdown (given enough calcium in the diet), and density increases to a maximum called peak bone mass. After age 35, however, breakdown exceeds buildup, and we slowly lose bone, perhaps as much as 1 percent a year. The goal then becomes holding losses to a bare minimum.

For women, menopause (around age 50) begins a unique danger zone of rapid bone loss—as much as 7 percent a year— for roughly five years. The cause? Declining levels of the hormone estrogen, which protects bone density in ways not yet fully understood. Depending on a woman's bone mass entering menopause, this is often the critical period when she crosses the line from strong bones to osteoporotic bones—bones that can fracture under only minor stress.

WHO'S AT RISK?

One way to predict who may develop osteoporosis is to look for risk factors—conditions of heredity, illness or lifestyle often associated with lower bone density. (To identify your own risk factors, see "Are You at Risk?" on page 144.) Women of northern European ancestry—Scottish, Irish and German, for example—may have a higher risk. So do small-framed women, who start out with less bone to lose.

Are You at Risk?

Women ages 35 to 50 should review their risk factors—characteristics research has linked to increased chances of osteoporosis—with their doctors. It's a great way to identify steps you can take now to reduce osteoporosis risks. There may be lifestyle changes you can make today to conserve as much bone as possible. Or your doctor may be able to adjust certain medications. But experts acknowledge that risk factors are not perfect osteoporosis predictors. You may have several risk factors and have strong bones, or have no risk factors and still develop osteoporosis. To be certain about fracture risk, you need a bone density measurement.

Hereditary and medical risk factors include:

• Female sex

• Caucasian ancestry—especially northern European

• Oriental ancestry

• Petite frame

• Family history of osteoporosis

• Over 40 years old

• No children

• Early menopause (from removal of ovaries, for example) without estrogen replacement

• Menopausal or postmenopausal

• Low testosterone level in males

• Insulin-dependent diabetes

On the other hand, you may have some bone assets as well. Women who get a lot of calcium—from drinking low-fat milk, for example—are likely to have stronger bones than those who

- Rheumatoid arthritis

- Long-term bed rest and/or enforced immobility

- Long-term use of these medications: corticosteroids (prescribed for asthma and allergic conditions, arthritic disorders, respiratory diseases and other conditions); antiseizure medications; furosemide diuretics (prescribed for edema associated with high blood pressure or kidney problems); thyroid hormone replacement (excessive dose); anticoagulants (blood thinners used against strokes and clots); aluminum-containing antacids

Lifestyle risk factors include:

- Low calcium intake

- Low vitamin D intake

- Excess caffeine intake

- Excess protein intake

- Excess salt intake

- Chronic dieting

- Anorexia nervosa to point of amenorrhea (loss of periods)

- Exercise to point of amenorrhea

- Sedentary lifestyle

- Smoking

- Excessive alcohol intake

don't. Not smoking and drinking only moderate amounts of alcohol can help protect bones, too.

So how does this add up? Risk factors are useful but far

from perfect predictors of who develops osteoporosis. The only certain way to establish the strength of your bones is with sophisticated medical testing. A high-tech device called a dual energy x-ray absorptiometer (DEXA for short) can be used to scan the bone mineral in the lumbar spine (the small of the back) and the top of the right hip where it joins the pelvis—two of the sites most vulnerable to osteoporosis. DEXA is fast (about five minutes for each view), noninvasive and ultralow in radiation.

Best of all, whereas standard x-rays reveal bone loss only after bone density is reduced 30 percent or more, DEXA is so precise it detects changes in bone density of as little as 2 percent. This means osteoporosis can be diagnosed in its early stages, giving you time to act—by exercising regularly, eating a nutritious, calcium-rich diet and, in some cases, taking estrogen replacements when menopause arrives, which can slow or stop further bone erosion.

THE EXERCISE RX

Getting regular exercise is a critical part of any osteoporosis management and prevention plan. "Actually, exercising and practicing good posture are what all women 35 to 50 should be doing to protect their bones, whether they have osteoporosis or not," says physical therapist Peggy Anglin, of Duke University's Osteoporosis Management Program.

Some studies have shown that midlife women who exercise regularly can maintain or even increase bone density. What's more, those who are sedentary can actually lose bone. Studies show that astronauts in weightless conditions and bedridden patients lose bone rapidly. "Remember," Anglin says, "if you don't use bone, you lose bone."

For the hip, wrist and lower spine—the three most vulnerable spots—you need weight-bearing exercises, which stimulate bones to maintain density by forcing them to carry the body's weight. Highly recommended for the hip and lower spine is brisk walking, a classic weight-bearing exercise that provides a simultaneous aerobic workout.

Also good are resistance exercises (working against an opposing force, such as gravity, weights or elastic exercise bands), which strengthen key muscles in the back and abdomen that hold the spine erect and protect it from undue stress. There's some evidence that resistance exercise also maintains or increases bone density. (Some experts think resistance is the most effective of the bone-bolstering exercises.)

How much exercise do we need to protect bone density? Though research hasn't yet yielded the definitive answer, Anglin advises a minimum 30 minutes of brisk walking—enough to reach an aerobic heart rate—plus 20 minutes of a variety of other weight-bearing and resistance exercises. Ideally, the walk and workouts should be done five days a week. This gives leeway to cover an occasional missed workout. For your busiest days, there's a streamlined 25-minute workout—20 minutes walking plus a quick 5 minutes of other key exercises—selected to hit most of the major bones and muscles you need to target for osteoporosis prevention.

SUPER SIX—BEST BONE EXERCISES FOR BUSY DAYS

For days when schedules won't budge, Anglin selected this streamlined routine to bolster all the bones most vulnerable to osteoporosis. Total time: about 25 minutes.

1. Walking to maintain hip and lower-spine density: Pound either pavement or treadmill briskly for 20 minutes.

2. Sitting push-up to maintain wrist and forearm bone density: Using a straight-back chair with arms, sit near the edge of the seat with your hands on the arms. Lift the weight of your body as high as you can comfortably, by straightening your arms and pushing up. Your feet should stay on the floor. Be sure not to bend forward; keep normal spine alignment. Hold for count of three with arms straight, then slowly lower, keeping weight through your arms. Increase repetitions to ten.

3. Modified push-up to maintain wrist and forearm bone density: Lie on your belly with a towel roll under your forehead, hands at the level of your shoulders and palms down. Let your arms and legs relax, then push up with your arms. Straighten your elbows as much as you can with comfort, never forcing them. Let your belly sag and pelvis stay down. Hold for count of three. Lower and relax. Increase repetitions to ten.

4. Prone trunk lift to strengthen back extensor muscles that support spine: Lie on your belly with a towel roll under your forehead. With your hands clasped behind your buttocks, lift your head and shoulders, pinching your shoulder blades. Hold for count of three. Relax. Increase repetitions to ten.

5. Arm and opposite-leg lift to strengthen back extensor muscles that support spine: Lie on your belly with a towel roll under your forehead, one arm overhead with elbow straight. Lift the arm, leading with your thumb. At same time, lift your opposite leg from the hip. Be careful to avoid lifting so high that your body twists. Hold for count of three. Relax. Increase repetitions to ten. Repeat with the other arm and leg.

6. Single-leg lowering with pelvic tilt to strengthen abdominal muscles that support spine: Lie on your back with your knees bent and a towel roll under the lower back. Press your back into the towel roll, using the abdominal muscles. (This is the pelvic tilt.) Hold the tilt as you straighten one leg up in the air. Maintain the pelvic tilt while slowly lowering your straight leg. Stop lowering as soon as you feel you may lose the tilt! Bend the leg and put your foot back on the floor. Now let go of the pelvic tilt and relax. Increase repetitions to ten. Repeat with the other leg.

Though the Super Six will safely bolster both low- and high-density bones, Sydney Bonnick, M.D., director of osteoporosis services at Cooper Clinic in Dallas, advises women whose bones are above the fracture threshold that research shows they may gain more bone-building effect from exercise that combines weight bearing with greater impact loading. For example, walking is a classic weight-bearing exercise to strengthen hips and lower back. But jogging, which subjects bones to many times the impact of walking, may stimulate them even more, some studies show. Other examples of weight-bearing impact-loading exercise: volleyball, tennis, basketball and some aerobic dancing.

POSTURE MAKES PERFECT

Remember your parents telling you to stand up straight? They were right. Habitual good posture—what Anglin calls neutral posture—turns out to be a prime strategy to protect the spine from the exaggerated curvature we recognize as dowager's hump, a classic image of osteoporosis.

When we slouch—letting back muscles give in to the weight of gravity and allowing our heads and shoulders to be pulled forward and down—we form a forward C-shaped curve with our spine that places undue stress on the vertebrae, especially the front edges. In contrast, neutral posture holds the vertebrae in the strong, resilient, S-shaped curve the spine is meant to form. The bottom curve of the S is the small of the back, where, if you're standing or sitting correctly, you should feel a slight hollow. "To find the right position," Anglin suggests, "imagine you're a marionette, with a string tugging from the top of your head to the ceiling."

Another benefit of great posture is that you just plain look better—and here the payoff is immediate. Good posture can alleviate back pain, too. Maintaining neutral posture may seem like work at first, requiring what Anglin calls postural awareness. But as back extensor and abdominal muscles strengthen and the position becomes automatic, neutral posture is much more relaxing than a slouch.

What's one of the worst enemies of good posture? A chair that doesn't fit your body—an all-too-common problem for women, Anglin says. Often the chair seat is too long, forcing us to scoot forward and sit on our coccyxes (tailbones)—putting our spines in the very C-shaped curve we need to avoid. Women with office jobs may endure well over a thousand hours a year slumped at their desks this way.

One solution is placing a small pillow in the hollow of the back—enough to bring you forward in the seat and maintain the upright S-shaped curve of the neutral spine. Better than pillows, which have a fixed shape and size, are rolled bath towels, which you can adjust until they're just right.

Another chair misfit for many women: The seat may be so high that your feet don't quite touch the floor unless you assume that stressful C-shaped slump again. To correct this, Anglin recommends using a four-inch-high footstool which lets you sit up straight while supporting your feet.

The best solution at work? Check with your office manager. Your desk chair may be adjustable, or you may be able to order a new, more posture-friendly chair and footstool. If not, use a towel and footstool that you bring from home.

Boning Up on Calcium

Besides exercise, the most powerful osteoporosis prevention tool for women ages 35 to 50 is a well-balanced diet—with lots of calcium. Sufficient calcium is essential for women of any age to balance natural calcium excretion and support bone mass. But after 35, when we begin to slowly lose bone mass (along with our capacity to substantially rebuild any lost bone), it's vital to take in enough calcium to hold losses to an absolute minimum, preserving as much bone as possible to help see us through menopause and beyond.

How much calcium do women need? According to the National Osteoporosis Foundation, 1,000 milligrams a day before menopause and 1,500 milligrams a day after. You say you can't get that much? Yes, you can—with a little "calcium calculating"!

1. Add up the calcium heavyweights you eat daily—foods with 300 milligrams or more per serving. Calcium heavyweights include:

- 1 cup Lactaid calcium-fortified milk (lactose-reduced; 1 percent fat)—500 milligrams

- 2 one-ounce slices nonfat cheese—400 milligrams

- 1 cup plain nonfat yogurt—400 milligrams

- 1 cup fruit-flavored nonfat yogurt—300 to 350 milligrams

- 1 cup nonfat milk—300 milligrams

- 1 cup lactose-reduced nonfat milk—300 milligrams

- 1 cup calcium-fortified orange juice—300 milligrams (Other high-calcium foods—such as broccoli and kidney beans—have less calcium per serving than the heavyweights. View them as nutritious extras only.)

2. Now, find the average over a week. Add to this the calcium content of your multisupplement, if you take one. Most multis contain 200 milligrams of calcium or less, although at least one brand packs in 450 milligrams.

3. Subtract the calcium you actually consume from the recommended amount: For most women, the difference is at

least 500 milligrams. If you can't eat more high-calcium foods, osteoporosis experts advise making up the difference with calcium supplements.

With so many supplement varieties, which is best? "Whichever is easiest for you to use," advises Robert Heaney, M.D., lead investigator of the largest-ever study of calcium absorbability (at Creighton University in Omaha). For many women, this may be calcium carbonate—"cheap, easily available, and you don't need a jillion tablets," Dr. Heaney notes. Another popular variety: calcium citrate. Three supplements to avoid: bone meal, dolomite and one type of calcium carbonate identified as "natural source" or "oyster shell." These three may contain too much lead.

To see how many tablets you need, check the label for milligrams of elemental calcium per tablet—the amount your body can use. Sometimes calcium is given as percent USRDA. To find milligrams, you add a zero to the percent number. (For example, 20 percent USRDA for calcium equals 200 milligrams.)

Then, to maximize absorption:

• Test your calcium tablets in a glass of warm water. Calcium tablets should disintegrate in one hour (swirl gently several times)—or they may not disintegrate in you, advises Dr. Heaney.

• Take calcium supplements with meals or use chewable calcium-carbonate antacid tablets. Avoid more than 500 milligrams elemental calcium in supplements at one time—spreading them over the day is best.

• Make sure you get 400 international units (IU) of vitamin D per day. This nutrient is an essential part of a strong-bones diet because it helps us absorb calcium into the bloodstream. Two major sources of vitamin D are exposure to sunlight (which causes our skin to make vitamin D) and vitamin D–fortified milk (100 IU per cup). To ensure a predictable supply, many experts now advise women to take a multisupplement with 100 percent of the USRDA for vitamin D, which equals 400 IU. (Don't overdo: Amounts of vitamin D above 1,800 IU may be toxic.)

Remember: Don't rely on supplements alone. Calcium

from food is best—for maximum absorption and for other nutrients that come with it.

Are there other diet habits that impact bone health? Experts say that too much caffeine, protein and sodium have each been associated in some research with excess calcium excretion in the urine. A sensible approach is to limit caffeine to no more than 300 milligrams per day (instant coffee contains about 75 milligrams per 8-ounce cup; brewed coffee, 140 milligrams or more per 8-ounce cup; one 12-ounce can cola, about 50 milligrams). For protein: Limit meat servings to 4 to 6 ounces per day. For sodium: 2,400 milligrams per-day limit.

ESTROGEN REPLACEMENT: IS IT FOR YOU?

After menopause sets in, women's most effective weapon to prevent rapid bone loss is hormone replacement therapy, or HRT—usually a combination of estrogen and progestin. Though calcium and exercise continue to be essential in the years after menopause, they are not enough by themselves to keep your bones from losing ground.

But not all women need HRT. Some have bones dense enough to sustain menopausal losses yet stay above the fracture threshold. Others need HRT to keep borderline bones from wasting into osteoporosis or to keep existing osteoporosis from getting worse. Getting a bone density measurement near the start of menopause will help you decide whether you need HRT—the sooner after menopause HRT is started, the more bone will be saved.

Here's the advice of endocrinologist Robert Lindsay, M.D., president of the National Osteoporosis Foundation.

• Women whose bone density already is low at the onset of menopause should start using HRT to prevent their existing osteoporosis from becoming more severe.

• Women with high bone density and women with borderline density, but no major osteoporosis risk factors, probably will not need HRT to protect their bones. (But because some menopausal women lose bone more rapidly than others, these women may want to monitor bone loss with another bone density measurement in one to three years.)

• Women whose bone density is borderline and who have some major risk factors, especially a mother with osteoporosis, should seriously consider HRT.

RISKS TO CONSIDER

In spite of HRT's power in preventing and treating osteoporosis, doctors estimate that less than 15 percent of women who could benefit from HRT use it. The main reason is women's fear of endometrial and breast cancer. What are the risks?

• It's known that estrogen given alone does increase rates of endometrial cancer in women with an intact uterus. But today's practice of prescribing estrogen with the hormone progesterone completely eliminates this concern.

• Does HRT raise breast cancer risks? "The bottom line is, we don't know," says Dr. Lindsay. Some studies show slightly increased risk, especially at high doses for ten years or more. Other studies show no increased risk, especially more recent studies that used today's lower estrogen dose (0.625 milligrams), which is about half the amount used in earlier studies, he points out. What's more, all studies have shown that women who get breast cancer while on HRT actually have lower rates of death than women with breast cancer who are not on HRT, possibly because estrogen users get mandatory annual mammograms, so breast cancer is detected early when cure rates are best.

Nevertheless, Dr. Lindsay does not advise HRT for women with a family history of breast cancer unless bone density already is low at the start of menopause, and only with careful counseling.

If a woman opts for HRT, how long should she take it? Dr. Lindsay believes HRT can continue for life, provided a woman gets an annual mammogram and pelvic exam and experiences no unacceptable side effects. Whenever HRT is stopped, he points out, rapid bone loss ensues within a matter of weeks.

However, taking HRT for one or five or ten years and then stopping is still of benefit, he says—delaying by that many years the period when a woman's bones may be at risk.

OTHER CONSIDERATIONS

Women should also evaluate their need for HRT in relation to its relief of menopausal symptoms and probable benefit to heart health, as well as potential side effects. Some conditions rule out HRT: known or suspected cancers that can grow faster on estrogen (no woman should begin HRT without first obtaining a negative mammogram); known or suspected pregnancy; undiagnosed vaginal bleeding; active liver disease; severe, uncontrolled high blood pressure; or an active blood-clotting disorder. Some disorders may be aggravated by HRT, such as migraine headaches, fibrocystic breast disease, gallbladder disease and lupus.

As an alternative to HRT, only one other drug, the hormone calcitonin, is approved by the Food and Drug Administration (FDA) for treatment of osteoporosis (though not for prevention—its efficacy for preventing osteoporosis is not well documented). Drawbacks are limited effectiveness in some women, high cost (two to three times as much as estrogen) and the need for daily injections. (A calcitonin nasal spray is up for approval by the FDA.)

Other drugs now in the investigational stage—which means further study is needed to determine long-term efficacy, safe dosage and any harmful side effects—include bisphosphonates, sodium fluoride, tamoxifen-class drugs, calcitriol (a powerful form of vitamin D), parathyroid hormone, and—far on the horizon—bone-growth factors. Unlike estrogen and calcitonin, which simply stop further bone breakdown, some of these drugs work by building back lost bone.

THE BOTTOM LINE

"It's never too late to improve your future bone health by making positive lifestyle changes," says Kristine Harper, M.D., medical director of the Center for Bone Disease at Duke. "My patients who do the best are the ones who go home and make these changes part of their lives. The ones who say, 'This is too hard,' just don't do as well."

Should every woman approaching menopause seek a physical therapist and nutritionist? Dr. Harper thinks that most women can adopt a strong-bones lifestyle just by reading and following the prevention guidelines such as those of the National Osteoporosis Foundation—the same guidelines taught at Duke. However, women below the fracture threshold can benefit from private counseling, particularly with a physical therapist to learn fracture-avoiding ways of moving and exercising.

Do all women need bone density measurements? Because of the expense, Dr. Harper normally advises them around the time of menopause only for women who would use the results to help decide whether to go on HRT or other medication. "If you've already decided to use HRT—or not to use it—then you wouldn't gain anything," she says. But she also advises DEXAs for any woman with several major risk factors. If bones turn out to be below the fracture threshold, it's important to avoid high-risk movements and exercise.

Uncramp Your Style

Get quick relief from monthly miseries.

Some women experience only a mild twinge. But many women suffer, doubled over in lip-biting silence, month after month. Usually, the pain is of mild to moderate intensity, which is bad enough. But occasionally, women swear their menstrual cramps are on a par with labor pains. (In fact, both are precipitated by the same body chemicals.)

Today, thank goodness, there's more to do than plug in the heating pad. Leading gynecologists recommend a plan of action that can often halt your menstrual misery even before you feel the first twinge.

The Prostaglandin Connection

Researchers aren't completely sure what causes painful periods, but most believe that hormonelike substances called prostaglandins are behind the problem. In addition to regulating other functions in your body, prostaglandins stimulate your uterine muscles to contract. In fact, doctors actually use prostaglandins to induce labor in pregnant women, says Toni Harris, M.D., chief of the Division of Gynecology at the University of California, Davis.

Before your period begins, the production of prostaglandins naturally rises. This makes the uterine contractions stronger—probably to help your body push the menstrual fluid out of your uterus, experts say. These contractions may be so mild that you don't feel them at all. But in some women, they can be very intense. The intensity may have to do with the amount of prostaglandins the women produce, researchers think. Indeed, studies suggest that the menstrual fluids of women who have cramps contain higher levels of prostaglandins than the menstrual fluids of women who don't.

Here's the good news. Prostaglandin production can be blocked with a common over-the-counter medication: ibuprofen. In fact, doctors used to prescribe ibuprofen specifically for painful periods before it was available over the counter. (If you have kidney problems, ulcers, nasal polyps or asthma, please consult your physician before self-medicating.)

To get the most benefit from ibuprofen, though, you have to take it correctly, says Susan Ballagh, M.D., director of the Stanford Women's Group at Stanford University Medical School. "Always anticipate the pain and try to get the medication on board before cramps begin, because ibuprofen works much better at preventing pain than it does in removing the pain once it's started," she says.

If your periods are regular or you have body signals like breast tenderness or bloating, it's easy to figure out when you're about a day away from your next period. That's when you begin taking ibuprofen at the dosage recommended on the label—two 200-milligram tablets every four to six hours—and continue that for about two days after you begin bleeding (or for as long as your cramps usually last).

Some women who have more severe pain might want to consider adjusting the dose to a maximum of three 200-milligram pills four times a day (with meals, to avoid side effects). That's equal to the dose used when ibuprofen was available only as a prescription, says Joanne Piscitelli, M.D., head of the Division of General Obstetrics and Gynecology at Duke University School of Medicine in Durham, North Carolina. "But make sure you're limiting it to the couple of days around your periods," she adds.

Ibuprofen may cause side effects, like stomach upset and diarrhea—even stomach bleeding—in some people. That may be doubly troublesome to women who commonly experience stomach problems along with their menstrual cramps. But you can usually avoid that by taking your dose along with meals and by strictly limiting the number of days you take it. To be safe, watch for dark stools, which signal abdominal bleeding, and report them to your doctor. (If you have stomach ulcers, you should avoid taking ibuprofen. Talk to your doctor about alternatives.)

THE NEXT STEP

If you don't find relief after three cycles on the above regimen, see your doctor for a pelvic exam. "If it's normal and there's no reason to suspect that there's a hidden cause for your menstrual cramps, the next step would be to consider taking low-dose birth control pills," Dr. Piscitelli says. Your doctor may even advise you to continue taking ibuprofen for added protection.

Today's commonly prescribed combination birth control pills (containing estrogen and progesterone) help reduce the amount of prostaglandin you produce by preventing ovulation and thinning the lining of the uterus. Some older studies suggested that oral contraceptive use may increase your risk of breast cancer. More recent, higher-quality studies have refuted that evidence, Dr. Harris says.

"The low-dose pills are remarkably safe. They even have some significant health advantages, like lower incidence of ovarian cancer and endometrial cancer, lower incidence of pelvic inflammatory disease and fewer ectopic pregnancies," she says. Women who have a history of heart attack, stroke, high blood pressure and blood clots in their legs or lungs or who have already had breast cancer, though, should avoid taking oral contraceptives.

If you're unable or unwilling to take the Pill, or if after two or three cycles on it your cramps still don't subside, your doctor may prescribe any one of a number of nonsteroidal anti-inflammatory drugs (NSAIDs) that work as "prostaglandin inhibitors"—like ibuprofen, but more powerful. They're prescribed for short-term use—for the day before your period begins and for the first day or two after you start bleeding. While they require less frequent dosing than ibuprofen, these NSAIDs are more likely to cause side effects. You may have to go through a couple of two-cycle trial runs to find a prescription NSAID that relieves your cramps and that you can tolerate, Dr. Ballagh says. It's extremely rare for prescription NSAIDs not to work for simple menstrual cramps, she adds.

SELF-CARE OPTIONS

Unfortunately, the research on self-care remedies for menstrual cramps is sorely lacking. Very often, women must rely on information from other women about what works for them. Our experts suggest that the following, while scientifically unproven, may have some merit in both preventing and easing those monthly woes.

Relax away the pain. There are dozens of good reasons to practice some form of stress management. Preventing and easing menstrual cramps may be one of them.

"Some studies suggest that elevations in stress hormones can increase your perception of pain," explains Dr. Ballagh. "So stress reduction around the time of your period may somewhat reduce your experience of the cramping."

Dr. Harris theorizes that prostaglandins may play a role, too. "There may be a stress component that either alters prostaglandin production or makes the uterus more sensitive to prostaglandin levels," she says.

Whatever the case, Dr. Harris often recommends medication together with relaxation techniques, such as yoga and meditation, to maximize pain relief.

Get moving. As a stress reliever, exercise can't be beat. Plus, there may be another reason it helps to ease menstrual pain. "Exercise does increase the level of endorphins—your body's natural painkillers—and that may have an effect on menstrual cramp pain, but we don't know for sure," says Christine Wells, Ph.D., professor of exercise science and physical education at Arizona State University in Tempe and author of *Women, Sport and Performance.*

WHEN PAINFUL PERIODS SIGNAL SOMETHING ELSE

Painful periods may occasionally signal a serious problem, such as endometriosis (a condition linked to fertility problems), pelvic inflammatory disease or fibroid tumors, says Toni Harris, M.D., chief of the Division of Gynecology at the University of California, Davis. The good news is that these conditions are simple to detect, if you're alert to their symptoms. Here's what to look for.

• Fever

• Vomiting

• An unusually painful period

• Pain that's located on the sides of the pelvis, instead of central, over your pubic bone

• Foul-smelling discharge

• Unusually painful intercourse

• Pain that starts more than a day or two before your period and continues to the end or beyond

While it's often said that menstrual pain should subside with age and after childbirth, don't worry if yours doesn't, Dr. Harris says. "But if you have a period that is really unusually painful—out of step with gradual changes you've been experiencing—you should definitely seek a medical evaluation." You should also schedule an appointment if the self-care measures described previously fail to provide relief.

So even if you're not feeling up to speed, try to stay active (unless, of course, you have severe nausea or are vomiting). If you feel weak in the legs, try something easy, like moderate walking, if you can.

"Sometimes, attacking the problem rather than lying on the couch and being a victim really makes a difference," adds Dr. Harris. Here are some tips for working out when you have cramps.

• Take it easy for the first 15 minutes of your workout. Then pick up the pace, if you feel good enough. If you don't, complete your workout at your warm-up pace.

• Avoid heavy lifting and intense abdominal work on "crampy" days. It's okay to do resistance training when you have cramps, but don't choose that time to increase weight or add new, unfamiliar exercises. Heavy lifting puts stress on your abdominal muscles, which may aggravate your cramps. For that reason, give yourself a couple of days off from stomach crunches and other belly-busting exercises, too.

Curl up—with the "Child's Pose." "Yoga can not only help you relax," says yoga expert Mary Pullig Schatz, M.D., of Centennial Medical Center in Nashville, author of *Back Care Basics*, "but certain poses—particularly forward bends—also allow a gentle compression of the pelvic organs that may also have a soothing effect."

She recommends the Child's Pose for cramp relief. It requires no particular yoga training. But if it causes you any back or hip pain, you should refrain from doing it.

Kneel on the floor, sitting back on your heels, arms at your sides. Bend over and rest your chest on your thighs, keeping your arms alongside your torso. Place your forehead on the floor, or turn your head to the side. Inhale deeply through your nose, exhale through your nose and pause a second or two before you inhale again. Hold the pose for as long as you're comfortable (up to several minutes).

If you're at all uncomfortable, try placing folded or rolled-up towels under your ankles to prevent excessive stretching, under your buttocks if you have trouble sitting back on your heels or beneath your head for cushioning or if you can't rest your head on the floor. If you feel any knee pain, place a rolled-up sock in the bend of each knee to create more space.

18

OUTSMARTING
OVARIAN CANCER

Take positive action with this lifetime protection plan.

"My wife Gilda was afraid of cancer all her life," recounts Gene Wilder in a public-service ad. "And even with wonderful doctors, no one discovered she had ovarian cancer until it was too late...."

The ad, sponsored by a renowned cancer treatment center, goes on to caution women: "If you have vague symptoms, like abdominal bloating, clothes that feel tight, backache and sudden fatigue, don't worry, they're normal. But if they don't go away—and especially if you have a family history of ovarian cancer—see your doctor right away."

Well-intentioned as it may be, this ad sent an untold number of healthy women into a state of near panic. We know this because several of our friends were among them. They confided to us that, after seeing that ad, they dashed to their gynecologists and insisted on pelvic exams, sonograms and CA-125 blood tests (just as the ad advised).

None, thankfully, had anything to worry about. But their experience may give reason for concern.

IN SEARCH OF BETTER SCREENING
GUIDELINES

Should every woman who notices these vague and common symptoms be concerned about the possibility of ovarian cancer and get tested? And more important, haven't better screening guidelines been established that can detect ovarian cancer in its very early stages, before symptoms develop?

Leading experts at America's best cancer centers and research institutions say that while the public-service message delivered by Gene Wilder, widower of the late *Saturday Night Live* comedienne Gilda Radner, is technically accurate, it is horribly misleading.

"Suggesting to a woman that if she has abdominal bloating she should see her doctor right away because it could be ovarian cancer is like saying if you have a headache, it's time to see a neurosurgeon because you probably have a brain tumor," says Michael Muto, M.D., head of the Familial Ovarian Cancer Center at Brigham and Women's Hospital, Harvard Medical School.

Nearly every woman has stepped into pants that won't snap. "But the percentage of women who have these symptoms and have ovarian cancer is very, very small," notes William Hoskins, M.D., chief of gynecology services at Memorial Sloan-Kettering Cancer Center in New York City.

Besides, treating ovarian cancer after symptoms develop is more difficult.

Detecting ovarian cancer before symptoms erupt is the best bet; at this early stage, women with ovarian cancer have an 80 to 90 percent survival rate, according to the American College of Obstetricians and Gynecologists. But, to date, there are no established screening guidelines for ovarian cancer, as there are for, say, breast cancer or cervical cancer.

Organizations like the American Cancer Society and the National Cancer Institute argue that because ovarian cancer is rare, mass screening of all women is not economical. The average woman has a 1 in 65 chance of developing ovarian cancer over her lifetime as compared with a 1 in 8 chance of getting breast cancer.

An even more compelling argument against mass screening is that the best available tests are unreliable. The CA-125 blood test, in particular, is notoriously inaccurate. Since the only way to confirm cancer is through a surgical biopsy, mistakenly abnormal results on a CA-125 blood test too often lead to unnecessary surgery.

WHAT'S A WOMAN TO DO?

Obviously, this is another area of women's health where medical research is sorely lacking. The question is: What's the best you can do to protect yourself now?

First, nearly every expert says to keep your concern in perspective. The fact is, ovarian cancer is a relatively uncommon disease. "There will be approximately 182,000 new cases of breast cancer diagnosed this year and 22,000 new cases of ovarian cancer," Dr. Muto explains.

"This is not a disease we should be in a panic about," agrees Susan Harlap, M.D., epidemiologist at Memorial Sloan-Kettering Cancer Center. "The vast majority of women are not at risk and needn't worry."

Of course, some of us may be at higher risk. And it's important for us to know that so we can channel our concern into positive action.

FOR WOMEN AT HIGH RISK

Experts agree that the number-one risk factor for ovarian cancer is a family history of the disease. Primarily, a woman who has at least one documented case of ovarian cancer in an immediate relative—a mother, sister or daughter—is considered at high risk. Having an aunt or grandmother ups her risk, too, but not to the same degree.

It's important to note, however, that having a family history of ovarian cancer doesn't mean you're born with a time bomb ticking inside. It means that there's a chance you may have inherited a flawed gene that could make you more vulnerable to the disease. Unfortunately, there's no way to tell whether you've inherited the gene. Not yet, anyway, though Dr. Muto anticipates that within the next five years genetic testing will make it possible to do just that.

In the meantime, if you know or suspect that anyone in your family had ovarian cancer, make an appointment with a women's cancer specialist (a gynecologic oncologist) for a risk assessment.

Cancer specialists say many women mistakenly believe their families carry hereditary ovarian cancer. "It sometimes turns out that the relative had another type of cancer that spread to the ovaries. Once you put the pieces together, it really isn't ovarian cancer," says Neil Rosenshein, M.D., director of the division of gynecologic oncology at Johns Hopkins University Medical Center in Baltimore.

Another consideration is that few cases of ovarian cancer are hereditary—only 5 percent, says Dr. Rosenshein. Having an immediate relative with ovarian cancer doesn't mean it's genetic or hereditary. It could be just chance. Short of obtaining permis-

THE BEST TESTS . . .
AT LEAST FOR NOW

Screening for ovarian cancer is a terribly imperfect science. That's why the National Cancer Institute is planning clinical trials to help evaluate the lifesaving value of the following tests. Until the results are in, here's what is known.

• *Pelvic exam.* A basic and essential tool in screening all women for ovarian cancer. In this exam, a physician inserts one finger into the vagina and presses on the abdomen with the other hand to palpate the ovaries for abnormalities. Another variation is to perform the same pelvic exam, with one finger in the vagina and another in the rectum.
According to Conley Lacey, M.D., at Scripps Clinic and Research Foundation, this allows for a more thorough assessment of the ovaries. Effectiveness depends, to a very large degree, on the experience and training of the physician and on the woman's build (excess abdominal weight can interfere with accuracy).

• *Transvaginal ultrasound.* Useful in combination with the pelvic exam to screen women at high and above-average risk. Also used to assess women whose pelvic exams are inadequate or suspicious. In transvaginal ultrasound (called sonogram), a probe is inserted into the vagina and high-frequency sound waves are bounced off the uterus and ovaries; the resulting image is trans-

sion to see your relative's medical records (which is definitely worth the effort if you're in doubt), the only clue that you may be dealing with a hereditary disease is the age at which your relative was stricken. Familial ovarian cancer tends to strike women ten years sooner, on average, than nonfamilial ovarian cancer. Also, a family tree strewn with multiple cases of ovarian cancer suggests a familial pattern.

mitted to a viewing monitor. The test can detect an enlarged ovary, which may suggest cancer.

But it's far from foolproof. As William Hoskins, M.D., at Memorial Sloan-Kettering Cancer Center in New York City explains, not every enlarged ovary is cancerous. Unfortunately, determining whether it is requires a surgical biopsy. Because of that—and the high cost of the exam (about $300)—transvaginal ultrasound is reserved as a tool for women at risk for ovarian cancer.

• *CA-125 blood test.* Too troublesome to use for screening. This blood test, which screens for antibodies produced by cancer cells, is notoriously inaccurate. It misses about half of the early ovarian cancers it should detect, says Dr. Hoskins. And according to a National Cancer Institute study, it sometimes suggests cancer in women who are disease-free; pregnancy, endometriosis, pelvic inflammatory disease, uterine fibroids, even menstruation can skew the test results. Besides, Michael Muto, M.D., head of the Familial Ovarian Cancer Center at Brigham and Women's Hospital, Harvard Medical School, points out, CA-125 has never been approved by the Food and Drug Administration for use as a screening test; its only approved usage is for assessing recurrences in women treated for ovarian cancer.

Experts agree that the highest hereditary risk is reserved primarily for women who have either two or more immediate relatives (mother, sister or daughter) with documented ovarian cancer or one immediate relative and multiple distant relatives (aunt, grandmother or other) with the disease.

Apparently, too, a woman has an elevated risk of developing ovarian cancer if (1) her family tree is laden with ovarian cancer plus breast cancer or (2) her family tree has a preponderance of colon cancer along with any of these: ovarian, endometrial (uterine), lung, pancreatic or prostate cancer.

However, some experts say that having just one immediate relative with the disease is enough to nudge you into the high-risk category. Often, however, it can be difficult to prove if what a relative had was really ovarian cancer. Unless you can prove beyond reasonable doubt that it wasn't, you'd be wise to take a cautious approach.

Being cautious means continuing to see a qualified gynecologist—preferably a gynecologic oncologist—for periodic checkups. As a woman's cancer specialist, a gynecologic oncologist has specialized training and experience to help you decide on a personal action plan.

Cancer specialists say the best advice for women at high risk would be to have a pelvic exam and/or a transvaginal ultrasound every six months beginning between ages 21 and 25. (See "The Best Tests . . . at Least for Now" on page 164.)

Dr. Rosenshein usually alternates these two tests at six-month intervals for his high-risk patients. Conley Lacey, M.D., head of gynecologic oncology at the Scripps Clinic and Research Foundation, tailors the tests to each individual. He gives his high-risk patients a pelvic exam every six months and makes liberal use of transvaginal ultrasound, particularly in women who are difficult to examine because of anxiety or excess body weight or when the pelvic exam findings are suspicious.

FOR WOMEN AT ABOVE-AVERAGE RISK

Although heredity represents the most significant risk factor for ovarian cancer, 95 percent of the women who develop the disease do not have a family history of it.

The search for reasons has led researchers to identify other possible risk factors. Two groups of women have emerged with above-average risk: women who have not had children and have not taken oral contraceptives, and women who have had breast cancer.

How many ovulations you have during your reproductive years appears to be a critical issue in determining ovarian cancer risk, explains Dr. Rosenshein. If you ovulate continually until menopause, without interruption by pregnancy, breast-feeding or the use of oral contraceptives, your ovaries are subject to monthly hormonal stimulation. This, experts believe, may increase cancer risk to the ovaries.

A woman who has had breast cancer is considered to be at increased risk for ovarian cancer as well, for reasons that are not exactly known. Like breast cancer, ovarian cancer is an age-specific disease, meaning that it's more likely to occur as you get older. The chance of developing ovarian cancer takes its biggest jump between the ages of 50 and 65, from about 28 cases per 100,000 to 54 cases per 100,000, and peaks around age 70 to 74 with 60 cases per 100,000 women. A woman at above-average risk (because of either uninterrupted ovulation or previous breast cancer) needs to be aware that advancing age may compound her risk.

If you fit the risk profile described here, take your concerns to a gynecologist (preferably a gynecologic oncologist) and discuss an action plan that's right for you. In addition to an annual pelvic exam, some experts offer their patients transvaginal ultrasound and suggest that it may be wise to have one once a year, beginning at age 35, as a precaution. However, they are quick to add that while transvaginal ultrasound is a valuable tool, it is not perfect. It can detect enlargements of the ovaries, but it cannot tell if they're due to cancer. So in coming up with a plan that's right for you, it's a good idea to discuss with a gynecologic oncologist the pros and cons of transvaginal ultrasound.

FOR WOMEN AT NONINCREASED RISK

Experts emphasize the importance of regular gynecologic care for women who are at no increased risk for ovarian cancer, since neither CA-125 nor transvaginal ultrasound is an appropriate test for the general population.

A careful pelvic examination at the time of a Pap test (to detect cervical cancer) should be performed by a qualified physician or health professional once a year beginning at age 18 (or sooner if a woman is sexually active).

"I urge women to have a pelvic exam and Pap test every year without fail, never to miss a mammogram and to examine their breasts every month," advises Dr. Muto.

To Remove or Not to Remove the Ovaries

That's a big question. And one that 295,000 American women say yes to each year. According to the National Center for Health Statistics, that's how many women surrender their healthy ovaries while having a hysterectomy—presumably to prevent ovarian cancer.

How many of those oophorectomies (ovary removals) are warranted?

Considering that ovarian cancer is rare and strikes just 22,000 women each year, it's fair to say that many healthy ovaries are removed unnecessarily. For most women, however, the fear of ovarian cancer overshadows the real risk-versus-benefit considerations.

"The trade-off is heart disease and osteoporosis," says Theodore Speroff, Ph.D. At Case Western Reserve University in Cleveland, Dr. Speroff conducted a careful risk-versus-benefit study of whether to remove or not to remove the ovaries in women in their thirties and forties. Compared with women who kept their ovaries, these women will suffer more heart attacks and hip fractures due to osteoporosis. Hormone replacement therapy can help protect against these serious problems, but compliance tends to be insufficient to offset the time spent without functioning ovaries. A woman who has her ovaries removed before menopause has to be willing to take hormones for the rest of her life. Also, some experts feel that estrogen provided by a pill or patch is not as good as what the body produces. "The ovaries provide a wonderful and continuous source of estrogen that I don't think can be easily replaced by estrogen therapy," says Dr. Rosenshein.

Most physicians agree, it's best to hang on to healthy, functioning ovaries if you can. Cancer experts would be reluctant to remove the healthy ovaries of a woman under age 40 unless she had a very strong family history of ovarian cancer (at least two immediate relatives) and had finished having children. According to Dr. Rosenshein, "As long as there is no good indication for removing them, I favor ovary preservation."

What if a woman is having a hysterectomy (surgical removal of the uterus) for other reasons? Should she consider having her ovaries removed at the same time? "After age 50, the ovaries have usually stopped functioning, so I recommend removing them," says Dr. Hoskins. "Between ages 40 and 50, it's entirely up to the patient. However, she needs to understand the pros and cons of removing them or leaving them in. The only reason to remove them is to prevent ovarian cancer, and most women are at very low risk for the disease. Personally I prefer not to take out the ovaries in anyone under the age of 45, except when there's a family history of ovarian cancer."

SHOULD YOU TAKE BIRTH CONTROL PILLS?

Birth control pills interrupt ovulation, just as pregnancy does, which appears to be a plus in preventing ovarian cancer. Even using the Pill for as little as one year can reduce your risk. After four years of use, risk is reduced by almost 50 percent. That's roughly the same degree of protection as having three full-term pregnancies, says Dr. Rosenshein.

Is that reason enough to suggest taking oral contraceptives as a preventive?

There's no simple answer. For some women, it's definitely not an option. The health risks for certain women (such as those with known heart disease, high blood pressure, active liver disease or a personal history of breast cancer, stroke or phlebitis) outweigh the health benefits, according to Paul Blumenthal, M.D., director of contraceptive research programs, Francis Scott Key Medical Center in Baltimore. Likewise, the Pill is not advised for women who smoke, especially if they're over age 35.

But for those who can safely take the Pill and are at high risk for ovarian cancer, "oral contraceptives are certainly a strategy to consider," says Dr. Rosenshein. "I personally have prescribed them for young women with a strong family history of ovarian cancer."

"The use of oral contraceptives for two years or more does appear to significantly decrease the risk of ovarian cancer as well as endometrial cancer—and the benefits are lifelong," says Dr. Hoskins. "I think it's reasonable to recommend them for primary prevention in high-risk women."

Whether child-free or infertile women (who are considered at above-average risk) should take the Pill for prevention is hotly debated, however. "Right now, I'd be a little reluctant to recommend birth control pills for someone who doesn't need them for contraception just because that person is in the moderate-risk category," says Dr. Hoskins. But he feels women should be given the facts about oral contraceptives' protective effect.

"I think it is something a woman needs to consider in her overall health care," agrees Dr. Lacey. "You need to tell her that she may be able to reduce her risk of ovarian cancer by as much as 50 percent. Then she can make a decision about using this as a preventive measure."

It's also unclear whether women over 40 who are at high or above-average risk can benefit from the protection of birth control pills. Despite this, several experts admitted that it's reasonable to recommend the Pill to women up to age 45 who are at risk.

For women at no increased risk, a decision to take oral contraceptives should be made strictly because of a need for contraception and not to prevent ovarian cancer.

Emotions

and

Your

Health

19
NATURAL GRACE

Let nature's tranquillity revitalize you in midlife and beyond.

Remember, as a child, your secret garden or woodland cove—your private nature retreat? There, you could tell a tree or a star your innermost feelings without fear of judgment or rejection. You could go to this place and be yourself and feel accepted.

In the journey toward becoming grown up, many of us abandoned the wisdom of our youth. It wasn't intentional. We just got busy establishing and juggling careers, families and homes. By the time we got a free moment to look up from our "to do" lists, two or even three decades had whizzed by.

All too often, we arrive at midlife overworked and overwhelmed, with spirits that ache for more.

"In midlife, we become aware of the need for simplicity, the need to decompress," says Ross Goldstein, Ph.D., a San Francisco psychologist and expert in the psychology of midlife, and author of *Fortysomething*. "We desperately long to slow down the manic pace, tune out the clamor of demands and find a source of silence, tranquillity and rejuvenation."

If only we would remember to turn our gaze to the awe of a child, we would recall that such a place exists within our grasp—in a garden, in a woods, by a stream. In nature, we would find what we're longing for: a beauty and stillness that lets the extraneous fall away and allows the essence of who we really are to emerge.

WAKING UP TO MIDLIFE

Like a tree sending roots deep into the soil, reconnecting with our true selves provides us with stability and equanimity in the face of midlife gusts. "The three big wake-up calls of midlife are disconcerting," says Dr. Goldstein. "They include the realizations that, one, you're not going to become president of the company (or, if you are president, it's not as fun as you thought it would be); two, your family life is never going to look like Ozzie and Harriet's; and three, you're not going to live forever."

The good news is that these painful realizations can prompt positive change and propel us to a new level of personal growth and fulfillment.

"Everybody does some soul-searching in midlife, but the degree to which people reorganize their lives and make significant changes varies," says Dr. Goldstein.

"Typically, people ask themselves 'Where am I going with my life? What should I do?' But midlife isn't just about what you do; it's primarily about who you are," Dr. Goldstein points out. "If we wish to embrace the second half of life with renewed vitality and vigor, we must devote some quality time at midlife to reassessing who we've come to be and who we'd still like to become.

"That process, we know from experience, does not happen spontaneously," he explains. "The inner voice that holds the answers cannot be heard against the din of everyday static. In order to hear it, we must stop and intentionally carve out a little quiet, contemplative time."

SUPPORT FROM MOTHER EARTH

Nature provides the perfect antidote to our hectic and complex existence.

"In the material, conventional world, we are pitting our own lives against a pace of existence that almost doesn't have room for our pace," says Mel Bucholtz, a therapist and co-director of the Returning to Earth Institute in Lincoln Center, Massachusetts, which hosts wilderness trips. "When we go back to the natural world, we start to see a time sequence that we fit into. Instead of pressure we feel acceptance." For once, we feel content not doing anything, just being.

"In the quiet of nature, you get the solitude and presence of mind to deal with the significant issues of your life," says Valerie Andrews, author of *A Passion for This Earth*. "It is when you allow the tide of your own activity to go out. And in the absence of all those activities, you gain wisdom and insight."

Compost for Personal Growth

Nature not only frees us from noise and distractions, but the natural processes and rhythms also provide valuable insights into our personal transitions.

One of the most difficult tasks of the midlife transition is learning to let go of old, outmoded life structures in order to move on to new ones.

"When you talk to people who are beginning the process, they talk about loss, about the things they have to give up, not about what they're going to gain," says Dr. Goldstein.

"Saying good-bye to an unrealistic image of yourself, to your dreams that haven't panned out, to careers, to people—friends, spouses, parents—inherently carries pain," he continues. "But you've got to say good-bye before you can say hello to whatever will be the next life structure that you're looking at.

"If you can't let go of those things and go into another cycle of risk and challenge, you just repeat the same thing over and over again and get stuck in old patterns of being," Andrews adds.

Nature helps people realize how to accomplish the transition. "Sitting next to a rotting stump, a person may notice new shoots growing out of the decay. That's a graphic example of transition," explains Bucholtz. "What people discover is that, as things decay, compost is created to foster new growth."

Taking lessons from nature helps us more gracefully surrender to the natural ebb and flow of life.

"The process of moving around obstacles is reflected beautifully against the backdrop of a natural phenomenon like a river or a storm," Bucholtz says. "When you see how a river changes course to continue its flow, or witness the way a landscape recovers after a devastating storm, you see how you can work in the way nature does with regard to change."

Submitting to the natural order induces a tremendous sense of relief because we no longer have to fight it. We can simply go with the flow.

One with Nature

There's also something very comforting in knowing you're connected to the whole of nature. You're not outside of it; you're a part of it.

"In a way, a lot of people feel as though they're coming

How to Get a Spirit Lift from Nature

Between concrete walls, shopping malls and city halls, it's darn hard to find open space anymore. Top that with a hectic lifestyle, and no wonder communing with nature gets the squeeze. Luckily, there are ways to creatively bring nature to your doorstep, even if you live in the city.

Take your fitness walks in a tranquillity zone. Instead of beating your feet along city sidewalks or suburban sprawls, treat yourself to a gentle path in a nearby woods or park. Tune into the seasonal changes, the play of sunlight and shadows and the movement of wildlife. Be a nature observer and explorer. Take a field guide with you on your wilderness walks and learn the indigenous birds and trees by name. Or discover a microworld of activity with a magnifying glass. Let the lens of a camera reveal new ways to look at familiar surroundings.

Get a dog. Rain or shine, Rufus gets you out of your four walls and into the open air. One inhabitant of Pasadena swears, "I've never been more in touch with nature than since I got my dog."

Find a secluded spot, sit and watch. At first, against the chaos of your mind's activity, it will seem that nothing is happening. But give the mental chatter time to wind down and your senses a chance to open up. Listen. Smell. Watch. Feel. Soon you'll begin to notice a fascinating universe of life around you.

Garden. Having even a small plot where you can dig, plant seeds and watch things grow is a powerful way of getting in synchronization with natural cycles. Window gardens can delight city dwellers, too.

Seek outdoor adventures close to home. Revive your thrill-seeking urge! Get the pink back in your cheeks with a refreshing challenge like inner-tubing down a river or hitting local trails on a mountain bike. Cap off your invigorating day with a relaxing picnic.

home when they're in the natural world," Bucholtz explains. "They belong in nature. They fit. They're an integral part of a system. That gives people we've seen a tremendous sense of personal relief."

"When I was going through my own midlife conflicts, I often rode my bike out to the ocean," says Dr. Goldstein. "I would be preoccupied trying to make decisions about my future and I would look out at the ocean and say, 'This has been here forever and it's going to be here forever,' and soon, the insignificance of my decisions would pale by comparison.

"At first, I'd feel my insignificance down in my gut. But then, that would be replaced by a tremendous comfort, a feeling of safety in just being a small cog in the larger works."

AWAKENING THE SENSES

Spending time in nature can also reinvigorate us by reawakening our senses and our creative spirits.

"In the urban environment, people tend to be mostly in their heads. They don't use their senses and end up missing very important information," says Jackie Farley, president of CenterPoint nature retreat center for women in Aspen, Colorado. "In nature, we become more present, more mindful, more aware of our surroundings."

To bring that concept to life, participants in Farley's retreats hike the Braille Trail, a nature trail near Independence Pass designed for the blind. The group walks the trail twice, first blindfolded and then with eyes open.

"What we discover is that as we overuse one sense, such as our eyes, we shortchange information coming from the other senses," says Farley. "When blindfolded, we hear more, we feel the sun as we move in and out of it, we smell the rich earth. As we gain access to all our senses, we become whole again.

"I don't see how we can be fully aware of our power to make decisions and to listen to our intuition unless we learn to use all the parts of ourselves as sources of information."

"As the aesthetic senses reawaken, people begin to talk about the reawakening of their sense of life in an almost artistic way," says Bucholtz.

Whether it's to invent an object, a painting, music, a social program, a new way of being in a relationship—whatever—people often feel inspired by the richness and diversity of the natural environment. Regaining the creative impulse is a found treasure—something many claim they'd lost years ago.

THE PHYSICAL CHALLENGE

Inspiration can come from watching a sunset, a snowfall, a tree turned gold in autumn. But it can also come from climbing a mountain or swimming against a swift river current. Meeting the physical challenges of nature has special meaning in midlife.

"We don't test our bodies very often," says Nancy Goddard, a leader of backpacking journeys into wilderness areas of the country. "A lot of people at midlife have given up on their bodies and succumb to aging without challenging themselves in a way that shows their physical strength and vitality."

As people then confront and triumph over physical challenges, they feel incredibly empowered emotionally as well, she adds. "Suddenly, they have a faith in themselves they didn't have before."

Dr. Goldstein agrees. "Tenacity as a character trait is ambiguous. But tenacity, as characterized by the ability to continue rowing a boat or hiking up a steep trail long past the point where you want to quit, is concrete. Seeing yourself in that light is very valuable." With nature to nurture us, midlife becomes a season of wonder and rejuvenation, when our lives really bear fruit.

THE HEALING EMOTIONS

Relaxing and reducing stress are key strategies in fighting heart disease.

It's 7:00 A.M. A morning mist envelops the San Francisco skyline, visible through the bank of windows, as our group quietly shuffles about, unfurling blankets on the floor. One by one, we lie down, our feet facing opposite walls and heads coming together along a center aisle. Within minutes, we are breathing in unison. Slow, deep breaths. One can almost sense the walls expanding and contracting.

"Take a nice deep inhalation . . . and as you exhale, feel that exhale sinking into the body, letting the entire body relax. . . ."

The voice of the yoga instructor flows over us.

"Be aware of any tension in the body. . . and with the next breath allow that tension to dissipate. . . and relax . . . now do a gentle hum . . . feel it vibrating your inner body. . . . Hummmmm . . . Ummmmmmmmmmmmmmm. . . ."

Welcome to Dr. Dean Ornish's "Open Your Heart" retreat. This special seven-day event, offered several times a year in Oakland, California, immerses participants in the lifestyle program that Dr. Ornish has proven can reverse heart disease, opening up blocked coronary arteries and greatly improving blood flow to the heart.

The program includes a nearly fat-free vegetarian diet, about 30 minutes a day of moderate aerobic exercise, such as walking, and advice to quit smoking. Perhaps the most intriguing part of the program, however, focuses on stress management and psychological issues. At the retreat, about four hours a day are devoted to this—two hours to yoga, an hour to guided imagery and meditation and another hour to group support.

"Sometimes people think of this as the California 'touchy-feely' aspects of what we're doing, even though from my perspective, it's probably one of the most important and powerful components of the program," Dr. Ornish explains to the 100-plus participants on the first day of the retreat.

"We have shown, using PET scans and angiograms, that people who practice some form of relaxation like yoga or meditation and meet regularly with a support group experience a greater degree of reversal than if they attack the problem only at a physical level, say with just diet or cholesterol-lowering drugs."

HEART AND MIND

Of course, Dr. Ornish believes all the components of his lifestyle program are important. But when it comes to fighting heart disease, the biggest battle is waged in the mind, he says.

He believes that that's where heart disease very often starts and where the healing process begins.   .

This may sound pretty radical, but Dr. Ornish doesn't have to convince this audience. Many have read his book—*Dr. Dean Ornish's Program for Reversing Heart Disease*—at least once. Some are already devouring his latest work, *Eat More, Weigh Less*. They've come here from all across the United States and as far away as India and Brazil; most either have heart disease or are accompanying someone who does. ·

There are even two hospital teams in attendance—from Beth Israel Hospital in New York City and Immanuel Hospital in Omaha—who intend to take Dr. Ornish's teachings back to their hospitals. This is evidence that this approach is gaining support among leading cardiologists who recognize that there's more to treating heart disease than bypass surgery and angioplasty.

To Dr. Ornish, bypass surgery is also a metaphor for an incomplete approach to dealing with a problem. "If you bypass the problem and don't also address what caused it, the bypass will tend to clog up over time," he says. "But by tracing the chain of events that leads to heart disease back to the beginning—to the cause—then the healing is often much more powerful."

Experts know that smoking, high blood pressure, poor diet and sedentary living, as well as certain things we can't control, such as age, gender and genetics, contribute to the problem. While important, those factors explain only about 50 percent of heart disease. Besides, says Dr. Ornish, "I don't think any of them go to the core of why people develop heart disease."

Decades of research have amassed mountains of evidence linking heart disease with emotional stress. (See "The Stress Connection" on page 180.) But it's not stress per se that's the problem. "Stress comes not so much from what you do but, more important, how you react to what you do," Dr. Ornish explains. "You can take two people, put them in the same job, with the same office, same responsibilities, and one may love it and thrive; the other may hate it and have a heart attack."

Why? Because some people react in a way that's driven by emotions like anger and depression. And studies have repeatedly demonstrated that people who harbor these emotions and react accordingly are prone to heart attacks. (See "Hostility, Hopelessness and the Heart" on page 182.)

THE STRESS CONNECTION

Spot a sinister stranger approaching you on a desolate street, and you'll feel your stress response kick in immediately. Your heart pounds. Pulse races. Blood pressure spikes. At the same time, adrenaline and steroids such as cortisol surge into the bloodstream to pump up energy and muscle strength. Other hormones are released to make your arteries constrict and your blood clot more easily to minimize blood loss.

You're ready to run like the wind or, if it comes to blows, to defend yourself mightily. Afterward, the heart settles down, the hormones recede and no harm's done.

But when the threat is emotional and ongoing (say, an intolerable work situation or interminable traffic jam), those helpful hormones can turn on you.

Medical researchers believe that, over time, excess cortisol and other steroids in the bloodstream may accelerate plaque formation along artery walls. At Bowman Gray School of Medicine of Wake Forest University in Winston-Salem, North Carolina, studies with monkeys, whose cardiovascular systems are very similar to ours, show that emotional stress (caused by the disruption of

At the core of the problem, he believes, is often a sense of social isolation. This became evident in his research; participants frequently described themselves as not feeling connected, of lacking support—that they're apart from rather than a part of a larger community.

"When you relate to the world from a position of isolation, it may lead to chronic stress and ultimately to illness," says Dr. Ornish. "In fact, there's increasing scientific evidence that people who feel socially isolated have three to five times the premature mortality rate not only from cardiovascular disease but also from all other causes."

By addressing the underlying emotional issues and recreating a sense of connection and community, however, we can the animals' social bonds) significantly increases coronary blockages. And this blockage occurs regardless of diet and blood cholesterol levels. And when the monkeys were fed a typical high-fat diet, emotional stress magnified the process of atherosclerosis 30 times! Research also suggests that cholesterol-encrusted coronary arteries tend to constrict in response to stress to a much greater degree than healthy arteries, seriously jeopardizing blood flow to the heart.

Furthermore, according to Thomas Pickering, M.D., professor of medicine at New York Hospital–Cornell Medical Center's Hypertension Center, there's mounting interest in "trigger factors," which are surges in blood pressure and heart rate—possibly caused by emotional stress—that some believe may cause the plaque in a coronary artery to rupture and a blood clot to form there, precipitating a heart attack.

"What appears to be clear now is that even people with relatively mild atherosclerosis can experience such an event and suffer a heart attack as a result," says Dr. Pickering.

---

transform anger to contentment and hopelessness to hope, according to Dr. Ornish.

What's more, he continues, when we deal with the emotional issues, people are more willing to change their behaviors for the better and to maintain them over the long run.

"Telling someone who is feeling unhappy and depressed and who feels that his or her life is out of control that they may live longer if they just give up meat or stop smoking isn't likely to motivate them. Many people who are unhappy don't want to live longer.

"If instead we help them address what's making them unhappy and show them how to regain control over their lives," he
(continued on page 184)

Hostility, Hopelessness and the Heart

Dean Ornish, M.D., director of the Preventive Medicine Research Institute in Sausalito, California, acknowledges that he isn't the first physician to connect heart and mind. More than a decade ago, two San Francisco cardiologists—Meyer Friedman, M.D., and Ray Rosenman, M.D.—established type A behavior as a coronary risk factor that rivals smoking, serum cholesterol and high blood pressure.

Type A refers to a pattern of behavior characterized by easily aroused anger, hostility and impatience. Type A people are always in a hurry; they talk fast, eat fast, drive fast. They can also explode in a rage at the least provocation.

Moreover, Dr. Friedman and his colleagues showed that by teaching angry, impatient type A heart patients to deal with stressful situations in a more appropriate and relaxed manner, subsequent heart attacks could be cut by 45 percent.

Since then, Redford Williams, M.D., has made similar observations. His years of research involving thousands of people established a link between hostility and increased risk of death not only from heart disease but also from all other causes. Dr. Williams, professor of psychiatry and director of the Behavioral Medicine Research Center at Duke University Medical Center in Durham, North Carolina, and coauthor of Anger Kills, characterizes this "hostility factor" as cynical mistrust of others and frequent feelings of anger, both of which can (and often do) erupt in emotional outbursts.

"The hostile person always suspects that others are out for themselves and can't be depended upon," he explains. "That's why he counts the number of items in the basket of the person ahead of him in the express lane. Or why he always checks up on his wife's projects around the house to be sure she's doing them right.

"It's no wonder he's often angered, irritated or annoyed," says Dr. Williams. "If you go around looking for people who are screwing up, you'll probably find enough to keep you pretty well ticked off most of the time."

Researchers in the United States and Canada point to another emotional tie to heart disease. At the Centers for Disease Control and Prevention in Atlanta, Robert Anda, M.D., exposed a clear correlation between feelings of depression and hopelessness and incidence of heart attacks among a random sample of nearly 3,000 people. In fact, the risk of both fatal and nonfatal heart attacks was nearly double among those who reported the strongest feelings of hopelessness as compared with those who reported low to no feelings of hopelessness.

Meanwhile, Nancy Frasure-Smith, Ph.D., and colleagues at the Montreal Heart Institute found that coronary patients suffering from severe depression were five times more likely to die within six months of their heart attacks than those who weren't depressed.

"We looked into the possibility that the depressed people may have been sicker. But even when we took severity of disease into account, the results were the same," says Dr. Frasure-Smith. "What we're finding is that depression is, in fact, a new risk factor for survival after a heart attack."

None of this comes as a surprise to James Billings, Ph.D., who helped Dr. Ornish develop his program. A psychologist and cardiovascular epidemiologist with 20 years of research experience, Dr. Billings has seen, firsthand, this spectrum of negative emotions among heart patients.

"Beneath the type A behavior lies a tremendous need to be in control. Part of what happens to people who have heart attacks is that there's a loss of control. That's what precipitates depression," says Dr. Billings. "When you feel helpless to deal with your situation and circumstances look hopeless, you're depressed. What people need then is something they can do that they believe is going to make a difference—to give them back their sense of control."

says, "people are more likely to make and maintain choices that are life-enhancing rather than self-destructive."

SHORT-CIRCUITING THE STRESS RESPONSE

Achieving this—or rather learning the skills that will help achieve this—is the reason so many people with heart conditions have come to the "Open Your Heart" retreat. Yoga, meditation, guided imagery and support groups—all part of the week's experience—are components of Dr. Ornish's master plan to short-circuit the emotional factors that may wreak havoc with the heart.

At 7:00 A.M. and again at 4:00 P.M., groups of 20 to 25 convene in quiet corners of Oakland's Claremont Hotel, the retreat's location, for an hour of delicious relaxation via yoga. We inhale slowly, deeply, feeling our abdomens expand, then our chests, and exhaling completely through the nose. We twist and stretch our bodies, tightening muscles we'd long forgotten. Then we release our tensions into the floor as we close our eyes and let our minds drift off to a safe and tranquil daydream.

The problem is that many people don't even realize how much tension they carry with them, explains James Billings, Ph.D., director of psychological services for the Preventive Medicine Research Institute in Sausalito, California, a nonprofit institute directed by Dr. Ornish. In fact, that anger, that tension, is stored in the muscles of the body. Yoga essentially stretches the accumulated tension out of the muscles in the body. "What happens, very often, is that people have their first sense of what it feels like to relax. The juxtaposition between relaxed and tense gives people very specific feedback—it's like biofeedback," he says.

Yoga breathing techniques are valuable, too. When people get angry or anxious, they very often stop breathing. This then causes a kind of desperate, panicky physiologic response, Dr. Billings explains. By training people how to breathe deeply, however, they learn how to recognize what it feels like when they're starting to get tense. Then they can take a moment to breathe deeply into their abdomens, which gives them some sense of control over what's happening.

While yoga stretches and breathing techniques act on a

physical level, meditation settles the mind. Some time during the day—usually in the evening, before bedtime, in a group or a private session—the retreat participants practice this technique. Seated in comfortable positions, we close our eyes, take a deep inhalation, then exhale. On this particular day, the voices and clanging of pots from the kitchen next door pierce the silence. At first, the unwelcomed noise creates tension and the natural inclination is to resist. But meditation leader Art Brownstein, M.D., suggests to us that we "accept" the sounds around us and "gently allow" our attention to come to our breathing.

Instantly, the mental shift from resistance to acceptance sends comforting waves throughout the body. Faces soften, shoulders relax, as our attention turns inward to "watch" the gently undulating air currents flowing through our body with every inhalation and exhalation. Dr. Brownstein offers a suggestion that we imagine the breath one color as it enters the body and another color as it leaves. Suddenly, the mind's eye is producing dazzling, abstract videos of these air waves. The experience is totally pleasurable, effortless. About 20 minutes later, he softly beckons us to become aware once again of the room around us and gradually open our eyes.

Like being asleep yet all the while awake, meditation gives the mind a nap. "Too often, people's brains are racing a thousand miles a minute, evaluating pieces of information for danger," explains Dr. Billings. "Once they lock onto one, they say 'Oh, my God, what am I going to do if . . . ?' They focus on it and ruminate about it. There's no solution that comes up that doesn't have consequences that outweigh the benefits. So they keep ruminating. This can lead people to feel depressed because they have a kind of panic that there's this thing that's going to happen to them that they can't do anything about. So they're moving once again toward feeling helpless."

Meditation can help interrupt this pattern of rumination, however. It helps you learn that you can control where your mind goes.

"While you're meditating, random thoughts will pop into your mind. But the key is to accept them. Don't let any one of the thoughts grab your attention," says Dr. Billings. "It's sort of like having a conversation with a friend while people walk by.
(continued on page 188)

THE BEST "WORST" CASE

To see Werner Hebenstreit today (more fit and energetic at 79 than most people half his age), you can hardly imagine that there was a time when he could barely cross the street without getting winded. Crippled by two heart attacks—and mad as hell that it happened to him—he was one of the sickest and most reluctant participants in the landmark study of Dean Ornish, M.D., director of the Preventive Medicine Research Institute in Sausalito, California.

"When I had my first heart attack, and I was asked by a cardiologist, 'Are you under stress?' I said, of course not. I didn't know what stress was; I thought my way of living was normal," Werner recalls. "In fact, I did have a tendency to flare up and lose my temper. An article in the morning paper could infuriate me so much that I couldn't eat my breakfast. If somebody cut me off in traffic, I tried to overtake the guy and curse him out. If I had a bad day at work and my wife asked about it, I would blow up, 'For heaven's sake, can't you leave me alone! I don't want to talk about it.'

"When I joined the Ornish study, the most difficult part for me was not the vegetarian diet or even the relaxation techniques; it was the support group.

"I didn't want to listen to other people air their dirty linen. What business is it of mine! I didn't want to disclose my personal stuff either. I didn't want people to know that I was always full of rage or that I was afraid of dying. It's none of their business.

"When I first got into the support group, I was quiet. I felt embarrassed. Eventually, when I did let go a little, I felt like a fool afterward. I came home and couldn't sleep. 'Why in hell did I let go?' I berated myself. 'Nobody's interested.'

"It took me a good six months, meeting twice a week, to begin to recognize the value in these sessions. Gradually, I began to discover new things about myself.

I realized, for example, that in flying off the handle every time something irritates me, I only harm myself. I started to make short entries into a little notebook whenever I had such a senseless explosion. On my very 'best' day, I counted 33 entries—33 times my blood pressure went up and 33 times my heart started to race in reaction to things I could not change in the slightest.

"Now when I feel frustration coming on, I do some deep breathing. Then I recall the former entries in my notebook, and I simply start to grin.

"Another thing I learned is to love my enemies. If I allow someone's behavior to infuriate me, then I empower that person. I empower him to make my heart beat faster. I empower him to raise my blood pressure. Why should I empower anybody to do that to me? So now if somebody cuts me off in traffic, I throw them a kiss.

"All this perception improved my entire personality and my marriage. I used to interrupt people because they didn't talk fast enough; now I have the patience to listen. I used to distance myself from people who didn't agree with me; now I've learned how to appreciate our differences.

"Before my transformation, I had the capacity to enjoy things, but I was not really happy and never really free. I was always burdened by emotional problems or deceptions, which made life not so easy for me. I really feel that once I was able to let go of those negative emotions—the fear and rage—my heart could start to heal.

"The support group made this possible. When I'm with the group, I feel 100 percent safe to say things I could never mention even in the midst of my own family. There's much more intimacy among us than in most families. We accept everyone as he or she is. We never give advice. We listen.

(continued)

The Best "Worst" Case—Continued

"The emotional unloading that takes place in the security of a support group is an incredibly healing process. This is my eighth year in the program, and I believe the support group was the most powerful tool for me in recovery, both mentally and physically."

Physically speaking, Werner had the best results of all the study participants. PET scans and angiograms bear this out; his blockage decreased from 53 percent at the beginning to 40 percent after one year, and to 13 percent after four years; and blood flow to his heart improved to the greatest degree.

"Before the program, I had to take an ungodly number of heart pills every day," Werner recalls. "Now I take just one baby aspirin every other day. And I have no limitations as to what I can do and would like to do. Strangely enough, as I get older, I get better."

You notice the people, but you don't look too closely at them. They're in the background.

"This helps you learn that basically you can allow your thoughts to run without engaging in them," he adds. "It's a way of helping you control how much you worry. And how upset you get."

THE CRITICAL CONNECTION

Perhaps the most powerful component of the Ornish program, however, is the group support. It's also the most difficult for many. It involves acknowledging personal feelings and sharing those feelings with a group of people you've never met before.

Each night after dinner, the participants split up into groups of about ten. Each group is joined by a trained facilitator. The ground rules are simple: Express feelings, not thoughts; everything said is important; and no advice allowed.

We began with a kind of minimeditation, closing our eyes and focusing our attention on our breathing. After a few moments, Dr. Ornish (who, along with his wife, Shirley Brown, M.D., is our group facilitator) asks, "How are you feeling? What's going on?"

There's no pressure to respond. But each person—as she feels comfortable doing so—identifies and expresses to the group what she is feeling. One woman discloses that she feels scared and anxious—even angry—because her husband had an angina attack this morning. Another expresses fear and apprehension about returning to a stressful home environment when the retreat is over.

"Try to understand how the other person feels," Dr. Ornish coaches. "Then examine your own experiences to see if you can find one that's equivalent or similar to the one being expressed. In that way, we can feel more connected to each other."

Dr. Ornish reminds us always to focus on our feelings, differentiating them from thoughts. "Feelings are true statements," he explains. "If I say 'I feel sad,' or 'I feel angry,' nobody can argue with the truth of that statement. Instead, if I express a thought—'I think you're wrong'—then we can argue about whether or not that's true."

When someone finishes speaking, another person might respond briefly, "I understand what is happening, and it makes me feel sad (or happy or worried or apprehensive)." Or another might comment, "I've never had that experience. Can you tell me more?" The goal is to emphasize ways in which you are the same—to give the people something of what you're discovering in yourself while you're listening to them. What's important is to acknowledge what the other person is saying. And never ever give advice, because it tends to make the other person feel diminished and unheard.

Amazingly, people find themselves sharing feelings that they admit they've never been able to share with their closest family members. There's safety, security and emotional support here, which, many people say, makes opening up remarkably easy.

In the beginning, Dr. Ornish recalls, "Those who were into sharing their feelings met with a lot of resistance from those who weren't. Some said, 'I didn't really sign up for this study to talk about my feelings. I want to get my cholesterol down. I want to unclog my arteries.'

"Over time, though, as people began to trust one another

and open up to each other, it became clear they had something in common besides heart disease," says Dr. Ornish. "I was struck by what a pervasive sense of loneliness and isolation existed in many of the people we worked with."

Not that these people lived alone or were physically isolated. In fact, most were married; many were active in social groups. Rather, it was an emotional isolation. A sense that they were different somehow, that they didn't belong.

"When you feel a sense of loneliness and isolation, it leads to a chronic way of relating to the world that's not a lot of fun," Dr. Ornish explains. "It became clear to me that people were hungry not just for information on how to lower cholesterol, but for a sense of connection and community and intimacy, as well."

"The world is very different today from the way it used to be," Dr. Billings concurs. "Not that everything was wonderful in the old days, but when most Americans were farmers, there's simply no question that they depended on each other. It had nothing to do with being weak or inadequate. Whether it was helping to get your barn raised or whether it was helping to feed your family in a bad year, they sort of shared responsibility for life.

"Today, we're alone, without those kinds of stable communities," he continues. "But in our program, we've found a little magical shortcut. That is, we've learned that if you share secrets with one another you essentially sidestep the need for 40 years of helping each other raising barns.

"In that moment of self-disclosure where someone tells you something that you have some empathic response to, there's a link. There's a bond between the two of you," Dr. Billings explains.

"People who are telling something that's important to them have a sense of openness and vulnerability. They're testing the assumption that something is wrong with them—that they are uniquely and systematically different. And what happens is that in the process of sharing the secret—and hearing back that the other person has felt that way, too—there is a connection.

"This makes you feel that you're a part of the world rather than outside of the world. That you're more like other people than more different," says Dr. Billings.

"Creating a sense of community within a support group may be the least high-tech treatment we offer," says Dr. Ornish, "but, in my view, it is one of the most powerful healing tools we've got."

21
WARD OFF
CHRONIC WORRY

Gain control with these helpful hints.

Asked the secret of longevity, comedian George Burns once put it this way: "My attitude is, if something is beyond your control—if you can't do anything about it—there's no point worrying about it. And if you can do something about it, then there's still nothing to worry about."

For most of us, unfortunately, the comedian's easygoing attitude isn't so easy to adopt. "We're a society that seems to worry a lot," says worry researcher Denise Person, Ph.D., of Pennsylvania State University in University Park. "If you watch the news, we go from crisis to crisis—one isn't even over before the next one starts."

Most of us don't have to look as far as a national crisis for something to worry about. Surveys show that the most common sources of worry for Americans are family and relationships ("What if she leaves me?"), job or school ("What if I fail?"), health ("What if I get sick?") and finances ("What if my check bounces?"). And then there's a miscellaneous category that includes everything from the environment to world peace.

While most people worry about 5 percent of the time, for some people, worrying becomes a way of life. Chronic worriers report that an average of 50 percent of each day is spent worrying, and some report as much as 100 percent, says psychologist Jennifer L. Abel, Ph.D., associate director of the Stress and

Anxiety Disorders Institute at Pennsylvania State University.

Worrying drains energies and can be a burden to family and friends. It can also cause physical problems. Researchers have identified a characteristic group of symptoms common among worriers: restlessness and feeling edgy; easy fatigability; concentration difficulties; irritability; muscle tension and aches; and restless sleep.

How to Stop Worrying

The good news is that worry has received a great deal of attention from psychologists. They have begun to develop a multifaceted approach to treating it, combining relaxation, behavioral changes and cognitive (thought) therapy to reduce unnecessary worry levels. Here are some of the effective techniques they recommend.

1. Learn to be a problem solver. Worrying may reflect a form of ineffective problem solving, says Timothy Brown, Psy.D., associate director of the Center for Stress and Anxiety Disorders at the State University of New York at Albany. "Examination of a typical chain of thoughts reported by worriers often reveals that the worrier is jumping from topic to topic without reaching a solution to any particular element."

Barry Lubetkin, Ph.D., director of the Institute for Behavior Therapy in New York City, concurs. "Probably the single best thing people who worry too much can do is learn to be good problem solvers," says Dr. Lubetkin. "The better you are at solving problems, the less of a worrier you will be. You need to learn to dispassionately and objectively confront a problem."

Dr. Lubetkin uses this exercise to help people determine if they're good problem solvers. "Draw a little picture on a piece of paper, cut it into six or seven jigsaw pieces, mix it up and try to put it together. While you're doing this, become aware of your thoughts. The people who aren't good problem solvers are telling themselves 'I can't do this, I'm not good at puzzles.' We want them to think like nonworriers, who are telling themselves 'The straight edge goes on the outside' and 'With time I'll get there.' "

If you're not a good problem solver, you can learn the skills. That's one of the goals of therapy. At the Albany anxiety clinic, therapists do what's called a realistic appraisal. If you're concerned about losing a job, for example, you and a therapist will evaluate your work strengths, weaknesses and techniques for improvement. You learn to focus on problem solving by consulting with a therapist or by taking courses and reading books on time management, personal organization and problem solving.

Of course, some problems—like world peace—are usually totally out of our control. It's important for worriers to practice what George Burns preaches—to learn not to worry about the problems that are out of their control.

2. Set aside a worry period. Interestingly, setting aside a daily worry period can reduce overall worry levels over time. How to do it? Leading worry researcher Michael Vasey, Ph.D., assistant professor of psychology at Ohio State University in Columbus, suggests setting aside 30 minutes a day, always at the same place and time, to worry. "Focus on your worry for the entire period and try to think of solutions to the problem." For example, if your worry is that you will be fired, imagine the whole scenario—the firing and the consequences—and don't let the image drift away.

It's likely that your first reaction will be an increase in anxiety. But resist the urge to distract yourself, says Dr. Vasey. "If you practice focusing on worries and thinking of solutions for 30 minutes each day for several weeks, your anxiety starts to taper off. You'll get better at generating solutions or realize it's not worth worrying about." Psychologists call this process desensitization.

Another benefit of worry periods: "During the rest of the day, when you notice that you're worrying, you can say 'I'm busy now; I'll worry during my worry period.' It frees you from worry for the rest of the day and teaches you how to let go of worries," says Dr. Vasey.

3. Visualize mastery. If you like, you can spend the last several minutes of your worry period imagining the best, not the worst. At the Albany clinic, therapists steer their clients through a visualization of their worst fear occurring. A half-hour is spent fixing on that image, and the other half-hour is focused on the client's ability to cope with the anxiety. Worriers learn to reduce their anxiety by rationalizing and dismissing their worst fears rather than worrying about them.

THE REWARDS OF WORRY

Despite the high price worriers pay over the long-term, researchers are turning up new evidence that worriers get short-term rewards for their worrying—psychologically and even physically. "Worriers find their worry very valuable," says Michael Vasey, Ph.D., assistant professor of psychology at Ohio State University in Columbus. "They seem to be saying that they would be more anxious if they didn't worry—and there's research to support that notion."

There is no evidence that worry causes disease. Research in the laboratory, measuring physical responses of worriers and comparing them to nonworriers, shows worrying may actually be a way to reduce more dramatic physical symptoms of fear, says Timothy Brown, Psy.D., associate director of the Center for Stress and Anxiety Disorders at the State University of New York at Albany.

"Under laboratory stressors, such as instructions to focus on an existing worry, worriers tend to respond more with muscle tension, whereas nonworriers may actually experience more autonomic symptoms, such as increases in heart rate, shortness of breath, light-headedness, dizziness and increased skin conductivity," says Dr. Brown.

4. Improve your thoughts. People who worry a lot tend to share the same ordinary concerns as nonworriers. The difference, says Dr. Vasey, is that worriers think that disasters are much more likely to occur. For example, if you ask nonworriers the likelihood that the elevator they are boarding will fall, they will accurately respond that it's extremely remote. But a worrier might rate the possibility at 20 percent or more.

Another difference between worriers and nonworriers: Worriers assume they won't be able to deal with their imagined

His hypothesis: Worry reduces autonomic arousal because worries are more thoughts than images. "Worriers process information in a thinking mode. If worriers stopped to dwell on images, their body would respond more," he says.

"But in the long run," Dr. Brown adds, "the cost may be high. Worriers can't concentrate, they get headaches and stomach upsets and may not be able to effectively confront and resolve their problems."

Dr. Vasey points out another, related incentive for worrying. For many, it provides the illusion of control. "When you worry, there's a feeling that you are doing something about a problem, when you're really not. Or for some, there's a sense that if the worst happens, at least you'll be prepared."

With these and other short-term "rewards" for worrying, it's hardly surprising that most people who are referred for therapy don't see worry as their primary problem. "It's often not worry that brings them to our clinic," says Dr. Brown. "They may come in because they developed some symptom related to worry, like insomnia, irritable bowel syndrome or frequent headaches. They may not immediately see what connection their worry has to these physical symptoms."

disasters. "They typically have a perception of not being able to cope," says Dr. Abel. They assume that if they lose their jobs, they'll wind up on the street, get sick and die. Nonworriers, on the other hand, assume that after a transition they'll find other jobs.

That's why a technique called cognitive therapy is ideal for worriers. It's a way of correcting negative, inaccurate thoughts and replacing them with more realistic, positive thoughts. Worriers are taught to detect the early cues that they're starting to worry. At the first hint of muscle tension or anxiety, for example, they ask themselves, "What am I telling myself that's threatening?"

The next step in this technique is to seek a more reasonable perspective, says Dr. Vasey. "Here the patient must question her assumptions. If she does just a little research, she'll find out that it's virtually impossible that the elevator will fall."

Dr. Abel notes that cognitive therapy is different from "positive thinking." "It doesn't mean seeing the world through rose-colored glasses. With worry, you tend to look at the world through cracked glasses—everything looks bad. Our goal is to give people clear glasses, so they see things more accurately."

You can try cognitive therapy yourself by carrying a notebook around for a week. Write down every negative prediction. Then do some research to come up with more realistic thoughts.

5. Breathe through the worry. Relaxing the body can relax the mind. Therapists teach worried clients techniques like meditation and progressive relaxation (relaxing the major muscle groups, from the legs on up, one by one).

Once they've mastered these techniques, says Dr. Abel, they can apply them as soon as they catch the first hint that their anxiety is starting to mount. When worry strikes, even taking a few long, deep breaths from the diaphragm can really help. (This relaxation technique is called diaphragmatic breathing.)

6. Focus on the moment. "Worry is almost always future-oriented," says Dr. Abel. "So if we can focus on what we're doing right now—the sentence we're reading, the tone of voice of the person speaking—rather than thinking about what someone might say next or our worries, we're better off."

7. Take a chance. Worriers usually have behaviors that reinforce the worry habit, says Dr. Brown. "A wife might call her husband at work several times a day to make sure he's okay. A parent might watch the kids at the bus stop every second, despite the fact that there's a chaperon there. In the short-term, those behaviors reduce anxiety. But over the long run, they reinforce the worry—you start to think that your call actually decreased the likelihood of something bad happening. Part of our treatment for worry might be to give worry behavior–prevention assignments, along with the cognitive technique of prediction testing, like 'Don't call your husband every day at work' and 'Don't watch the kids every second,' " Dr. Brown explains. Then set a prediction on what could happen if you don't call your husband or you do leave the kids alone, and compare the prediction with the actual outcome. "Eventually, people learn that the dreaded consequences still aren't occurring, and that reduces worry levels."

GETTING HELP

Can people cure themselves of worry without undergoing some kind of therapy? Some people do, experts say. But if it's a lifelong habit, says Dr. Abel, "You may not be able to control it on your own. Treatment provides relief for most worriers." Look for a therapist or program that specializes in cognitive therapy and applied relaxation, she adds.

And by the way, most experts agree that medications are usually not an effective treatment for chronic worry. "They may help some people for a while, but when a person goes off the drugs, there's a high chance of relapse," says Dr. Brown. "With behavioral and cognitive programs, clients may actually learn techniques that last a lifetime."

BRUSH AWAY
THE COBWEBS

Here are six physical reasons your mind may seem a little mushy.

Thinking's easy. You do it all the time, and you've gotten pretty good at it. In fact, you could do it with both frontal lobes tied behind your back. Lately, however, the noggin's been nodding off. You're losing car keys more often, and when you find them, you spend 20 minutes in the mall parking lot searching for your car. Amid the missed appointments and the mistakes in your checkbook, things seem a little foggy, and life is getting a little confusing. Call it cognitive cobwebs.

Relax. You may be losing keys, but you probably aren't losing your mind. There may be physical reasons—unexpected or overlooked—for your fuzziness. In fact, you may be unwittingly mushing your mind in ways that could easily be prevented or treated.

MEDICINE CABINET MUSHINESS

Behind that mirrored door is a collection of potential mind-muddlers. "Impaired mental performance caused by drug side effects is an underestimated problem among the general population," says Rodney Richmond, of the Drug Information and Pharmaco-Epidemiology Center at the University of Pittsburgh. "Sedation, dizziness, drowsiness and fatigue are common, but reversible, although they can become bad enough to cause a dramatic reduction in your overall performance."

Some of these problems can be egged on by Father Time. "As you age, your body finds it harder to process medication," says Arthur I. Jacknowitz, Pharm.D., professor and chair of the Department of Clinical Pharmacy at West Virginia University School of Pharmacy in Morgantown. Antihistamines, for example, can cause sedation and grogginess. They impair the function of cholinergic neurons, which are used in thought processes. "Since cholinergic neurons become less functional as you age, the drugs offer a double whammy," says Dr. Jacknowitz.

"Kidney function also declines with age in many people, and that, combined with drugs, can affect cognition," says Dr. Jacknowitz. "Certain drugs taken for peptic ulcer disease—cimetidine, for example—may not be metabolized as efficiently due to poor kidney function and may accumulate to higher-than-desired levels." These increased levels may lead to some cognitive impairment that can, in rare cases, reach dementia-like proportions.

"Many of the nonsteroidal anti-inflammatory drugs can impair blood flow to the kidneys in some people, thus increasing the risk of memory loss, inability to concentrate, confusion and personality changes in older people taking these agents," says Dr. Jacknowitz.

Because they enter the central nervous system, some blood pressure medications can also have mind-fuzzying effects. "Beta-blockers and calcium channel blockers may also cause fatigue by slowing your heart rate," says Richmond.

"Of course, if you're experiencing some mental impairment, and you think it may be due in part to any medication you're using, see your doctor or pharmacist immediately," says Richmond. You may not need to stop taking your medications—just change dosage or switch to another drug at your doctor's advice.

Take note, too, that mind-mushing side effects can sprout even from milder over-the-counter (OTC) medications. "If you're taking any OTC drugs, read the labels carefully and ask your doctor or pharmacist what certain ingredients can do," says Richmond. "Mental impairment from OTC drugs isn't extremely common, but it's possible that it could be at the root of your cognitive trouble." Some possible mind-numbing OTC drugs:

Antidiarrheal agents. "Some of the ingredients found in these OTC products contain opiates and anticholinergic agents and can have sedative properties," says Richmond. "Some products contain an opiate called paregoric, while another (loperamide) is chemically related to a certain psychotropic drug, which can have potential for drowsiness and fatigue."

Analgesics. Nonsteroidal anti-inflammatory drugs (such as ibuprofen) can cause some drowsiness or dizziness in 3 to 15 percent of users. "Some analgesics and other sinus-allergy-headache products contain antihistamines that may compound the effect," says Richmond.

Antitussive agents. The cough suppressant in some popular OTC cough syrups may be codeine, while others may contain dextromethorphan, a mirror image of codeine. "Both can have sedative effects in some people," says Richmond. "Other products may contain diphenhydramine, which may have sedative effects in up to 50 percent of adult users."

And others can double as bar fare. "Any OTC using the title 'elixir' contains alcohol—as much as 5 to 10 percent," says

Richmond. "Some elixirs, however, can run as high as 25 percent alcohol—more than a hearty wine." Of course, the amount of alcohol in a typical dose is small and may not affect a 175-pound man. However, it may have an entirely different effect on a 50-pound tyke. "If it's for your child, that's even more reason to check the alcohol content," says Richmond. Further, alcohol can compound the sedating effects of any sedative drug. Look for alcohol-free products out on the market now.

Antiemetic agents. "Some antinausea drugs can cause sedation in roughly half the people using them," says Richmond. Some of these OTC products contain meclizine or dimenhydrinate, which can have sedative-like effects.

Sleeping agents. "Most OTC sleeping medications contain antihistamines, which can stay in your body much longer than you'd like them to," says James Walsh, Ph.D., director of the Sleep Disorders and Research Center at Deaconess Health System in St. Louis, Missouri. "They can remain active for 12 to 15 hours, so 4 hours after you've gotten up, they're still trying to put you to sleep." Some sleeping aids also carry the above-mentioned diphenhydramine, which may affect your daily performance of repetitive tasks.

UNFITNESS FOG

Evidence suggests body fitness may enhance brain fitness. If that's indeed the case, then the opposite may also be true—that being out of shape may lead to a foggy state of mind.

Mental metabolism. "While you're improving your body's metabolism through exercise, you may also be boosting your cerebral metabolism," says Charles Emery, Ph.D., assistant professor of psychiatry at Duke University Medical Center in Durham, North Carolina, and exercise and cognition researcher. Although research in this area is in its infancy, exercise may help increase blood flow to the brain, which carries more oxygen to help boost function. Exercise may lead to changes in neurotransmitters in the brain as well. This mindful metabolism may also help accentuate glucose transport to the brain, packing the lobes with much-needed fuel for thought.

Cognitive confusion. The speed at which you might process material—and what Dr. Emery calls sequencing, or your ability to follow instructions—could be hampered by a lifestyle of inactivity. "Sequencing is the way you would think if you were following directions," he says. Taking a wrong turn may in part result from a lot of time being sofa-bound instead of walking or jogging.

Life's demands. If exercise prepares you for the rigors of reality by making you stronger, then it makes sense that lack of exercise may leave you overmatched by your daily activities. "Life demands a proportion of effort on your part," says Bryant Stamford, Ph.D., director of the Health Promotion Center at the University of Louisville in Kentucky and author of *Fitness without Exercise.* "If your energy capacity is only equal in proportion to what's demanded from your daily activities, then you'll be tapped out. If your energy capacity outweighs the demand, then you'll have a reserve of energy, so you won't feel tired." To enlarge your fuel tank for living, you need to exercise regularly. As exercise eases the demands of living, alertness and mental vigor won't be undermined by physical fatigue.

Just one bout of exercise may work as an on-call cobweb cutter. If your mind is mush—or oatmeal—a brisk walk may stir it up. "I take a 20-minute walk in the afternoon to help reinvigorate myself," says Dr. Stamford. It may be the change of scenery that works. Exercise may also trigger an endorphin release—chemicals in the brain that may boost your mood. And because cognitive function may be hindered by depression or anxiety, improved cognitive function may come about from enhanced psychological well-being.

BRAIN BURNOUT

If you're stressed out from being overworked—and you're reading this sentence—chances are your mind has already strolled off this page. "Your ability to concentrate and make decisions, along with short-term memory, may be one of the first areas of mental functioning hit by stress," says Paul J. Rosch, M.D., president of the American Institute of Stress. "Some of this stems from information overload. The constant flood of information we now have to process and sort out for personal relevance may become too much to handle."

Loss of control. In a review of 82 studies and articles conducted by the Naval Training Systems Human Factors Division in Orlando, Florida, "perceived control" was the major factor implicated in good or bad performance due to stress. "When there's a sense of loss of control, it can lead to high levels of job stress, cardiovascular disease and burnout," says Dr. Rosch.

In one study, 24 women were put through four hours of continuous mental activity, during which cortisol, a stress hormone, was tested. A test of their cognitive performance then followed. Women with elevated cortisol reactions—indicative of stress—scored much lower in attention during the cognitive testing. Of course, stress is an unavoidable part of life—and up to a point, increasing stress or demand increases productivity at work. "But there's a limit—once you exceed it, productivity plunges downward and mental and physical fatigue results," says Dr. Rosch. Stress is much like the tension on a violin string. If you don't have enough, it's going to produce a dull, flat sound. If it's excessive, the tone will be harsh or shrill; or worse, the string may break. "But with the right amount of stress, or tension, you can make beautiful music," he says.

Changing your perceptions. "Many stressful events aren't necessarily stressful, but it is rather our perceptions that cause problems," says Dr. Rosch. "Often we can change or correct faulty perceptions and regain control." Sit down and list all of the things at work or home you consider stressful and divide the list into those items over which you have no control and others where you can exert some influence. "Use your time and talent to change those things where you can make a difference, and learn to accept or avoid those things you can't do anything about," says Dr. Rosch.

BLOOD SUGAR

"For people with diabetes, low blood sugar clearly affects awareness, attention and other aspects of cognitive function," says Alan Jacobson, M.D., staff psychiatrist at the Joslin Diabetes Center in Boston. "Short-term memory and attention—the ability to stay focused—get hit first." Because glucose functions as fuel for your brain, when it dips low, what your brain does best—thinking—may suffer. Staying alert or following complicated instructions can become Herculean tasks. "This problem can go on for some time and you won't even be aware of it," says Dr. Jacobson. That's because these very symptoms keep you from recognizing them.

Friends as cognitive watchers. "Because fuzzy thinking may keep you from realizing you have a problem, it's key for your friends and family to be aware," says Dr. Jacobson. "These warning signs need to be heeded before blood sugars dive to a more dangerous zone." The unclear responses and slowness may be a tip-off that blood sugar is low. Treatment may be as simple as a glass of orange juice to get your sugar raised. (And obviously, blood glucose monitoring is key for all people with diabetes.)

The sweet slump. For people who do not have diabetes, eating habits may mush you up by lowering blood sugar. "The human body wasn't designed for consuming a whole bunch of rapidly absorbed processed sugar," says Jay Kenney, R.D., Ph.D., nutrition research specialist at the Pritikin Longevity Center in Santa Monica, California. "It's doubtful a sweet snack will knock you out at your desk, though in a few people, a snack of colas and candy bars may raise blood sugar levels quickly, causing their bodies to produce so much insulin that their blood sugar temporarily plummets, leading to a short period of grogginess or feeling weak. If this occurs infrequently, munching on a piece of bread or fruit will bring you back to normal within 10 to 15 minutes.

"However, if this reaction occurs frequently, and particularly if it's accompanied by anxiety or sweating, it may be a 'reactive hypoglycemia.' If it occurs consistently after eating a meal or snack high in refined carbohydrates, you need to have your blood sugar checked when you have the symptoms. If your blood sugar is very low, your physician may need to do other tests," says Dr. Kenney.

Graze past the daze. The "Thanksgiving-dinner effect"— eating a large meal—may also cause a drop in energy level. "This is a normal physiological response to a very large meal and probably occurs because blood is shunted to the digestive tract to get all those extra calories transported and stored," says Dr. Kenney. "Eating two or three large meals a day may work for our schedules, but may not be best for our bodies." Dr. Stamford adds, "To keep your function steady, eat in smaller amounts and choose from high-carbohydrate, unprocessed foods." By eating smaller meals more often (grazing), you may keep your blood sugar level and not hit the postmeal need-to-nap switch.

CAFFEINE ROLLER COASTER

What we use to stay alert can turn us into "grog monsters." "Some—though not all—people often experience the symptoms of caffeine withdrawal, which include faintness, irritability and shakiness when the caffeine level in their blood drops," says Dr. Kenney. Considering that 75 percent of the U.S. population uses caffeine, there may be a whole lot of shakin'—and yawnin'—going on.

Getting mugged. Because caffeine's half-life in the body is roughly 3½ to 4 hours, by late afternoon, the morning buzz has finally made it out of your system. So, 6 to 8 hours after those jolts of French roast, you're sliding into your chair. Because that cognitive dip comes after you've eaten lunch, you may blame it on what you ate. In truth, the main cause may be caffeine withdrawal.

A study of 62 regular-coffee slurpers underlines caffeine's seesaw effect. Coffee drinkers abandoned their mugs and instead got their caffeine in capsule form for two days (an amount equal to about 2½ cups of java). During a second two-day period, they received a dummy pill containing no caffeine. No one knew which pill they were taking during the study. During the caffeine-free period, half of the group experienced extreme fatigue, lack of concentration and impairment of motor performance. To measure work performance, the group performed tapping tasks. No surprise—they performed poorly when going through withdrawal.

Other caffeine fiends. Colas, tea, chocolate and some other soft drinks have caffeine, too—only in lesser quantities than coffee. Even some OTC analgesic and antihistamine medications contain 75 to 200 milligrams of caffeine per dose— roughly equivalent to a six-ounce cup of coffee. Have a cup of coffee, followed by a candy bar and a cola for a snack (plus a combination analgesic for your headache), and you're setting yourself up for a big fall. Severe symptoms of withdrawal—like those seen in the study mentioned above—can begin 12 to 24 hours after the last use, peak at 20 to 48 hours and last roughly one week.

How much is too much? The study suggests that anyone who gulps just two or more servings of caffeine-containing beverages can be at risk. If you think your fuzziness is due to caffeine withdrawal, you might consider trying to wean yourself off the bean—slowly. Reduce the intake incrementally—halving portions and mixing them with decaf. Follow that strategy and you'll be off the buzz completely.

BEDROOM BEDLAM

If your sleep is screwed up, chances are you won't know it. The only sign that something is awry at night, then, is what's going on the next day. "Sleep disorders can cause lapses in attention and fatigue in the daytime, especially when you're faced with repetitive tasks requiring complete attention," says Peter Hauri, Ph.D., administrative director of the Mayo Clinic Sleep Disorders Clinic in Rochester, Minnesota, and author of *No More Sleepless Nights*. "The more attention demanded by the job, the greater effect lack of sleep can have on your performance." Here are some common sleep problems that may mush you up in the daytime.

Insomnia. "Insomnia isn't a disorder, but a symptom of other problems, from stress to depression or chronic arthritis," says Dr. Walsh. "How much sleep is disrupted will dictate how severe the grogginess is during the day." And that grogginess can turn dangerous. "Insomniacs have roughly 2½ times more accidents than normal sleepers," says Dr. Hauri.

"Because insomnia can be caused by any number of things, your first step is to pinpoint the underlying problem," says Dr. Walsh. "If you can narrow it down to one to three contributing factors, most insomniacs can be helped within a few weeks. Sleep medications can provide temporary help—but they won't address the root cause. If arthritis is the real cause, then sleeping pills won't help—the illness must be treated first."

Plus, you can do a lot to promote good sleep without drugs. "Exercise, but do it at least three hours before bedtime," says Dr. Walsh. That's because exercise stimulates you initially, leaving you wide awake instead of sleepy. "The same thing goes for mental stimulation," he adds. Have a cooldown period—a very calming presleep routine for 30 minutes—before bed.

"Go to bed at the same time and get up at the same time every day," says Dr. Walsh. On weekends, limit the extra sleep that might cause Sunday-night insomnia and the following Monday mushiness. "Sleep is partially controlled by your biological clock," says Dr. Walsh. "A regular sleep schedule can reinforce that rhythm to improve sleep."

Sound sleep means avoiding caffeine products at night. But aim for an earlier cutoff point. "Even at 4:00 P.M., caffeine can still be disruptive," says Dr. Walsh. And while alcohol may help you fall asleep, the net effect is a negative one. It's metabolized fast and your brain ends up rebounding in the second half of the night, leaving you stimulated.

Sleep apnea. Because breathing obstruction is the calling card of sleep apnea, causing sufferers to wake up to catch their breath 40 to 60 times an hour, they'll often demonstrate impaired daytime performance due to sleep loss. "Most people won't remember waking up—so their only signal is their daytime grogginess," says Dr. Hauri. Your most important step: If your spouse reports that you regularly stop breathing during loud snoring, see a physician for a professional evaluation. Sleep apnea can be life-threatening.

"Once apnea is diagnosed, however, the treatment is successful in a vast majority of cases," says Dr. Walsh. For people who experience sleep apnea only when they sleep on their backs—while breathing fine on their sides or bellies—a custom-made nightshirt might help. It has a pocket that allows you to fit tennis balls along the spine—keeping you from rolling onto your back. Weight loss is also encouraged if the sufferer is obese.

More serious cases may require a CPAP (continuous positive airway pressure) machine. It's a bedside compressor connected to a face mask that delivers a steady stream of pressurized air into the nose throughout the night. Surgery is another option for more serious cases.

Unrefreshing sleep. These insomniacs think they sleep okay at night, but don't. Their sleep is very shallow, or "unrefreshing." "Those folks don't know that their daytime fatigue is due to light sleep," says Dr. Walsh. "They may wake up 10 to 15 times an hour and remember only a few. This sleep fragmentation results in a lot of time in the light stages of sleep, without real slumber." Stress, pain or discomfort due to arthritis or other chronic conditions might cause this. "Circadian rhythm disorders—mismatches between the time you sleep and the time your brain wants to sleep—can cause it, too," says Dr. Walsh.

Periodic limb movements. Many people experience a constant twitching of their legs throughout the night. "The typical patient will have a leg jerk once every 30 seconds for hours and hours during the night," says Dr. Walsh. And, like sleep apnea patients, they tend not to remember many of these awakenings and feel tired the next day. "Although many people experience normal limb activity during the night, once it gets over 100 to 200 times a night, you've got a problem." The cause of this ailment isn't known, but it could be due to some shenanigans in the spinal cord or brain. "And it may be triggered by anemia or kidney failure," says Dr. Walsh. A drug containing levodopa and carbidopa, normally used in combination for Parkinson's disease, seems to work in most patients.

Sleep cheats. You may also just be cheating yourself knowingly of slumber, causing your mushiness. "We're a nation of sleep skippers, and that courts disaster," says Dr. Walsh. "Thousands of accidents can be attributed to lack of sleep. You have to realize you need sleep to lead a productive life."

"Experiment with your sleep schedule," says Dr. Hauri. Try seven hours each night for one week. If toward the end of the week you're tired during the day, add an hour. "Just seeing how well one night of sleep works isn't enough—your body needs to adapt," says Dr. Hauri. If you feel you may have a sleep problem beyond your control, talk to your doctor about seeing a sleep specialist.

SOLITARY EXCITEMENT

Make the most of private moments.

Taking time out from normal routine for periods of solitude is not a luxury; it is as much a necessity as food, water, oxygen and intimacy. For reasons we may be unaware of or unable to explain, we sometimes feel periodic urges to go off by ourselves, to find both the space and the time to be alone. Each of us has our own threshold of overdosing on social interaction and togetherness, times when we have had our fill of human contact—after a particularly hectic day at the office, a week of houseguests or increased socializing during the holidays. At such times we develop a deep longing to be alone.

When the pressure becomes too much, solitude allows us to withdraw temporarily in an effort to compose ourselves. In solitude we find a freedom of thought and movement that is not obtainable through other means. We can contemplate every facet of our existence that offers either pleasure or confusion. Solitude helps invigorate our spirit and infuse ourselves with renewed energy and enthusiasm.

GEOGRAPHY OF PRIVATE MOMENTS

Your ability to appreciate your solitude is influenced greatly by the opportunities for privacy and physical seclusion that are available. Yet surprisingly, the places you can go to be alone are rather limited.

For a number of people, private time is limited to fleeting moments of solitary travel in an automobile. However, since the advent of the car phone, this sacred solitude is rapidly dwindling. No longer can you expect to escape the pressures and demands of home and office as you drive along. One moment you are off inside your own world, cruising down the road, and the next moment the ringing phone brings you back to the land of obligations.

The price we pay for this permanent umbilical cord to the fast lane of life, of course, is greater stress and considerably less tranquil solitude. One consultant who travels a lot refuses to give in to pressure from his colleagues to install a telephone in his car:

"I can't imagine having a phone in my car. I sit perched on my seat, watching the scenery flow by, a landscape that is forever changing. I love to sing along with the radio. And I love to talk to myself. If I ever feel the urge to talk to somebody else on one of my long trips, I like to make tapes on a recorder I carry with me. I conduct these long monologues. I feel so uninhibited talking to someone who is not really there. I can easily fill up a 90-minute tape just chattering away about what

LESSONS IN LIVING ALONE

For some, living alone can be stressful, boring and lonely. But with sufficient practice and motivation, solitary living can become quite comfortable. In *Why Do I Think I Am Nothing without a Man?*, a book for women who feel helpless, angry and frustrated without a partner, author Penelope Russianoff suggests that a change in attitude might make a difference.

Living alone is just like being married, except the relationship you are having is with yourself. Like marriage, living alone has its ups and downs. Sometimes you hate yourself and sometimes you love yourself; sometimes you're at odds with yourself. There are days you find yourself fascinating and days you find yourself intolerable. And here is where this little analogy falls apart because one thing you can't do alone, as in marriage, is to stalk into the other room and slam the door in your face.

People who like living alone report a special appreciation for quiet and relaxation. They enjoy the restful solitude of reading the paper with their feet propped on the table. No intrusions, no distractions, nobody crying for attention. They feel a sense of pride in solitary ownership, knowing that who they are and what they have is the result of their own labors. They develop inner resources and feel satisfaction in their independence and ability to take care of themselves. People who live alone enjoy greater privacy to be thoroughly themselves. They feel more natural and act with fewer inhibitions.

Those who don't live alone can learn a lot from those who do, especially with regard to taking care of needs and listening to one's own rhythms. In a respectful, open, caring relationship or family structure, it is possible to negotiate time for solitude without sacrificing the quality of other relationships.

is going on in my head or my life. My friends appreciate getting these tapes in the mail because they are so honest and spontaneous."

FREEDOM OF NATURE

The type of mental solitude you can achieve is enhanced when you are out in nature. There your inner solitude is matched by an external aloneness. You have no one to be concerned about but yourself, no voices to listen to but your own. No telephone, no television, no neighbors, no noise.

In the quiet of a hillside, wooded path or mountaintop, it is easier to hear yourself think. Many people have reported that one of the primary benefits of spending time alone in nature is that they are able to attain a state of real mental clarity.

Liberated from external demands and schedules, you are free to focus your attention wherever you like. You can choose any direction to think, to walk, to explore. You can dress however you like. (The trees and birds don't care.) You can eat when you feel like it, wash if you want to and generally follow the body's natural rhythms.

Under these conditions, in the woods or wherever you feel most natural and unobserved, you will find it easier to do any of the following:

• To consider aspects of your life that are in need of attention

• To relive experiences from the past that bring you the pleasure of learning

• To be more aware of your unfulfilled desires

• To enjoy tranquillity and self-renewal

• To seek adventure and take risks that can only be accomplished alone

• To plan the future—where you are headed and how you intend to get there

THE JOY OF SOLITARY EXPERIENCES

According to Abraham Maslow, Ph.D., a pioneer of humanistic psychology, and many other experts on mental health, the most well-adjusted individuals are those who are able to seek out and enjoy their time alone. They are able to experience peak moments of joy on a consistent basis, especially when they are in their own company. One social science teacher uses his summer vacations to decompress from the year's pressures and rediscover his inner world. One summer he took a solo cross-country trip by motorcycle; another year he bicycled around the Great Lakes.

Recently he took a month by himself to wander through Europe.

"It is such a great feeling to be completely free of schedules and programmed days. Among the most significant experiences of my life is hiking in the mountains. I recall one instance of being in the Alps. I walked up trails through trees, rocky cliffs and meadows gleaming with flowers in yellow, white and purple. Snowy peaks rose in the distance. I don't think I've ever heard such total quiet. The only sounds were of my labored breathing and the wind blowing through the trees. After a while I would start to hum to myself, just to hear a sound. But the most amazing thing is how my brain shuts down. You have to understand I am always thinking about stuff. But once in that atmosphere, I just seem to lose myself in what I'm experiencing."

Certain other activities, especially outdoor ones that involve movement or communion with nature (hiking, skiing, horseback riding), also lend themselves to complete immersion in the moment.

Solo Exercise

Exercising alone also gives you the time to consider issues you find fascinating and problems you find perplexing. And like any meditative process, exercising increases your capacity for self-discipline in other areas of your life.

Many people like to run by themselves because it gives them time to think. They plan the day that lies ahead and go over the previous one. There are few activities as tranquil yet invigorating as a long walk by yourself.

Take a look around. Maybe you'll see clouds gathering and wonder if you'll get back home before it rains. You might even decide to walk in the rain. Don't be alarmed when the first drops start to fall. Say to yourself "Why not enjoy it?" See the droplets on the trees that look like little crystals. Taste the rain coming down your face. See the rocks glisten all around you. Don't be surprised that you feel somehow special—as though you're part of something bigger than you.

Whether you are alone in the woods, your car or the bedroom, solitude provides opportunities for self-reflection. Just as you have a definite need to be with others, you have a desire to be with yourself, to have peak experiences without feeling lonely and alienated. A contented life is one that is filled with a balance of intimacy and solitude; without one, the other feels hollow. Solitude helps improve your productivity, inner wisdom and independence; it allows you to face yourself without the need for distractions.

Healing

Breakthroughs

24
KNOCK OUT
ARTHRITIS PAIN

You can protect your joints from this crippling disease.

Here's some good news you may have thought you'd never hear: Top arthritis experts now say that symptoms of the most common type of arthritis (which causes literally millions of people to give up activities such as tennis and gardening and gives them trouble just getting through the day) aren't inevitable.

"Despite the changes in your joints that occur naturally with age, you may be able to prevent the pain and disability of arthritis," says Kenneth D. Brandt, M.D., professor of medicine and director of the Multipurpose Arthritis and Musculoskeletal Disease Center at Indiana University Medical Center, in Indianapolis. He doesn't mean you'll merely be able to limp through another couple of tennis seasons. The latest medical research reveals some simple—and surprising—ways you may be able to buy yourself an entire lifetime of pain-free activity.

This research concerns osteoarthritis—the most common type of arthritis by far—which affects almost 16 million Americans, most of them over the age of 45. Although it also strikes the hands, hips and spine, osteoarthritis is most disabling when it affects the knees.

Osteoarthritis is characterized by the breakdown of cartilage, the resilient, spongelike material that coats the ends of your bones, keeping them from rubbing together. Some of this cartilage wears away naturally with age. But that deterioration doesn't necessarily bring with it the aches and pains that may freeze up your joints. In fact, Dr. Brandt says, "you may have severe pain and disability with only mild changes seen on an x-ray, while the next guy with precisely the same amount of damage (as seen on an x-ray) has only minimal difficulty, or no problems at all."

Experts don't fully understand why that happens. One study suggests that up to 30 percent of people with severe, crippling symptoms of generalized osteoarthritis may have a genetic defect that causes the disease process. But even in these cases, as with run-of-the-mill osteoarthritis, there are strategies to help those who don't yet have clinical osteoarthritis to keep their joints healthy for a longer period of time, as well as to avoid serious progression of existing osteoarthritis symptoms.

STRATEGY 1: LOSE WEIGHT

Researchers have long seen a higher incidence of debilitating osteoarthritis in people who are overweight. In a landmark study by researchers at the Boston University Arthritis Center, women who lost an average of 11 pounds over the ten-year study period were almost half as likely to develop knee osteoarthritis as women who weighed the same as, or more than, they did at the outset of the study. "This is the first study to suggest that you can prevent the initial occurrence of knee osteoarthritis by just losing a moderate amount of weight," says David Felson, M.D., associate professor of medicine and public health at Boston University School of Medicine and one of the authors of the study.

Exactly how being overweight makes you more prone to osteoarthritis isn't fully understood. "In normal circumstances, most of the load when you walk and run is borne by muscles and tendons—your built-in shock absorbers," Dr. Felson says. "But being overweight isn't a normal circumstance. It may be that so much of a load is transmitted that your muscles and tendons just aren't quite capable of serving as good shock absorbers, and the load is transmitted directly to the cartilage." The fact that the overweight-obesity link is much stronger in women than men leads experts to believe that hormones may have something to do with it, too.

Another theory suggests that when you're overweight, your bones may be so dense that they become stiff. "They may be too stiff to yield under load," Dr. Brandt says, "and that may be detrimental to the overlying cartilage."

Whatever the reason, there's convincing evidence to lose weight, if you're overweight, to significantly improve your odds against getting osteoarthritis. And there's a good chance you don't have to reach your "ideal" weight to do that. "In fact, it's likely that many of the women in our study were still somewhat overweight, even after the 10- to 15-pound weight loss," Dr. Felson says.

The best way to lose weight and keep it off is by setting a realistic goal to lose one pound a week. That means creating a 500-calorie "deficit" each day. You can do that easily by cutting back on fat in your diet and by burning more calories through regular exercise, such as walking.

STRATEGY 2: EXERCISE

Exercise isn't just good for calorie burning. It's also one of the prime osteoarthritis-prevention strategies because it actually keeps your joints healthy—a fact that may surprise you because it has long been fingered as a cause of arthritis. It was thought that high-impact activities, such as long-distance running, caused joints to wear out faster. But research disproves that theory. In one study, researchers at Stanford University looked (over a two-year period) at the knee x-rays of 51 men and women who ran about three hours a week. Part of the group decreased their weekly activity during the study. The others either increased or maintained their levels of exercise. When the researchers compared the two groups' knee x-rays, they found no significant differences in the number of "bone spurs"—tiny, lumpy growths on the joints that are the prime sign of osteoarthritis.

That means that regular exercise—even high-impact exercise—doesn't accelerate the deterioration of the joints, says James Fries, M.D., associate professor of medicine at Stanford and one of the authors of the study. In fact, his 25 years of research on runners who log a whopping 40 to 100 miles a week reveal that people who exercise are better off—much better off—than their sedentary counterparts. "You'd expect that the runners' x-rays would be worse than nonrunners', but they're not—they're exactly the same," he says. "What's more, runners have much less pain and disability than sedentary people."

That's because exercise appears to feed the cartilage with important nutrients that it wouldn't otherwise get (because it has no blood supply like most other tissue), Dr. Fries explains. "When you bear weight on a knee joint, you squeeze all the water and waste products out of the cartilage, just like the water squeezes out of a sponge when you press down on it. When you let up on the pressure, it fills up again with water and oxygen. That exchange nourishes the cartilage cells and keeps them alive."

The best exercises for preventing arthritis in healthy joints are ones that move them, pain-free, through their natural rotation, he says. For the knees and hips, that means walking, rowing, swimming, cross-country skiing and cycling, which keep the joints moving in a forward direction and nourish the cartilage.

Running gets the okay, too, as long as you're not overweight. It does, however, carry with it a high risk of injuries, such as ankle sprains and strains. If you've never exercised regularly, you haven't worked out in a while or you're currently overweight, Dr. Fries suggests you stick with brisk walking and other low-impact activities. The basic exercise prescription for total health is 30 minutes of sustained activity, three to five days a week.

But if you want to work out more, go to it, he says. "There's no evidence that any of these exercises are going to hurt your joints, no matter how much you do." Just make sure you don't take on too much too fast. He suggests increasing your time spent exercising by no more than 10 percent a week.

STRATEGY 3: PROTECT YOURSELF

The upshot of Dr. Fries's research—and the consensus among arthritis experts—is that exercise doesn't cause arthritis. Certain serious injuries sustained during exercise, however, can set you up for arthritis pain later. Minor problems like bursitis, tendinitis and strains and sprains are nothing to worry about, the experts say. It's traumatic injuries, like a torn knee ligament or torn cartilage, that put you at risk for osteoarthritis.

Those injuries are most common in "pivoting" sports—sports that require you to twist, turn and torque your joints into unnatural positions. They include soccer, football, skiing and court sports, such as basketball, volleyball and tennis.

Just because there's a risk of injury, though, doesn't mean you have to sit on the sidelines. "It's not the sport itself that's the risk factor. It's the injury you sustain playing that sport," Dr. Brandt says. And you have more control over your chances of injury than you may think. Here's your anti-injury insurance plan, with expert advice on how you can protect your body from serious damage on the field and on the courts.

Adopt a preseason resistance-training program. Before the tennis or ski season begins, lift weights three times a week to build strength in the muscles around your joints and make your ligaments and tendons more resilient. Maintain your strength during the season by cutting back to once or twice a week.

Building the surrounding muscles can make the joints more stable, Dr. Brandt says. Make sure you maintain balance in your resistance-training program—don't, for example, strengthen the quadriceps muscles in the front of your thighs and neglect the hamstring muscles in the back of your thighs. There's some evidence that muscle imbalance may increase risk of injury.

Choose the proper shoes. It's not only a fashion faux pas to wear your old running shoes on the tennis court, they can make you slide when you don't want to slide, as well. Choose shoes that are appropriate to your sport and the surface you're playing on. (Your local sporting goods retailer should be able to help guide your selection.) Also, replace your shoes when they're worn out. If there are bald spots or holes on the upper, the sole's probably about ready to give way, too.

Warm up. Just before game time, warm up with some light aerobic activity, like brisk walking or jogging, gradually increasing your pace. Then do some simple stretches, like arm circles and seated toe touches. (Avoid stretches like deep knee bends and full squats, which put too much stress on your joints.) Simple stretches help loosen your muscles, tendons and ligaments, so they can better absorb the shock of stopping short and turning on a dime.

Start slowly. If, for example, you're a tennis player, don't sign up for a multiday tournament at the beginning of the season. Settle, instead, for one- or two-set outings for the first couple of weeks, with at least a day's rest in between. Doing too much too soon leads to fatigue, and that can transform you from sure-footed to sloppy and set you up for injury.

Cool down—and stretch. Use your cooldown to really work on your flexibility. Choose a sequence of stretches that gets at all the major muscle groups, particularly the ones you use most in your sport. Perform each stretch three to five times, easing into each one slowly and holding for 10 to 20 seconds. Here are a few examples of some helpful stretches.

• For your lower back and hips, lie on your back and bring one knee up to your chest. Hold and repeat four or five times with each leg.

• For your abdomen and chest, lie facedown on the floor and push the upper torso back with your arms as far as you can while keeping your lower torso on the ground. You should hold your head up and look straight ahead.

• For your legs and hips, sit on the floor with your legs spread as far apart as feels comfortable. Keep your knees straight. With your back straight, lean over one leg, reaching your hands toward your toes. Hold for 10 to 20 seconds, then repeat on the other side.

• For more legwork, stand on your right foot while holding a chair or wall. Bend your left leg and grab your left ankle with your hand. Hold, then repeat on the other side. Don't pull your foot way up—keep it at least 12 inches away from your buttocks.

25
MEDICAL CARE UPDATES

These 15 tests can save your life.

If every woman followed established guidelines for breast cancer screening, some 15,000 lives would be saved each year. Screening for colon cancer could save many thousands of women's lives. Even simple things like having blood pressure checked and blood cholesterol levels measured and controlled regularly could prevent up to half of the 250,000 heart attack deaths and the 100,000 stroke deaths among women each year.

Besides making healthy lifestyle changes (like quitting smoking, eating a healthy diet and exercising regularly), following established guidelines for medical screening tests and self-exams is a key to prevention. Most women do get the basic screening tests, such as annual blood pressure and cholesterol measurements.

But there are some areas—particularly those specific to women's health—where we could be doing better. According to one survey:

• Breast self-examination rates are disappointing; only 47 percent of the respondents said they performed them monthly.

• Older women need special encouragement to ensure they get annual mammograms. Only 69 percent of respondents ages 55 to 64 get annual mammograms—this despite the fact that increasing age is the primary risk factor for breast cancer.

• Annual Pap testing rates aren't very good for mature women. Rates to screen for cervical cancer were good for women in their thirties and forties (around 80 percent), but dropped to 62 percent for women over age 65.

Why the gaps? Some of these screening tests are inconvenient or uncomfortable, so only the most motivated of women go. Another obstacle is expense: Public and private insurances don't pay for every vital test, like bone scans for osteoporosis.

But the biggest barrier to needed screening tests isn't motivation or cost, asserts breast cancer expert Janet Rose Osuch, M.D. She places most of the blame squarely on the shoulders of her fellow physicians. "Doctors are not doing a good enough job reminding women to get the tests they need," says Dr. Osuch.

She points to mammography as an example. "In research studies, the most commonly cited reason by women for not having a mammogram is that their doctor didn't tell them to do it."

Indeed, a study by the Massachusetts Institute of Behavioral Medicine in Boston is one of many that bears her out. The researchers interviewed 630 women, half of whom had had at least one mammogram, though none of them were getting them as regularly as they should. In that study, the women who reported physician encouragement were four times more likely to have had mammography.

Doctor encouragement was more closely correlated with having a mammogram than any other factor, including age, education, income, health status or attitude.

It's not that physicians have bad intentions. Often, they're just too busy to address preventive care measures with every patient. In fact, a national study found that the average time a doctor spent talking with each patient was a meager 11 minutes.

What's more disturbing is that many doctors are less likely to encourage senior women to get screening tests. In the above study, for example, women age 55 and older were more likely than those between 50 and 54 to report that their doctors didn't suggest breast self-examination or annual mammography to them. Yet about 75 percent of women who get breast cancer are 55 or older. And the older a woman is, the greater her chances for developing the disease. What's a woman to do?

FINDING DR. RIGHT

One of the most important steps for a woman to take to protect her health is to find a primary-care physician who takes time to talk about preventive care and who is sensitive to women's health issues. "If a woman does not have a good primary-care physician, it can jeopardize her health," says women's health expert Lila Wallis, M.D., clinical professor of medicine at Cornell University Medical College in New York City.

Dr. Wallis says too many women rely on specialists, like gynecologists, for primary care. This is especially true of young women. The survey found that more than a quarter of women under 34 consider their gynecologists to be their primary-care doctors. That's better than not seeing a doctor at all, says Dr. Wallis, but women need someone with a wider perspective.

Dr. Wallis says that most women's best bet for primary-care physicians are general internists with special training in women's health. "They're more likely to offer preventive counseling on many different health issues. Even their waiting rooms are more likely to have literature about screening tests."

Ideally, that doctor should be well-informed about women's health. That's a little tougher for a patient to investigate, though Dr. Wallis says if the doctor herself is a woman, she may be more attuned to women. One big clue to whether the physician is informed about women's health is if she does careful breast and pelvic exams during the annual physical.

Another clue is whether the physician asks about issues that are particularly important to women at each stage of life. For example, Dr. Wallis says, young women should be asked about body image, eating disorders and calcium intake. For women in the middle years, it's especially important to ask about multiple stresses from caring for elders and children, sleep and weight changes, and coping with menopause; for seniors, bone health, social contacts and abuse by spouse or caregivers are examples of issues to which physicians should be particularly sensitive.

It's important to remember, however, that reeducating doctors won't do the whole job. "We need to teach women how to be responsible partners. With health reforms on the horizon, physicians may spend even less time with each patient. So women need to be even more assertive."

KEEP YOUR OWN MEDICAL LOG

Are you the kind of person who thinks you had a Pap test a year ago, but when you check you find out it was in 1989? That's why it's a good idea to start a notebook in which you list every major screening test you have had or might need. Next to each entry, write down the date you had the test. It's also a good idea to write down the results of the test. Call your doctor after each test to discuss it. (This practice has the added advantage of forcing the doctor to look at your test results.)

Take your logbook with you when you visit your doctor. It's a good idea to discuss your screening schedule at least once a year with your primary-care physician. Changes in screening guidelines or in your personal risk factors might suggest that your screening schedule needs updating. Says Dr. Osuch, "Most doctors are not going to get upset by a gentle reminder to talk about medical screening tests—they're going to be grateful. The patient's not just saying 'Do you think I need a mammography?' Another statement that's implicit is 'I'm willing to go get one, and I'm asking for your expert advice.' "

Which medical screening tests should you have regularly? Each woman's needs are different, based on her age, genetics, medical history and lifestyle. Use the following information to help you and your physician determine a screening schedule that's best for you. Keep in mind that these are general guidelines for women. Nevertheless, the list is a good starting point for discussions with your physician.

1. Blood pressure test: A measurement of blood pressure taken with an inflatable cuff (sphygmomanometer).

- Once every year if you are age 19 to 40 with no heart disease risk factors and are not taking oral contraceptives.

- Twice or more every year if you are over 40; or take oral contraceptives; or have borderline high blood pressure (140/90 or greater); or have a personal history of high blood pressure or heart disease; or are taking blood pressure–control medication; or have a family history of high blood pressure and/or heart disease; or smoke; or are very overweight; or regularly take over-the-counter nonsteroidal anti-inflammatory medications (analgesics); or other reasons, at a physician's recommendation.

Note: A healthy blood pressure reading should be less than 140 systolic over less than 90 diastolic.

2. Blood cholesterol test: A small blood sample is analyzed at the doctor's office or in a lab. The test is done after a 12-hour fast because triglycerides are very sensitive to diet.

- Once every year at any age if you are in good health. "Even screening in childhood may be of benefit and should be continued lifelong," says cardiologist Debra Judelson, M.D.

- Twice or more every year if you have recently gained a great deal of weight; or have become sedentary; or have become ill; or have borderline high cholesterol (about 200 to 240); or have high cholesterol (above 240); or are on cholesterol-lowering medication; or have diabetes or kidney disease; or have HDL (good cholesterol) levels below 35; or have undergone removal of the ovaries; or have recently undergone menopause; or have heart disease or symptoms of heart disease; or other reasons, at a physician's recommendation.

Note: Healthy readings for women should be approximately: total cholesterol 160; HDL 50 or higher; LDL below 120; and triglycerides below 110.

3. Exercise stress test: Requires exercise on a treadmill while the heart is monitored externally.

• One screening test, possibly followed by repeated tests every two to five years if you: are over age 40; or are over 30 and have strong risk factors for heart disease, such as high blood pressure, diabetes, significant obesity, smoking, family history of heart disease; or have had your ovaries removed; or have high cholesterol; or have symptoms of heart disease; or other reasons, at a physician's recommendation.

Note: For 40 percent of women who take the exercise stress test, the result is a false-positive—in other words, it indicates problems when there are none. When the finding is abnormal, the physician refers a patient for more sophisticated tests, like a stress echocardiogram, involving exercise and ultrasound, or a nuclear medicine test, involving an injection of radioactive material. If a woman is at a high risk for heart disease, a physician may skip the exercise stress test and go directly to the more sensitive tests.

4. Breast self-examination: The careful self-palpation of each breast, preferably the week after a woman's monthly menstrual period, to check for any unusual lumps or masses.

• Once every month if you are over age 16. By that age, most women's breasts are fully developed, and doctors say it's best to learn breast self-exam (BSE) when you're young, so it becomes a lifelong habit.

Note: To learn BSE, ask your doctor for guidance or check with your community hospital or women's health clinic for classes or your local American Cancer Society office.

5. Breast examination by a health professional: Visual examination and careful palpation of the breasts and underarms by a qualified physician or health professional. The practitioner should examine your breasts both while you are sitting up and lying down.

• Once every two to three years if you are age 16 to 39 and have no risk factors for or symptoms of breast cancer.

• Once every year, or more frequently, if you are over age 40; or have lumpy breasts that are difficult to self-examine; or if you do not perform monthly breast self-examination; or have risk factors for breast cancer, such as a family history of the disease, no children before age 30, breast biopsies that show atypical epithelial hyperplasia or a personal history of breast cancer; or for other reasons, at a doctor's recommendation.

6. Mammography, low-dose breast x-ray: The apparatus compresses the breast firmly between two plates, which may cause discomfort. Usually two or three views per breast are required for a complete screening.

• One baseline test, followed by additional tests every one to two years if you are ages 40 to 49 and don't have risk factors for or symptoms of breast cancer.

• Once every year if you are age 50 or older; or have risk factors for breast cancer (see number 5 on page 224) regardless of your age; or at a doctor's recommendation.

Note: Most physicians recommend women schedule their mammography for the week after their menstrual period, to minimize discomfort.

• There is controversy over whether most women under age 50 need regular mammograms. Some studies suggest that mammography in younger women doesn't significantly reduce death rates. However, Dr. Osuch points out, even if that unproven contention is true, early detection through mammography does give younger women more treatment options, like breast-saving lumpectomy. Until there's more data, it may still be a good idea for women to begin getting regular mammographies at age 40.

• All suspicious lumps should be biopsied for a definitive diagnosis regardless of what the mammogram shows. There is a 15 percent false-negative rate for mammography.

7. Pelvic examination: A manual examination by a qualified physician or health professional of a woman's vaginal area to check for abnormalities of the uterus and ovaries. Usually, the doctor places—carefully and gently—two gloved fingers in the vagina while the other hand presses on top of the abdomen.

• Once every year if you are over age 18.

8. Pap test: After a speculum is inserted into the vagina and opened to reveal the cervix, the doctor takes a scraping of cells from the cervix and the cervical canal and smears them on a slide. The sample is sent to a laboratory to examine for signs of cervical cancer.

- Once every year if you are over age 18.

Note: Cervical cancer has been linked to certain strains of the human papillomavirus. This virus can be transmitted through sexual intercourse, but any woman can develop cervical cancer at any age, regardless of sexual activity. "I've seen cancer of the cervix in nuns," says Dr. Wallis. Seniors still need to be tested regularly, even if they don't have a partner. This is true after a hysterectomy if the cervix is left intact. (If the cervix is removed you still need Pap tests, but not as often.)

- The Pap test's reliability depends on the skill of the medical professional and the laboratory that analyzes the slide. You should seek a board-certified health practitioner for your test.

9. Transvaginal ultrasound: An ultrasonic probe is inserted into the vagina, transmitting images of the uterus and ovaries to a monitoring screen. It's sometimes used as a screening tool to detect changes in the lining of the uterus and the ovaries that might suggest cancer.

- One screening test, possibly followed by others at the recommendation of a physician if you are at or past menopause and have the risk factors for endometrial cancer (see number 10, below). May also be used for women of any age who have a strong family history (in first-degree relatives—mother, sister or daughter) or other significant risk factors for ovarian cancer.

10. Endometrial tissue sample: A thin instrument is inserted through the vagina and cervical opening to remove a tiny tissue sample from the lining of the uterus. Also called an endometrial biopsy or aspiration, the procedure can cause cramping.

- One screening test, possibly followed by others, at intervals recommended by a physician if you are past menopause and are considering or taking hormone replacement therapy; or are taking tamoxifen; or eat a very high fat diet; or have a history of infertility; or have a history of not ovulating; or are very overweight; or have a family history of endometrial cancer; or exhibit abnormal uterine bleeding; or other reasons, at the recommendation of a physician.

Note: Endometrial sampling should always be performed by an experienced physician, in order to avoid damage to the uterus.

11. Digital rectal exam: With a gloved finger, a physician feels inside the rectum for abnormalities.

  • Once every year if you are age 40 or over.

12. Fecal occult blood test: A stool sample is obtained at home and brought to a physician's office, hospital or clinic for analysis. (The stool sample could also be obtained in the doctor's office.) The test seeks blood as a possible symptom of colorectal cancer.

  • Once every year if you're age 50 or over.

Note: This test has been criticized because of the high rate of false-positives (wrongly indicating a possibility of cancer) and false-negatives (it misses the cancer when it's really there). But it's important to remember that while a positive result may not mean cancer, it can indicate ulcers, hemorrhoids or other problems. For a definitive diagnosis of colorectal cancer, more sophisticated tests are required (see below).

13. Sigmoidoscopy: A thin, hollow, lighted tube is inserted into the rectum and lower part of the colon to look for precancerous polyps and remove them before a cancer develops. Flexible sigmoidoscopes are preferred because they cause less discomfort than rigid scopes.

  • Once every three to five years if you are age 50 or over, without colorectal cancer risk factors or symptoms.

  • More than once every three years, at the discretion of the physician, if you have a personal history of colon

polyps, chronic inflammatory bowel disease, or colorectal
cancer; or have a family history of colon polyps or colorectal cancer, especially if a first-degree relative—parent, sib-
ling or child—developed colon cancer before age 50; or
have symptoms of colorectal cancer, such as diarrhea, constipation, or both, blood in the stools, very narrow stools,
unexplained weight loss, frequent gas pains and general
stomach discomfort; or a feeling that the bowel does not
empty completely; or have a history of breast, endometrial
or ovarian cancer; or other reasons, at the recommendation
of a physician.

14. Bone scan: The scans are performed by machines that use
low-dose radiation. The woman sits or lies on a table with the
machine's energy sources above and/or below her; depending
on the technology, the painless procedure may take five minutes to a half-hour.

• One baseline screening test just before menopause or
very early in menopause; one more test a year to 18
months after menopause. In specific cases, more follow-
up tests may be required. Older or younger women may
also require testing, depending on their risk factors for
osteoporosis (family history, steroid use, low-calcium
diet, sedentary lifestyle), at the recommendation of a
physician.

Note: A bone scan can show women who are approaching
menopause whether they are at risk for osteoporosis and
should take estrogen or other medication (like salmon calcitonin or etidronate) to prevent further bone weakening.
It also provides a baseline measurement, so that a year
past menopause, a repeat scan can determine whether you
have lost too much bone and need to begin medication or
adjust your current dosage.

• Several different technologies are available for measuring
bone density, including dual energy x-ray absorptiometry,
dual photon absorptiometry, single photon absorptiometry, quantitative computed tomography and radi-
ographic absorptiometry. All of the techniques are
capable of detecting low bone mass and diagnosing osteoporosis, according to Sandra C. Raymond, National Os-

teoporosis Foundation executive director. She points out that "some experts believe that for predicting fracture risk, the specific bone at risk for fracturing should be measured."

• It's not always easy to find a facility for a bone density test. The National Osteoporosis Foundation suggests checking with a local academic health center, a major hospital or the local branch of the American Medical Association.

• Even major medical centers may not perform tests accurately. "It's a problem all of us recognize and are trying to improve," says Sydney Bonnick, M.D., director of osteoporosis services at the Cooper Clinic in Dallas. In the meantime, ask the technician whether he's had several years of experience with bone scans. And make sure the physician will be reviewing the test and providing a written interpretation—don't settle for a computer printout–based diagnosis. Raymond emphasizes that "a bone-mass measurement should be performed in the context of a total medical assessment by a qualified physician."

15. HIV (human immunodeficiency virus) test: A blood sample is taken for analysis. Results are returned in 10 to 14 days. Private physicians may return results sooner.

• One screening test. Follow-up tests at three to six months after last possible exposure to the virus, if you had a blood transfusion between 1977 and 1985; or if you have had sexual intercourse since 1977 with any partner whose sexual, transfusion, or drug-use history from 1977 is uncertain; or if you have ever injected drugs with shared needles.

Note: For the vast majority of people, an HIV test at least three months after the last possible exposure indicates whether HIV is present. However, in very rare cases, the telltale antibodies to HIV don't show up in the blood until six months after the last exposure. One suggestion: Take a test at three months, but continue to abstain from sex or practice safer sex (limiting activity to nonpenetration, or careful and consistent use of condoms) until a test after six months from last possible exposure.

• Many people are reluctant to get an HIV test through their physician because of concerns about anonymity. Fortunately, there are anonymous tests sites in every state. They never take names, identifying clients only through a number. To locate these sites, call your state health department and ask for the HIV/AIDS department. Or call the Centers for Disease Control and Prevention's toll-free national AIDS hotline, at 1-800-342-AIDS. Spanish speakers can call 1-800-344-SIDA (7432).

26
WHEN CANCER HITS BELOW THE BELT
The Best Options for a Man's Trouble Spot

If you've been watching television, listening to the radio or reading your local paper lately, you've probably been caught up in the whirlwind of media attention surrounding—not a pop star—but a walnut-size gland nestled at the base of a man's bladder.

The prostate gland is news, and prostate cancer is the focus. Unfortunately, much of this media attention seems to generate more heat than light. And the flood of new scientific information about prostate cancer can be overwhelming and scary. But be reassured. There are ways to cut through the confusion. And the threat of prostate cancer, though serious, may not be as fearsome as many men think.

"Half of all normal men will have some microscopic prostate cancer found at autopsy, but only 13 percent of men will actually be diagnosed with it during their lifetimes," says Patrick Walsh, M.D., chairman of urology and director of the Brady Urological Institute at Johns Hopkins Hospital in Baltimore. Translation: Chances are that natural causes will get you well before prostate cancer does.

That said, prostate cancer is still no walk in the park. While one prostate tumor may be meek as a mouse, another can roar like a lion. Biopsies of prostate tissue show that there are two types of cancer cells: a slow-growing kind unlikely to cause big problems and an aggressive type that will. While the majority of tumors may be of the slow kind, it's very difficult for doctors to tell the difference accurately. Plus, even if you don't develop an aggressive type, the slower kind can end up creating troublesome symptoms that require treatment.

The key, therefore, is effective screening to catch any disease early, followed by the best possible treatment to cure it.

EARLY DETECTION

Death from prostate cancer is sneakily increasing—2 to 3 percent per year among the population—due in part to our longer life spans. In 1994 an estimated 200,000 men were diagnosed with it. And while prostate cancer is primarily a disease of men over age 65, it could claim 38,000 lives this year, making it a leading cancer killer of men—second only to lung cancer.

You can avoid that fate, though, if the cancer is caught early enough to be cured. "Early detection is the key to beating this cancer," says William Catalona, M.D., chief of urologic surgery at Washington University School of Medicine in St. Louis. "The earlier you detect it, the better your cure rate is and the lower your risk will be for encountering serious complications from the treatment you choose."

Not too long ago, the only office test doctors had for detecting this cancer was the digital rectal exam. The doctor simply uses his gloved finger to probe the prostate for firm nodules and other areas of hardness. The problem is, however, small cancers can be missed—the kind of imperceptible growths that may be at the ideal, curable stage. One study, in fact, found that using digital exams alone may catch only about one-third of patients with organ-confined disease—the stage allowing the best chance for cure.

Enter the prostate-specific antigen (PSA) test. With this simple blood test, PSA—a protein that only the prostate makes—is measured. As the disease progresses, the amount of PSA in the blood should rise. Generally, a reading is considered abnormal if the PSA level rises above 4 nanograms per milliliter (ng/ml).

This test dramatically improves a doctor's ability to detect signs of early disease—detecting almost twice as many cases of organ-confined prostate cancers as the digital method. One study, in fact, found that death from prostate cancer occurred in 33 percent of the men diagnosed one year after a previously normal digital exam.

Still, the PSA has flaws. It can mistakenly suggest cancer because PSA can rise due to other, less serious problems, like benign prostatic hyperplasia (BPH). "Conversely, some cancers can fool the cellular machinery so that the PSA protein doesn't signal its presence at all," says William R. Fair, M.D., chief of surgical urology at Memorial Sloan-Kettering Cancer Center in New York City. In fact, 20 to 40 percent of patients with early prostate cancer may have normal PSA levels.

Despite the imperfections of both tests, though, experts agree that PSA screening combined with the digital exam is the best strategy for catching curable tumors. A recent study found that the PSA/digital combo significantly increased the detection rate for early prostate cancer compared with using these tests alone.

"It used to be that seven out of ten men had their cancer diagnosed when it was too advanced," says Dr. Catalona. "Now it's reversed. By using both tests, seven out of ten men are diagnosed when their cancers are in curable stages."

WHAT'S YOUR PSA?

Because it is normal for PSA to increase with age, a normal PSA level for one man may not be normal for another. "In the prostates of older men, more PSA cells are available to make PSA, as well as more inflammation," says Joseph E. Oesterling, M.D., professor and chairman of the division of urology at the University of Michigan in Ann Arbor and editor-in-chief of the journal *Urology*.

The PSA concentration can go up roughly 3.2 percent per year even in a healthy older man with no prostate cancer. To help predict or rule out the possibility of cancer, some top doctors are now using age-specific guidelines as another tool to improve the ability of PSA to detect cancer.

Instead of the typical cutoff of 4 ng/ml, a lower cutoff would be used for younger men and a higher one for older men.

"These age-specific ranges have the potential to make serum PSA better at detecting truly significant cancers in older men and finding potentially curable cancers in younger men," says Dr. Oesterling, who first published the age- specific cutoffs.

Your PSA level may be considered abnormal if it's above the cutoff point for your age—leading you to more testing. "Measurement errors can occur, too, which is why repeating your PSA test is valuable," says Dr. Fair. No doctor should rely on a single PSA test: Repeated testing always paints a more accurate picture.

WHEN SHOULD YOU BEGIN SCREENING?

The American Cancer Society recommends screening annually with a PSA test starting at age 50. You should begin having digital exams earlier, at age 40 (which also screens for other illnesses, such as rectal cancer). If you're African American or have a strong family history of prostate cancer, then you should start the PSA screening earlier—at age 40.

Most experts agree that after age 75, PSA is not suggested as a detection tool—just the digital exam. However, Dr. Oesterling sets the upper limit at age 79 for healthy men with an extended longevity. "The cancers the PSA finds then probably will not impact your life," says Richard Babaian, M.D., professor of urology and director of the prostate detection clinic at the University of Texas M.D. Anderson Cancer Center in Houston. The digital exam should be continued, because it helps catch larger tumors and also aids in detecting rectal cancer.

Family doctors and internists can do extremely good rectal exams. But they don't do as many as urologists. "If you're concerned, seek out a urologist with a prostate specialty who does rectal exams and PSA testing on a daily basis," says Dr. Oesterling. This makes even more sense for someone at high risk.

THE NEXT STEP

If either your digital or PSA exam comes out abnormal, your doctor will use other tests to help make sure it is—or isn't—a serious problem. Some doctors, for example, try to get a better view of what's going on by employing a transrectal ultrasound, which uses sound waves to view the prostate and determine its volume. Some doctors, however, may skip that option, but rely on others to see if the earlier tests were correct. Here are some other diagnostic tools you should be aware of.

• PSA velocity. Doctors may gather more information by looking at the rate of change of your PSA over time—what's called PSA velocity. "Because cancer grows faster than BPH, and serum PSA rises along with it, a man with cancer should have a higher yearly change than a man with BPH," says Dr. Walsh. "A telling sign may be if your PSA rises on average 0.75 ng/ml per year three or four times in a row, especially if it was elevated to begin with." This may play a role in deciding how quickly you should treat the cancer and what therapy to use.

• PSA density. Your doctor may also measure your PSA in relation to your prostate's size. "A high serum level may not be a cause for alarm if the man has a large prostate," says Dr. Fair. So if your earlier PSA test comes out high, you may have a PSA density test—using ultrasound—to measure prostate size and its relationship to serum levels.

PSA density may help you avoid unnecessary treatment by helping to figure out if a tumor is aggressive or not. In a recent study, Dr. Walsh and colleagues looked at the removed prostates of 157 men to see how much cancer was really in the prostate. They compared these findings with preoperative test results to see how accurate the tests were in identifying men whose cancers were not big enough to need surgery. They found that 16 percent of the men who were operated on had small, insignificant tumors.

"By comparing PSA levels with the size of the prostate, we were able to establish pretty accurate guidelines on who should be treated," says Dr. Walsh. "A good candidate for surgery may be a man with a PSA more than 10 to 15 percent of the total weight of the prostate gland or with adverse pathology—cancer in three biopsy samples, cancer in 50 percent of tissue in one biopsy sample or other indicators." While each patient must still be looked at individually, Dr. Walsh and his colleagues feel these are useful guidelines. "Although this is new, it's my hope that other centers will try it and have similar success."

• Free versus complex PSA. Researchers have now found that PSA exists in the blood in two forms: by itself in a free state or bound to other proteins in a complex state. According to Dr. Oesterling, in cancer patients, the ratio of complex to free PSA is higher than for men who don't have prostate cancer. Assays are becoming available to distinguish the free form from the complex form and help make PSA a better marker for cancer.

• Biopsy. To really know if you have cancer, a biopsy is a must. It sounds scary, but it's relatively painless. It can be done in a doctor's office and usually doesn't require anesthesia.

A thin needle is inserted into the suspected area through the rectum or the skin near the anal opening. Your doctor may use ultrasound to guide the needle into the right spot. A small sample of tissue is withdrawn and sent off to a laboratory for examination. Antibiotics are used before the procedure and for the next day or two afterward to prevent infection.

Repeat biopsies may be done to verify or predict the extent of disease. If the initial biopsy turns out fine, your doctor may take another look in six months to a year using the same regimen. If the biopsies point to cancer, then the doctor will check the cells to see how fast they may be growing and check what stage the tumor is in.

THE BEST TREATMENTS

If early screening and prompt diagnosis picks up cancer, chances are you've caught it at a stage where it's curable. Your next step is choosing the right treatment. Following are the best options based on your age and other factors. The younger you are, the more likely you can handle more aggressive treatment, but your overall health may ultimately dictate your decision. That means sitting down with your doctor and evaluating your whole body—not just your prostate.

"Once a localized prostate cancer is found, the physician and patient, working as a team, must decide on the preferred treatment or management. Depending on the tumor's characteristics, the patient's age and health and the patient's preference, one of three options may be pursued: surgery, radiation therapy or watchful waiting," says Dr. Oesterling.

• If you're under 65. If your tumor is confined to the gland and you're in good health, then surgery is your best bet for a cure. "At that point, there's no better treatment than removing the

CHECK YOUR CANCER RISK

Here's the latest on the risk factors that may or may not play some role in your getting prostate cancer.

• *Getting older.* "Age is the single most important risk factor—as you get older, your odds for developing prostate cancer go up," says Joseph E. Oesterling, M.D., professor and chairman of the division of urology at the University of Michigan in Ann Arbor.

• *Race.* Prostate cancer incidence is 30 percent higher for African-American males than for white males.

• *Relatives.* Men with a family history of prostate cancer take note: "Your odds of getting prostate cancer if a first-degree relative (father or brother) has it are two to four times higher, and with two first-degree relatives, risk can go up to six to eight times higher," says William R. Fair, M.D., chief of surgical urology at Memorial Sloan-Kettering Cancer Center in New York City. "Across the board, though, roughly 10 percent of prostate cancer is familial or genetically linked."

• *PIN.* "There may be an association between cancer and an abnormality found on biopsy, called prostatic intraepithelial neoplasia (PIN)—which may be a precursor of cancer," says Dr. Fair. "We don't know if PIN leads to cancer or that it develops along with it, but nonetheless, these patients should be followed extra carefully."

• *Vasectomies.* Although some studies have suggested a mild correlation between vasectomies and developing prostate cancer, most experts maintain that the data so far are weak. "Anytime you have two common phenomena occurring—vasectomy and prostate cancer—people are bound to think a link exists," says Dr. Fair. "But really, there is no real evidence that the former may increase the risk for the latter."

gland," says Dr. Walsh, a surgeon who regularly performs these "radical prostatectomies."

Experts predict that of the men who undergo radical prostatectomy, 90 to 95 percent can expect a cure—living recurrence-free for up to ten years and more. If a tumor is found at this younger age, it may very well be the more aggressive type—as opposed to one caught, say, when you are 75. That makes the case even stronger for surgery. "Simply put, if you remove the prostate when the tumor has not already spread, you remove the cancer," says Dr. Oesterling.

Surgery, you should know, does have possible serious complications—incontinence, impotence and, in rare instances, death. A recent surgical advance, though, has markedly reduced the chance for these occurring—what's loosely called nerve-sparing surgery, pioneered by Dr. Walsh.

"The surgery controls blood loss so the surgeon can better see what he's doing," he says. That enables him to assess the extent of the tumor and preserve the nerves involved in sexual function. (In some cases this can't be done—the tumor may be too bulky and peeling it off the nerve may risk leaving cells behind.) Finally, it allows reconstruction of the bladder and urethra to avoid incontinence.

Thanks to this nerve-sparing technique, a large majority of patients undergoing surgery can retain sexual function, no more than 10 percent become incontinent and the death rate drops to near zero.

Age, however, does determine surgery's effect on sexual function and the severity of other complications. "A man, say under 50, may have a 90 percent chance of having sufficient erections," says Dr. Walsh. (But it'll take 12 to 18 months before he can enjoy sex comparable to before the operation.) That rate drops to about 75 percent for those ages 50 to 60 and to about 60 percent for those ages 60 to 70. After age 70 only one-fourth of the men may escape impotence. And remember—these statistics can vary, depending on tumor size, and are based on the hands of expert surgeons, so they may run a bit lower when surgery is performed by less-expert surgeons.

• If you're 65 to 75. As you get older, your health may start playing a bigger role. You may have developed other conditions making you less likely to handle surgery, and radiation may become the best option. If you're still in great shape and have no other health problems, however, surgery may be what you're after. "Patients who get surgery should be in good shape to withstand the operation," says Gunar Zagars, M.D., a radiation oncologist at the University of Texas M.D. Anderson Cancer Center in Houston. "That's not a criterion for radiation—we get many patients who have heart trouble and other medical conditions." Radiation is usually the best option at that point.

The most effective form of radiotherapy is external beam radiation, in which a focused beam of x-rays from a machine bombards and destroys cancer cells. "When it's given properly, you can have an excellent life expectancy with few side effects," says Dr. Zagars. Another form of radiotherapy exists, called interstitial radiation, which involves implanting radioactive seeds into the prostate. This therapy is still experimental, however, and comparison with other treatments is needed.

External beam treatments can last seven weeks or more. "Most of the men we treat take an hour off or so every day to come in for their treatments and then go back to work," says Dr. Zagars. A patient may experience side effects during treatment, such as mild diarrhea, rectal discomfort and bladder urgency, which go away over time.

But the therapy also has long-term side effects. "Roughly two out of five men become permanently impotent over time," says Dr. Zagars, though that statistic can vary. And again, like surgery, the effectiveness of radiotherapy depends in part on the person administering it. "Of the men I've seen who were potent before treatment, 70 percent were still sexually functional after one year," says Gerald Hanks, M.D., chairman of radiation oncology at Fox Chase Cancer Center in Cheltenham, Pennsylvania. Incontinence is so rare that Dr. Zagars has seen no cases of it in the more than 700 patients he has treated.

Some damage to surrounding tissues also occurs, but newer technologies may lessen that side effect as well as make external-beam radiotherapy more effective.

In three-dimensional conformal therapy, for example, a computer reconstruction of the patient's pelvic anatomy is made using a CAT scan. To fine-tune the radiation attack, a three-dimensional model of the prostate is created to help plan the best angles for the radiation beams. "That way, you end up treating just the prostate and very little of the tissue around it," says Dr. Zagars. "That allows us to give a higher dose without worsening the collateral damage. In theory, that should eradicate the cancer more effectively."

• If you're 75 or older. At this point, if you're in poor health and the tumor is small and hasn't spread, then your doctor may suggest another option, called watchful waiting. This means monitoring the cancer with follow-up testing every 4 to 12 months using the PSA and other tests—and treating if the condition worsens. Most experts agree that the ideal candidate for watchful waiting would be an older man, 75-plus, with other serious health problems and a relatively tame tumor as determined through biopsy.

A man with chronic heart disease, for example, may be unlikely to withstand the rigors of prostate surgery. And because these heart disease problems may be a more urgent concern than a cancer known for slow growth, removing the prostate may be unnecessary. Instead, the patient and doctor may agree to let the slow-growing cancer dawdle on and to treat it when needed. That tumor, one hopes, will take much too long to grow to have any effect on the patient's quality of life.

Roughly 40 percent of these patients, however, experience progression of disease serious enough to call for hormonal therapy. Hormonal therapy reduces the body's testosterone production to slow tumor growth. This can be done by regular, monthly injections of hormone analogues or by an operation called an orchiectomy (removal of the testicles). Newer, less-invasive therapies like cryosurgery—in which the cancer is frozen out with liquid nitrogen— might also be considered.

So while watchful waiting may seem to imply doing nothing, it's not. "A patient must make a commitment for life to be followed closely by his doctor with regular checkups and to undergo various treatments if needed," says Dr. Oesterling.

Generally, surgery may not come into play for a 75-year-old man, but there are exceptions. "If the patient is an active, healthy, older man who looks like he's got a long life ahead of him, then he may want the cancer out of him completely," says Dr. Walsh.

27

SMALL OPERATIONS

Advances in "keyhole" surgery can reduce pain and speed recovery.

When magazine researcher Cemela London had surgery on her sinuses five years ago, the operation was, as she says, "something out of the Dark Ages. A terrible experience. Horrible." In order to reach the deeply buried, badly infected vaults of her sinuses, the surgeon had to punch a small hole through her cheekbone, just beneath her upper lip, and two others near the bridge of her nose. The surgery left her with permanent scars around her eyes, was so painful "my whole skull ached" and produced such profuse bleeding that her nasal passages had to be packed with what she remembers as "37 feet of mummy stuffing."

After two separate operations and a bill of over $16,000, she was out of work for six weeks. But even two months after the operations, she still didn't quite feel herself. "I can actually smell now, and I don't have headaches anymore, but the process itself was hell," she says.

Too bad she hadn't found out about endoscopy!

Because today, due to this technological marvel, sinus surgery has become a much softer, gentler sort of operation. Sinus surgery is still not exactly breakfast in bed, but the new way of doing things "allows us to do much more careful, meticulous surgery, damage less tissue, cause less bleeding and make no external incision at all," says Donald Leopold, M.D., associate professor of otolaryngology at Johns Hopkins University School of Medicine in Baltimore. For the patient, that means less pain, no external scars, no punching through bone and, perhaps best of all, reduced recovery times.

For minor sinus surgery, patients can go back to work the next day; for more extensive procedures, in a week. In fact, most patients don't have overnight hospital stays at all. Compared with what Cemela went through, that's about as traumatic as skinning a knee.

What's made the difference in sinus surgery and other procedures is the endoscope—a lighted, often flexible tube that allows surgeons to peer directly into the darkness inside the body. (Strictly speaking, an endoscope used to peer inside a joint, like the knee, is called an arthroscope; one used to penetrate the abdomen, a laparoscope.) Rather than opening an incision large enough to actually view a diseased gallbladder or kidney or sinus cavity, endoscopic surgeons require only a hole large enough to pass the viewing tube through the skin, plus a couple of other punctures through which to slip tiny surgical tools. It's almost like operating through a keyhole.

One of the great practical advantages of "keyhole surgery" is that, besides leaving much smaller scars, the procedure causes less pain and hastens recovery. It's the incision itself—particularly the severing of muscle tissue—that causes much of the trauma of conventional surgery, doctors say. "When you cut from the skin on down, it's almost like cutting all the way through a deck of cards just to cut the 52nd card at the very bottom. You damage a lot of tissue to get where you're going," says James Chow, M.D., clinical assistant professor of orthopedics at the Southern Illinois University School of Medicine in Springfield. "In endoscopic surgery, we're cutting from the bottom up."

NINTENDO SURGERY

The amazing lighted tube has swept through nearly all the medical specialties. Specialized scopes are now being used in gynecology to remove lymph nodes and fibroid tumors and to treat endometriosis; in thoracic surgery to remove lung tumors while causing only a fraction of the pain that used to be associated with chest incisions; in abdominal surgery to repair hernias and remove kidneys and to take liver biopsies; and in many other areas.

Some endoscopes are rigid, like a sea captain's spy glass; others are flexible bundles of light-transmitting fibers, allowing surgeons to peep around corners and into otherwise hard-to-reach nooks of the body. Endoscopes are also often equipped with tiny ports through which various specialized tools are slipped—grabbers for steadying an organ about to be operated on; forceps for taking tissue samples for biopsy; surgical scissors for cutting; snares to remove growths and polyps. The tip of an endoscope may also have outlets for air, water or gas to inflate the body cavity for better viewing.

An endoscope is usually attached to a camera, providing surgeons with a clear, greatly magnified image of the ongoing procedure on a video monitor. This Nintendo surgery, as it's sometimes called, requires tremendous hand-eye coordination because it forces surgeons to do their work without watching their own hands. Also, they're using only a two-dimensional video image to go by.

INTO THE SINUSES

For sinus surgeons, endoscopes have been a blessing because "they give us a dramatically better look" at these obscure, inaccessible crannies, says Dr. Leopold.

The sinus cavities, he says, are actually "like a tall, narrow hallway down the middle of the head, with rooms—the sinuses—out to the sides." Because of this labyrinthian layout, it's almost impossible to get a clear view of the sinuses—and even more difficult to operate.

In conventional sinus surgery, surgeons had to operate with limited visibility, in a tricky area close to the eyes and the brain, where any surgical misstep can be disastrous. And the only way to enter the sinuses and surgically remove the blockage (caused by nasal polyps, or growths, infections, scarring or other obstructions) was fairly crude, as in Cemela's case.

In the 1990s, endoscopes have revolutionized all that. A patient is likely to be put under sedated local anesthesia (meaning that she's drowsy, but awake) rather than general anesthesia. Then the surgeon gently slips a slender, rigid endoscope up a nostril. The scope is equipped with tiny lenses that allow the surgeon to view things from various angles. In effect, "The surgeon can basically climb right inside the nose and get a great, highly magnified view of the sinuses," says Dr. Leopold.

This might not be your idea of a good time, but it has saved thousands of patients from enormous pain, discomfort and disfigurement. "One of the biggest advantages to patients is that the surgery can now be done on an outpatient basis," says Fred Laine, M.D., assistant professor of radiology at the Medical College of Virginia, Virginia Commonwealth University in Richmond. "Sometimes the procedure itself takes only an hour or so."

ENDOSCOPES IN GYNECOLOGY

Gynecologists were among the first medical specialists to take to the endoscope in a big way. As early as the mid-1960s, they were using them as diagnostic tools to probe for the source of pelvic pain and other problems. And since the early 1970s, many OB/GYNs have used them to do sterilization (tubal ligations, or "tube tying") by passing a scope through an incision in the belly button. Over the past three or four years, laparoscopes have been applied to a whole array of gynecological surgeries.

"Now we are using laparoscopes for tubal pregnancies, to take fibroids off the uterus, to remove ovarian cysts, treat endometriosis, do hysterectomies—almost every kind of pelvic surgery," says Paul Underwood, M.D., chairman of the Department of Obstetrics and Gynecology at the University of Virginia Health Sciences Center in Charlottesville.

One of the newest developments is laparoscopically assisted vaginal hysterectomy. In a traditional abdominal hysterectomy (the most common type), a woman's uterus (and sometimes her ovaries and other parts of the reproductive system) is removed through a six- to eight-inch incision in her abdomen. This usually requires four to six days in the hospital, followed by four to six weeks of at-home recovery.

In perhaps a quarter of all cases, however, surgeons are able to remove the uterus through an incision in the vagina (a vaginal hysterectomy), which spares the patient a belly scar and speeds recovery time. But even in the conventional way of doing this simpler procedure, surgeons are operating with a restricted field of vision.

But with laparoscopically assisted vaginal hysterectomy, patients generally require only one or two nights' stay in a hospital, followed by a week or less of recovery time. And the only physical evidence of the experience the patient's left with are three barely noticeable scars on her abdomen.

The scars are the result of three tiny incisions the surgeon makes in order to pass a scope and surgical instruments into her abdominal cavity. Once inside, the surgeon detaches the uterus (and other parts of the reproductive system). In the second stage of the procedure, these organs are slipped out through an incision in the vagina, much as they would be in a vaginal hysterectomy.

The operation itself takes longer than a conventional abdominal hysterectomy. And endoscopic surgery is also a bit more expensive. Even so, in some cases, "a woman can go home the same day or the next day (although there may still be discomfort) and go back to work in a week or so. That's one of the big things that's driving this new surgery: reduced hospitalization," Dr. Underwood says.

FAST RELIEF FOR CARPAL TUNNEL SYNDROME

Another promising application is in the treatment of carpal tunnel syndrome, the numb, tingling fingers caused by repetitive wrist motions, such as typing on a computer. The wrist's carpal tunnel is like the narrow point of an hourglass, through which pass nine tendons and one nerve (the median nerve). When the tendons become inflamed and swollen, they compress the median nerve (which runs to the fingers). The resulting tingling, numbness or pain can be so severe it sometimes results in permanent disability.

In conventional surgery, orthopedic surgeons open a two- to four-inch incision from the palm up through the forearm, laying open the whole structure to work on it. Besides leaving a nasty scar, the operation can take six or eight weeks' recovery time.

But in the new surgery, only two tiny cuts are made: a half-inch incision at the wrist to slip in the endoscope and a quarter-inch incision in the palm (too small to require even a single stitch) through which surgical implements are slipped. By doing it this way, "there's just a lot less trauma to the body," says Dr. Chow, a pioneer in using endoscopy to treat carpal tunnel syndrome. "And the less trauma to the body, the better off you are."

In competent hands, the operation seems to be very effective. Dr. Chow has done over a thousand such operations and had minor complications in only three (though eight or nine other patients had relapses and had to repeat the surgery). As with every other type of endoscopic surgery, recovery times are also dramatically shortened. "For example, I operated on an orthopedic surgeon—I did both his hands—and six days later he did a total hip replacement," Dr. Chow says.

STREAMLINED GALLBLADDER SURGERY

In order to remove a gallbladder using a laparoscope, the scope is passed through a tiny port (which looks like a plastic drinking straw) inserted in the belly button. The surgeon and one or two assistants then operate by passing their instruments through three other incisions in the abdominal wall—some so small they can be closed with nothing more than a surgical bandage. The detached gallbladder is then pulled through the opening in the belly button.

"In the old days, there was significant pain associated with gallbladder surgery—we used epidural anesthesia and what we call patient-controlled analgesia (PCA, IVs that allow patients to give themselves more pain medication)," says Charles Itzig Jr., M.D., staff surgeon at Schumpert Memorial Hospital and Physicians and Surgeons Hospital in Shreveport, Louisiana. "But with laparoscopy, a huge number of our patients require no narcotics at all."

When 31-year-old Mary Louise O'Rourke had her gallbladder removed, it wasn't exactly a day at the beach. But compared with what her mother went through 25 years ago, it was really like a warm sea breeze.

A gallbladder operation then was major abdominal surgery famous for its pain, scarring and slow, gut-wrenching recovery. In the mid-1960s, Mary's mother spent more than a week in a hospital heavily sedated with pain medication and another five or six weeks recovering at home, and was left with a six-inch scar on her belly.

By contrast, Mary Louise had her operation on a Thursday night and went home Saturday morning. What little pain she felt went away in a few days, and a couple of weeks later she was back at work. Her only souvenir of the experience was four scars on her belly so tiny that several didn't even require a stitch.

In fact, Dr. Itzig says, Mary Louise's experience was rougher than most: 90 percent of his patients don't even stay in the hospital overnight. Early risers who come into the hospital for surgery at 7:00 A.M. can go home by 1:00 that afternoon.

The gallbladder removal operation (called laparoscopic cholecystectomy, or a "lap choly") was one of the first laparo-

HOW TO FIND A GOOD SURGEON

Glittering new technologies like video-aided laparoscopy seem wondrous, almost miraculous. But all this high-tech wizardry can be as dangerous as it is wonderful if the surgeon who does your operation lacks the skill or training to use it. "Sometimes surgeons have rushed into this without proper training," says Charles Itzig, Jr., M.D., staff surgeon at Schumpert Memorial Hospital and Physicians and Surgeons Hospital in Shreveport, Louisiana. Part of the problem is the dizzying speed at which the new technology has swept into operating rooms across the country.

In one hospital, for instance, in the space of a mere 22 months, endoscopic surgery to remove gallbladders went from being an experimental procedure to one that was used in 90 percent of all operations, according to a report in *Archives of Surgery*. But that's too rapid a change to be entirely safe. In fact, a number of studies have shown that endoscopic gallbladder operations performed by inexperienced surgeons are more likely to result in serious complications (like injuries to the bile duct, arteries or bowel) than if the operation had been performed the old-fashioned way.

How do you tell if your surgeon is experienced enough to perform endoscopic surgery?

"One thing you can do is simply ask the surgeon how many times he's done the procedure," says Dr. Itzig. "I'd say the learning curve on gallbladders is about 25 procedures. If a surgeon has done that many—or, preferably, more—he should probably have his sixth sense about it and be competent to do it."

As for laparoscopic hysterectomies, "ten procedures is too few, without any question," says Paul Underwood,

scopic surgeries to be adopted widely in the United States. In fact, though it was only first performed in this country in 1988, it's now considered the gold standard therapy for gallstones, re-

M.D., professor and chairman of the Department of Obstetrics and Gynecology at the University of Virginia Health Sciences Center in Charlottesville. "If I had to pick a number, I'd say you'd have to do 25 to 30 of these procedures to become reasonably competent, though naturally this number would vary according to the skill of the surgeon."

It's also important how frequently the surgeon has been doing the operation. "If he's been doing three or four a year, I'd say that's not much, but if he's doing two a week, I'd feel much more confident," says Donald Leopold, M.D., associate professor of otolaryngology at Johns Hopkins University School of Medicine in Baltimore.

It's likely to be difficult to find out from the hospital or medical center how many endoscopic procedures a given surgeon has done, Dr. Underwood says. You'll have to ask the surgeon.

Also, ask about what sort of formal training in endoscopy the surgeon has had. "Any resident who finished in the past five years is likely to have done 20 to 30 endoscopic procedures and be ready to go," Dr. Leopold says. Older surgeons are likely to have taken courses in the technique, which are now widely offered. It's important to know if they've kept their knowledge and training up-to-date.

There is a medical board (the Society of American Gastrointestinal Endoscopic Surgeons, or SAGES) that establishes standards of training for abdominal endoscopic surgeons. But most states do not require any special licensing for surgeons who are performing endoscopic surgery. That means the burden is on you to make sure your surgeon knows what he is doing.

placing the operation that had been considered the best treatment for the previous 100 years.

It's become so popular partly because the gallbladder is

such a perfect candidate for removal with an endoscope. The gallbladder is a pear-shaped little thing, about three inches long, that's tucked under the right lobe of the liver.

"When I tell people I'm going to take their gallbladders out through their navels, people are amazed," Dr. Itzig laughs.

EASY HERNIA REPAIR

Even though it's one of the most common major surgeries performed in the United States, routine hernia repair has never been particularly pleasant. A hernia, of course, is the often painful bulging-out of internal organs through a weak spot in the abdominal wall. (That's the most common kind, at least.) The traditional approach has been to go in and sew the weak spot by suturing the muscle back together. This may require general anesthesia (other times it can be done under local anesthesia), a five- or six-inch abdominal incision, a day in the hospital and up to six weeks of restricted activity. On top of all that, there's a less than 5 percent chance that the hernia might burst open again due to pressure on the sutures.

Nowadays, though, laparoscopy has taken a good deal of grief out of the whole thing. A scope is slipped through an incision in the navel, then the abdominal cavity is pumped full of gas so it blows up like a balloon. This provides an unrestricted view of the area in question. Finally, surgical tools are slipped through two other slits. Also, rather than sewing the muscle together, a polypropylene patch is sewn over the weak spot. This makes recurrences less likely, because there's no tension on the patch. (The surgery is so new that reliable, long-term studies of it are not yet available.)

The best part: It generally takes less than an hour, there is minimal discomfort, and recovery lasts just three to five days.

RISKS AND COMPLICATIONS

The endoscope, in short, is a marvelous new tool. But it hasn't taken all the risk out of surgery. One study of 600 laparoscopic gallbladder operations, for instance, showed there were major complications in a little less than 2 percent of cases. That's roughly the same complication rate as with the old-fashioned, open surgery. Typically, says Dr. Itzig, complications involve injuries to the main artery that supplies blood to the liver, bile duct or bowel.

There's also a chance that a gallbladder operation that begins with a dainty little laparoscopic slit will wind up being "converted" into an open operation, complete with six-inch incision, if things don't go well. One study of 1,518 operations showed this happened in about 5 percent of cases and was especially frequent among advanced cases and those with acute infection.

Laparoscopically assisted hysterectomy, despite all its advantages, is not without risk, either. "There are still many complications occurring with this surgery—the most common being injuries to the ureter and the big blood vessels," Dr. Underwood says. "The whole technology is in a growth period. Some people are still doing this without adequate training." So it pays to make sure that your surgeon knows what he is doing. (See "How to Find a Good Surgeon" on page 246.)

It's also possible that you may not be a candidate for laparoscopic surgery, no matter how ardently you may wish to be. If you've had a lot of previous abdominal surgery, are too medically unstable to undergo the open operation, or have a good deal of scarring around the organ in question, you may not be a good candidate for laparoscopic surgery, doctors say. So it's important to ask your doctor whether you're a candidate before you get your heart set on it.

Beautiful

Forever

28
YOUR LOVELY SKIN

*Exfoliation stimulates your skin, making it softer,
smoother and fresher.*

If a fresher complexion sounds appealing, exfoliation (removing dead skin cells) may be just the thing for you. When
used properly, it's a terrific, freshening beauty treatment. Unfortunately, on the wrong complexion or in the wrong hands, it
can be a disaster. Here are the basics.

EXFOLIATION BASICS

As your skin matures, the turnover of epidermal (upper-
layer) cells slows down. Because the dead skin cells cling together to the surface instead of being pushed off, your
complexion may appear dull and pallid, with a rough texture.

"Basically, by exfoliating properly, you can increase the epidermal cell turnover and therefore make your skin look
smoother again, and pinker, and generally improve its appearance," says Diana Bihova, M.D., clinical assistant professor of
dermatology at New York University Medical Center. Exfoliating not only removes the dead cells that make your complexion
look ashen and uneven but it also helps stimulate the production of young epidermal cells.

The first of the two basic types of exfoliants are the mechanical ones—those that work by rubbing or abrading the
skin. Washcloths, sea sponges, exfoliation sponges (such as
Buf-Pufs), loofahs, pumice stones, cleansing grains and scrubs
all fall into this category. Not all tools for mechanical exfoliation are created equal, however. "The principle behind a face
cloth and a loofah is the same. What can be very different is
the degree of exfoliation," says Dr. Bihova. "This we control
not only by what we use but also by how we use it."

In the other broad category are the nonmechanical exfoliants, which run the gamut from cosmetic masks that work only
on the skin surface cells to tretinoin (Retin-A) and chemical exfoliants (such as the alpha hydroxy acids). Depending on the

concentration used and the amount of time on the skin, these can penetrate to the living tissue. Chemical exfoliants should be used only under a dermatologist's supervision.

Both mechanical exfoliating tools and masks can be used effectively at home if you have the right type of skin and follow directions carefully.

THE MECHANICAL WAY

Mechanical exfoliants work by stimulating the skin. This can be rough—in fact, too rough if you have very sensitive skin. "People whose skin is extremely sensitive or people who are prone to broken blood vessels would harm themselves more than they would benefit," says Dr. Bihova. "These people usually tend to have fair, thin skin. If you touch that skin, it reddens.

"To give you an example of what can happen, a woman came to me with hemorrhages on both cheeks. They were a result of rubbing too hard and too long with a washcloth. This is normally a gentle exfoliation tool. But the best things in life can become the worst if you use them excessively." The moral here is, if it hurts, stop.

People with acne should probably not use mechanical exfoliants, either. If you have whiteheads or closed comedones (blemishes that are below the surface), they have no way out when you apply pressure or stimulate those areas by rubbing them. As a result, they can rupture inside the skin, leading to more inflammatory acne.

Exfoliation works best for people with healthy, normal or dry complexions. It can also be great for people with dull, sun-damaged skin or skin with a tendency to form blackheads. Even thin skin can benefit from the milder exfoliants, as long as there are no broken blood vessels. If you've had acne but now are acne-free, mild exfoliating can help keep the pores unclogged and actually help keep your complexion healthy.

"It's a very delicate line between exfoliating and seeing the benefit, and exfoliating and harming yourself," says Dr. Bihova.

NONMECHANICAL PLOYS

Among the nonmechanical exfoliants, masks never work deeper than the dead, superficial layer of your skin, and chemical peels can vary in strength according to the chemical used and its concentration. Chemical peels should be used only under a qualified doctor's supervision.

Today, light chemical peels are a "hot" treatment at many facial salons. These treatments, however, can be far stronger than store-bought treatments. Because of this, the Food and Drug Administration is looking at them to determine whether these peels should be done only in a doctor's office.

Masks are a cosmetic product and are made in different formulas, including clay and botanicals, that provide a suitable mask for every skin type.

THEMES AND VARIATIONS

Let your skin be your guide. "Generally, you can't exfoliate the same way all year-round," says Dr. Bihova. "The skin changes depending on the season, the temperature and so forth, and you must change your routine to meet your skin's needs. In the summer, for instance, skin has more moisture, while in the wintertime your skin is drier, and you won't want to use your exfoliant of choice as often."

Restrain yourself. "The main problems that I have seen have occurred in women whose attitude was that 'If a little is good, a lot will be even better.' This is definitely not the case with exfoliants," says Dr. Bihova. Generally speaking, the mildest exfoliants are the sea sponge, the face cloth and cosmetic masks labeled for dry or sensitive skin.

A complexion brush along with some moisturizer can work well to exfoliate if you use the brush gently in circular movements. (Please, don't use occlusive or heavy moisturizers—they'll clog your pores.)

For normal to thick skin, sea sponges or exfoliation sponges (especially the mildest ones) can be used effectively to exfoliate. Treat yourself no more than three times a week and in the winter once a week, for two to three minutes.

BODY EXFOLIATION

Body exfoliation is acceptable for everyone. Just avoid rubbing any area where you have inflammatory acne. Backs, shoulders and chests can be affected by blemishes, as well as your face, and the result of rubbing would be the same.

"Exfoliation is especially great for knees and elbows, because when you then apply your moisturizer right away, you've created an ideal situation for the moisturizer to penetrate," says Dr. Bihova.

Self-tanners also give a much more even coverage when applied to exfoliated skin. If you shave your legs, you don't have to worry about exfoliating them. The razor does it for you.

29
A NEW WRINKLE IN SKIN TREATMENTS

Restore smoothness and luster from the inside out.

Some wrinkles seem impossible to iron out. Those deep vertical frown lines between your brows, for instance. No amount of moisturizers, masks or mud packs budges them. The only line of action seems to be plastic surgery, and even that doesn't always yield ideal results. But a new use for an old drug may help erase the problem.

ALL LINES ARE NOT CREATED EQUAL

Wrinkles divide into two broad categories: those that are caused by the skin's aging and those that we euphemistically refer to as expression lines. It's this second category that is most resistant to treatment.

"Our facial expressions are caused by muscles that attach on the undersurface of the skin. When they contract, they pull the skin in, causing a line," says Monte Keen, M.D., director of facial, plastic and reconstructive surgery, Columbia Presbyterian Medical Center in New York City. "Certain muscles, such as those that control the frown lines between the brows, can contract even when the muscle is at rest, eventually causing deep furrows."

The traditional lines of attack on frown lines include dermabrasion, chemical peels, forehead lifts and collagen implants. The plus side for the first three is that they're considered permanent—but they all have their downsides as well. The downsides are that they don't work well on deep wrinkles and expression lines, and they may cause undesirable pigmentation changes in the skin. "Both dermabrasion and chemical peels are exfoliators and work better for fine wrinkles," says Dr. Keen.

A forehead lift, while permanent, is an expensive surgical procedure. Essentially the surgeon stretches the frown line and cuts the muscle that causes it. "The downsides are expense, it's an invasive surgical procedure, and you can have side effects such as a permanently numb forehead. In short, I think that if you have only one or two frown lines, it's a long run for a short slide," says Dr. Keen.

Collagen injections are considered a filler and are not permanent. The collagen is injected to bloat the wrinkle out. "A problem with collagen is that there can be an allergic reaction, and it lasts only from one to three months," says Dr. Keen. Like all cosmetic procedures, the success of collagen implants relies heavily on the skill of the doctor. If the collagen isn't put in the right place, it's bumpy. And since it's a series of needle sticks, it can really sting.

ATTACKING THE PROBLEM AT ITS SOURCE

A new therapy has begun to be used in the treatment of these stubborn frown lines. The drug, Botox, has been used for 15 years by neurologists to treat people with neuromuscular disorders of the head and neck, but its cosmetic applications have just begun to be explored. Botox works in a totally different way. It's not a filler, and it doesn't stretch or damage the skin. Botox is a nerve-paralyzing agent that totally blocks nerve impulses to the muscle, relaxing the muscle tension on the skin, thus erasing hyperkinetic wrinkles (lines that are caused by muscle contraction).

"If you can pinpoint the muscle that's causing the wrinkle, you can weaken it, and the wrinkle will just flatten out," says Dr. Keen.

It's vital that the doctor target the muscle precisely, and it's only the right combination of technology and technique that gives the best results. "We use a special needle, which is hooked up to an EMG (electromyograph) machine, so it's both a needle and an electrode," says Dr. Keen.

"We ask the patient to frown; then we put the needle in where we think the muscle is. We turn the machine on. When the patient frowns and the muscle moves, the machine tells us if we're in the middle of the muscle. If we're not, we move the needle until we're in the right place. We then put a very small dose of the drug directly inside the muscle so we weaken the frown muscle without weakening the muscles next to it. There is a very small amount of diffusion of the drug, but it should not be enough to cause the rest of the brow to droop," says Dr. Keen.

The average frown line needs two injections. The injections take about five minutes in the doctor's office, and the results become apparent in three to five days.

Botox works best on lines where you don't need the muscles, such as the frown muscles. "To avoid a droop or loss of expression, we don't inject within a half-inch of the brow," says Dr. Keen. "With EMG control we can put the drug exactly where we need to put it." There has been some criticism of Botox on the grounds that you could lose the ability to express yourself facially by paralyzing the muscles. "That's simply not true, because you're injecting only the muscle that is causing the frown," says Dr. Keen. "So you can still have your range of facial expression minus the frown." Botox is minimally invasive. "You're not cutting something or putting a filler in; you're getting rid of the cause of the wrinkle," says Dr. Keen.

The results last between three and six months. The paralysis itself lasts three months, but the weakening of the muscle tone (which is what erases the wrinkle) lasts up to six.

SOME LIMITATIONS

Botox is a leap forward, but it's not a panacea or a miracle drug. "Because it doesn't work for several days, you don't always know exactly how much to use, so you may want to see the patient back in a week to put a little more in to even things out," says Dr. Keen.

"Also, there's a theoretical chance that people could develop antibodies to the drug—we know this because it has been used for years to treat neuromuscular disorders, and it has happened, but only at doses a hundred to a thousand times the doses we're using. Those antibodies don't affect the people except to make the drug useless for them."

Botox doesn't work well for wrinkles that are intrinsic changes in the skin caused by age or the environment, so don't think you can abandon your regular use of both sunscreen and moisturizer. In fact, it's an incentive to a regular skin care regimen because the drug's greatest success is in people in their thirties to mid-fifties or those who have taken good care of their skin.

How available is this treatment? "There are not yet a lot of people using this procedure," says Dr. Keen. "First, there aren't that many who have an EMG machine. (These are generally used by neurologists, not surgeons.) And second, the published research is just coming out and shows that Botox works well for the upper third of the face."

The Food and Drug Administration has approved Botox for use in disorders of the facial nerves. As for wrinkle removing, use of this drug is still considered experimental.

"We've been injecting people for cosmetic purposes for only 2½ years, but we have 15 years' worth of data on the drug," Dr. Keen says. "We're confident that its cosmetic use will become widespread because it just works so well with only a minimal downside."

To find where this procedure is being done, call the American Academy of Facial, Plastic and Reconstructive Surgery at 1-800-332-FACE.

30
BOTTLED RAYS

*Self-tanners provide the benefits of sunshine
without the risks.*

There's only one safe tan, and that's an artificial one from a bottle or tube. If this conjures up images of orange, streaky skin, think again. Today's self-tanners are easily applied, look natural, take only minutes and don't harm your skin.

How Tanners Work

A suntan is the result of your body's attempt to protect itself from the punishment of the sun's ultraviolet rays. Your skin reacts deep within its layers by producing more of the dark pigment called melanin to absorb the damaging rays. The result is your darkened skin tone.

Cosmetic self-tanners work without exposure to the sun. The main active ingredient, dihydroxyacetone (DHA), acts only on your skin's stratum corneum epidermis. "They work mainly on the very superficial cell layers of the skin. When the DHA combines with certain amino acids and keratin in your skin's stratum corneum, it produces natural golden color," says Yveline Duchesne, international training director of Clarins Cosmetics. The only drawback to this is that a "fake" tan fades as you shed your dead skin cells, usually in only a few days.

Tanners' Bonus Benefits

The color of a tan without its hazards is the raison d'être for self-tanners. But with each new generation of products, extra benefits are added. One benefit is added sunscreen. Depending on the brand, this ranges in sun protection factor (SPF) from 0 to 15. "While self-tanners add color, they do nothing to protect your skin from UV radiation unless they have added sunscreen ingredients," says Duchesne. But while the self-tanner's color can last several days, as soon as you wash, you lose the protection of the sunscreen.

Another plus is added moisturizers. This is especially helpful since the DHA in self-tanners can be somewhat drying. With added moisturizers, your tan will last longer; the more your skin is hydrated, the longer it takes for cells to flake off. Since self-tanners are now used in the winter when a moisturizer becomes a must for your skin, this can be a real plus.

To attract the sensitive-skinned customer, there are also special formulations that are fragrance-free and allergen tested. Says Duchesne, "As with any new product, the customer with sensitive skin should test the product before she buys."

Don't Forget to Protect

Even among those self-tanners with sunscreen, few contain the recommended SPF 15. When using these products, the best way to protect is by also using a sunscreen with an SPF of 15 or greater.

To keep you safe in the sun, your sunscreen should offer a broad spectrum of protection (such as oxybenzone, titanium dioxide, zinc oxide or parsol 1789). Apply your self-tanner at least several hours before going out, preferably the night before. Then apply your sunscreen at least an hour before you go outside.

Says Joyce Weisbach Ayoub of the Skin Cancer Foundation, "Don't forget to protect areas that aren't covered by protective clothing, such as hands, the back of the neck, ears, lips and balding spots on the top of the head."

Self-tanners themselves need a bit of protection. "The self-tanning formulation is still somewhat fragile," says Duchesne. "It should be used within three months of opening. Because DHA degrades quickly, try to keep it away from heat."

For the Tan You Want

Even with the improved formulations, know-how is necessary to ensure the most natural tan. The following self-tanning tips are from Patricia Agin, Ph.D., sun-care project manager at Coppertone's Solar Research Center in Memphis, Tennessee.

• Exfoliate before you apply. It's a bit like sanding before you paint. DHA can take unevenly in areas where there's a buildup of dead cells. Areas to be sure to include are hands, elbows and knees.

• Start at your forehead and work down, covering all exposed areas. Natural color means even application. This includes ears and under the jaw. Skip the eyebrows, though—color can get too dark there. And some brands say to avoid the eyes; so be sure, as always, to read the label.

• Use a moisturizer on areas like elbows and knees and apply self-tanner on these places with a light touch. Because of their wrinkles and dryness, they tend to develop more color.

• Don't reapply before you've seen the final results. The depth of color is determined by how often you reapply—not by how much you put on. It can take from three to five hours for a self-tanner to develop fully.

Since tanners can stain fabric, wait at least 30 minutes for the self-tanner to dry before you get dressed or go to bed. While some brands take less time, you can't go wrong waiting 30 minutes.

Wash your hands after you've applied a self-tanner or you'll end up having tan palms.

CROWNING GLORIES

Experts reveal the secrets of beautiful hair.

The media bombard us with images of models' shining hair. How do those models do it? We asked hair specialist (the scientific term is trichologist) Philip Kingsley and master stylist Kenneth of Kenneth's Salon, New York City, for their expert advice on how to have the hair you've always dreamed of.

COMING CLEAN

Photographers can adjust the lights and camera to maximize appearance of shine. The goal of your hair care program should be to provide the right surface for light to reflect off your hair naturally.

The surface of each hair is composed of cells layered on top of each other, like shingles on a roof. "Only when those cells are clean and lie flat and tight can they reflect the maximum light," says Kingsley, of the Philip Kingsley Trichological Centres in London and New York. When hair is dirty or damaged, the cells lift and separate, deflecting light rather than reflecting it clearly.

"I'm a great believer in daily hair washing," says Kingsley. "Consider how dirty your face is at the end of a day; well, your hair gets just as dirty. It's not immune to the smoke and environmental pollutants that assault the rest of your body."

Many people, especially those with dry hair, have the misconception that daily shampooing dulls hair. "In fact, it does the opposite if you use the correct shampoo," says Kingsley. Washing dry hair enhances rather than detracts from it, because hair is dry due to loss of moisture, not loss of oil. "If you wash your hair with a remoisturizing shampoo," says Kingsley, "you're actually helping your hair repair itself. The right shampoo can correct your hair's balance, whether it's dry or oily."

Unfortunately, choosing the right shampoo can be a matter of trial and error, because what's best for you isn't necessarily right for someone else with similar hair.

"I suggest that instead of choosing a shampoo that says oily, dry or normal, choose your shampoo according to your hair's texture," says Kingsley. Also try buying shampoo in the small sample sizes until you've found one you really like.

Permed or colored hair also benefits from daily washing, even though it tends to be drier than untreated hair. Each process causes the hair to tangle more, and if you've had both processes, your hair is doubly apt to tangle. A remoisturizing shampoo and a richer conditioner can help keep treated hair looking great.

Daily washing does, however, create a time problem if you don't have a style you can manage easily yourself. If your morning time expenditure causes you to skip a wash, it's time to think about trying a lower-maintenance style.

HANDLE WITH CARE

The second important factor in attaining shining hair is to keep the cuticles lying smooth. "Processes such as perms and overcoloring are among the main cuticle offenders," says Kingsley. "But even overbrushing can damage your hair." Teasing or back-combing the hair not only scrapes the cuticles in the opposite direction to which they normally lie, but also interlocks the cuticle cells to give the hair height. Continuous teasing weakens the cuticle to the point that it can even be stripped from the hair shaft.

Anything that chemically damages your hair detracts from its shine. This includes sun exposure, chlorine in the water—anything that alters the composition of your hair.

"Excessive chemical processes on the hair (perm, color or straightening) are a major mistake," says Kenneth Battelle, creative genius behind Kenneth's Salon at the Waldorf Astoria in New York City. "It's best to decide which you feel makes you look the best and then do only that one.

"When making the choice of a perm or color or any chemical process, do it only because it makes your hair perform and look better to you, not to follow the latest fashion gimmick," adds Kenneth.

HEALTHY SCALP, HEALTHY HAIR

Hair follicles are nourished via your scalp, yet most of us give the scalp little thought. Scalp massage can contribute to your hair's health. It improves circulation and blood supply to the scalp and exercises it. The best time to massage is either before or during shampooing because the massage helps to encourage more oil flow and the shampoo can remove any excess.

Don't scrub or rub your scalp. You press the scalp with your fingertips and knead it. Actually move the skin on the skull beneath. Starting at the front hairline, use a circular movement and work toward the back.

PERFECT CONDITION

There are two basic types of conditioners: daily conditioners and intensive, deep conditioners that are used only occasionally. Daily conditioners are used mainly to detangle, which helps prevent mechanical damage to the hair's surface.

Intensive conditioners usually need to be applied only once or twice a week or less. For the optimum effect and maximum convenience, apply a deep conditioner before you wash your hair. Allow it to be absorbed for a few minutes, while you gently work it into the hair with your fingertips. You can apply before you shower, then shampoo and use your regular conditioner afterward as normal. Chemically treated or damaged hair usually responds best to a weekly deep conditioner. Moderately dry hair probably only needs it once or twice a month.

"The main drawback is the boredom of doing it. There's no doubt that your hair looks better if you deep-condition regularly," says Kingsley. "Other errors are too much conditioning or using the wrong conditioner, especially if your hair is porous. It can make hair limp and greasy and lie flat on your head."

THE DIET CONNECTION

What you eat can't affect existing hair. The only thing that affects that is external conditions—sun and chlorine damage, for example. Although you can't affect old hair by what you eat, your diet can disrupt its growth cycle and hair-cell reproduction.

"The classic example of a poor diet's effect is thinning hair such as I've seen in anorexics (people with an eating disorder)," says Kingsley. Eating three healthy, well-balanced meals and eating at regular times can help give your hair the proper start. Missing meals on a regular basis—such as always skipping breakfast or lunch—drains your energy levels, and the nutrition requirements of your hair follicles aren't met.

"An interesting sidelight is that the hair follicle is one of the most prolific cell reproducers in your body," says Kingsley. "But the hair follicle is nonessential tissue. So if there's anything going wrong nutritionally, your hair follicle is one of the first things to suffer and the last to benefit because your body uses up all the nutrients for essential functions first."

FOR BETTER OR WORSE— IT'S UP TO YOU

There are no scientific tests to determine which hair care product might be the best one for you. What you can do is to pay attention to what works and what doesn't.

"I truly believe that great-looking hair comes mostly to the client who understands her own hair as well as or better than her stylist does," says Kenneth. "A personal hair care regimen followed daily can help anyone have model hair."

Fit

for

Life

32

SWEAT SUCCESS

A little exercise—even very little—is terrific for your health.

You don't have time to exercise. You've never been able to stick with it. Your home is too small for fancy equipment. The health clubs are too snobby. And even if you wanted to join, you can't afford the membership. So why bother getting in shape?

Because you don't have to spend half your life at a fancy fitness center to reap major physical and emotional benefits from exercise. You can improve your health and fitness—and look and feel a lot better—by incorporating just a little more physical activity into your life. You hardly have to break into a sweat.

Ridiculous, you say? Not at all. Just read the latest findings from the nation's leading exercise researchers. "The fitness gurus used to insist that we had to punish ourselves with strenuous aerobic exercise for at least 30 minutes three times a week to become fit and healthy," says Bryant Stamford, Ph.D., director of the Health Promotion Center at the University of Louisville in Kentucky and author of *Fitness without Exercise.* "But the latest studies show major benefits from exercise so modest that it doesn't even feel like a 'workout.'"

A study of 102 women ages 20 to 40 at the Cooper Institute for Aerobics Research in Dallas showed that the kind of exercise that leaves you panting isn't necessary to improve health. Strolling a 20-minute mile—a lap or two around the typical mall—significantly decreases blood pressure and cholesterol, which reduce risk of heart attack, stroke and high blood pressure. A study at Columbia University in New York City of 344 women ages 20 to 69 showed the same results: Light exercise just once or twice a week is surprisingly good for the health of your heart.

"For lowering cholesterol and blood pressure, low-level exercise works just as well as strenuous exercise," says John Duncan, Ph.D., associate director of the Cooper Institute and senior coauthor of the study. "The more out of shape you are, the more you benefit from low-intensity exercise."

266

In addition, a study at the University of Massachusetts Medical School in Worcester showed that walking reduces tension and anxiety no matter how fast or slow you walk. "Fast, medium or slow, everyone felt less stressed after walking," says study author James M. Rippe, M.D., director of the Exercise, Physiology and Nutrition Laboratory there.

These studies and others have spurred the American Heart Association to promote modest exercise a few times a week as a great way to significantly reduce the risk of heart attack, one of the country's leading killers.

"The health benefits of low-level exercise are great news for sedentary Americans," Dr. Duncan explains. "Intensity doesn't matter. What's most important is regularity. If you become just a little more active, and stick with it, your health improves significantly."

A LITTLE EXERCISE: BIG BENEFITS

Even modest regular exercise is a major boon to both physical and emotional well-being. Physically, exercise:

• **Helps control weight.** In addition to burning extra calories while you're exercising, physical activity boosts basal metabolic rate, the rate the body burns calories while at rest. When you're physically active, you continue to burn extra calories even after you stop exercising. "You may not lose 20 pounds taking leisurely strolls," Dr. Duncan says, "but you'll be better able to maintain your current weight, and you might lose a little."

• **Reduces risk of heart disease.** Heart disease is a leading cause of death. Exercise helps prevent it by strengthening the heart, by reducing blood pressure and by lowering cholesterol.

• **Reduces risk of stroke.** High blood pressure is a key risk factor, and exercise helps reduce blood pressure.

• **Helps preserve bone.** Regular moderate weight-bearing exercise (such as walking, gardening and dancing) helps prevent bone-thinning osteoporosis, a major health problem for women over age 50.

• **Builds strength, flexibility and stamina.** As you exercise, your muscles become stronger, your joints become more sup-

YOUR BEST EXERCISE INVESTMENT: GOOD SHOES

Forget expensive health clubs, exercise equipment and designer sweats. You don't need them. But good shoes are a boon to even modest exercise programs based on everyday activities. You have to buy shoes anyway. Why not have them help you exercise? You don't have to spend a fortune. Just shop smart. Here's how.

• Check your feet. If you have flat feet, you need extra arch support. If you have a high arch, you need extra shock absorption. If you have weak ankles, consider high-tops.

• Check your old shoes. Notice where they're most worn and look for shoes reinforced in those areas.

• Get a good fit. Experts say there should be about ¼ inch between your toes and the end of the shoe. And try on both shoes: Feet can be different sizes.

• Check the weight. Usually, the lighter the better.

• Check the traction. Shoes should not slip on any surface.

• Test them. Shoes used for exercise should feel comfortable in the store. They shouldn't require any breaking in. Jump up and land on your forefoot. In well-cushioned shoes, you should feel almost nothing. Rock from side to side. You shouldn't wobble. Pivot in different directions. Your shoes should feel flexible.

ple and you can remain active longer without tiring. In other words, the more you exercise, the more you can exercise.

• Helps people quit smoking. Exercise feels invigorating, which helps replace the nicotine high of smoking. Exercise also helps ex-smokers stay that way.

• Helps manage arthritis. Exercise moves the major joints through their full range of motion, which helps keep them pain-free.

• Provides significant emotional benefits. Most experts agree that regular exercise can boost self-confidence, provide a feeling of accomplishment and help you cope with stress and anxiety. It can even result in greater sexual pleasure! That's what a survey of 8,000 women ages 18 to 49 showed. Once they began exercising, 40 percent said they became aroused more easily and 25 percent experienced increased ability to experience orgasm.

WHAT'S STOPPING YOU?

Even modest exercise has so many benefits, everyone should want to do it, right? Everyone wants to, but too often, obstacles get in the way. Do any of these excuses sound familiar?

"I'm too busy." Of course, you're busy. You lead a hectic, stressful life. That's why you need to exercise—to build the stamina, strength, flexibility, confidence and self-esteem you need to cope with all the demands you face.

"I hate exercise." Don't do anything you dislike. Ask yourself what kinds of physical activities you like and do them regularly. You don't have to run, do sit-ups or use a stair-climbing machine. Bicycling, gardening, folk dancing, bowling, roller-skating and table tennis can be great exercise.

"I've never been active. It's too late to start now." It's never too late. One study shows that even 90-year-old lifelong couch potatoes gained significant physical and emotional benefits from modest, regular exercise. No matter how long you've been out of shape, you can get back into shape. Just start now.

"I don't have half-hour blocks of time to exercise." "You don't need them," Dr. Rippe says. "Sporadic exercise adds up. If you take just three 10-minute walks a day during breaks, you're exercising 30 minutes." What kind of physical activities do you already engage in? Shopping, housework, cooking, child care? Just walk a little more briskly while shopping. Stretch, bend and lift a little more during housework and cooking. And play more physically with your children.

"I feel self-conscious. I hate looking ridiculous." You don't look ridiculous. You look like someone who's taking control of her life and health. You look good. No, you look great!

"I never seem to improve." Chances are you just don't notice. Chart your progress. Make a chart showing how many blocks from work you're parking, or how many flights of stairs you can climb before you feel winded—anything that's measurable. Plot your progress weekly, and you'll see how far you've come.

"I never stick with it." You're not alone. Half of those who start exercising quit within six months. To keep from being a quitter:

• Be realistic. For every year you've been out of shape, it takes a month to get back in shape. It takes about eight weeks to start feeling the physical and emotional benefits of exercise, and longer to lose weight.

• Start slowly, and don't overdo it. You should be able to carry on a conversation while exercising. If you become breathless, you're overdoing it.

• Only do things that feel fun. If something isn't fun, switch to something else.

• Find a buddy and exercise together. Support each other.

• Vary your activities so you don't get bored.

Easy Everyday Shape-ups

You don't have to turn your entire life upside down when starting a new exercise plan. It's better to start simple. For example:

Take the stairs instead of the elevator. If you're out of shape, start simply by walking down. When you feel ready, start walking up partway, then all the way. When climbing stairs no longer leaves you winded, climb a little faster.

Park a few blocks farther away. Walk the extra distance to work, the mall, the movies, church or friends' homes. As you gain stamina, park even farther away and walk more briskly.

Take a walk before lunch. You may find you eat less afterward.

Stash a pair of walking shoes at work. Slip them on for walks at lunch and on breaks.

Buy a backpack. Instead of driving to all your errands, walk as much as possible and use your backpack for purchases.

Cancel "food dates." Instead of meeting friends for lunch, coffee or dessert, make dates to take walks, go dancing or go for bike rides. Or make a date to visit a health club. Most clubs allow free one-time visits to check out the facility. Try several.

Make breaks count. During breaks at work or television commercials, get up and stretch or walk around. Organize your co-workers and housemates to join you.

Make the most of phone time. Don't sit while talking on the phone, pace. Invest in a longer handset cord so you can walk farther, or get a cordless phone. If you must stand in one spot, march in place, raising your knees up high. Or rise to tiptoes. Do this five times. When you feel ready, do ten.

• Curls: With your arm straight, hold your weight down by your hip. Then bend your elbow and bring the weight up to your shoulder.

• Presses: With your arm in the curled position, straighten it over your head. Do five of each. When you feel ready, do ten.

Make the most of "microwave minutes." Don't just stand there watching the time wind down. Pace, stretch or do some weight lifting.

Mow the lawn. Pushing a power mower is good exercise. Or retire your power mower and invest in a push model.

Tend a garden. Digging, weeding, raking, cutting and hauling are great exercise.

33
MUSCLE UP YOUR BODY AND SOUL

Regular exercise boosts your energy and outlook.

"Get that chicken fat back to the chicken. . . ." The memory of those lyrics filling phys ed class may have you chuckling today. But back in the 1960s, few would describe calisthenics as an uplifting experience. This may explain why so many of us approach midlife lacking a passionate commitment to exercise. And this lack is definitely our loss, because life in the fast-but-sedentary lane begins to exact a big toll, physically and emotionally, in our middle years.

"Inactivity is an unnatural state for human beings," says Keith Johnsgard, Ph.D., psychologist and author of *Exercise Prescription for Depression and Anxiety*. "All of our body's systems function best with exercise being an integral part of our daily regimen. Without it, these systems go to hell. We gain weight, our muscles atrophy, our cardiovascular systems suffer and, to make matters worse, we feel depressed and anxious."

The role exercise plays in emotional health is nothing short of amazing. "Daily activity makes us feel better, have more energy and sleep more deeply," asserts Dr. Johnsgard. That leads not only to greater physical health but also to deeper emotional and spiritual well-being.

EXERCISING CONTROL

Very often, it's the act of building muscle and losing weight that leads to positive emotional changes.

"At first, a person witnesses the physical change. 'I do this movement, and I increase that muscle's strength and endurance,' " says Sandra DiNatale, exercise physiologist at Green Mountain at Fox Run in Ludlow, Vermont. "The payback is immediate. For someone who's been inactive, that's incredibly empowering."

This sense of mastery then becomes the foundation for personal growth. After experiencing the physical benefits of their effort, people inevitably apply that confidence in emotional and relational situations.

"I've seen it hundreds of times," DiNatale says. "Once a person experiences success with exercise, she goes on to say, 'You know, I need to renegotiate this situation or that relationship,' and has the confidence to do it." Someone who has felt very out of control of her life is suddenly, through her own effort, in control.

The weight loss that typically accompanies exercise also gives a firm boost to self-esteem.

"When I moved from my position as a counselor on a college campus into the health-club field, I was astounded at how losing five pounds did more for a person's mood and self-esteem than six months of counseling," says Annharriet Buck, director of the Golden Door health spa's mind/body program in Escondido, California. "Combining the two is really ideal. Self-esteem rises a lot faster when people are active and losing pounds and inches."

ANTIDOTE
TO DEPRESSION

Another wonderful benefit of exercise is that it shields us from depression. "If you administer personality tests to active and sedentary middle-age men, the biggest single difference between the two groups is depression," says Dr. Johnsgard. "And study after study has shown that the cause and effect is in the direction of activity reducing depression and anxiety."

How exercise works so effectively against depression is, no doubt, complex. Some suggest it distracts people from their problems; others say it increases recall of pleasant memories. Whatever the reasons, it doesn't take much to bring about a positive effect. A brisk half-hour walk three or four times a week is enough.

An added bonus is that exercise helps to dissipate anger, says Dr. Johnsgard. And anger is a natural step in the grieving process when coping with the painful losses of midlife. "I see women and men get very angry at their bodies," says Joan Borton, licensed mental health counselor and author of *Drawing from the Women's Well: Reflections on the Life Passage of Menopause.* "They can't do as much as they used to, and they feel their bodies are letting them down. I see that as being up against a real spiritual opportunity—to change the things you can and accept the things you can't."

With so much of our lives in transition at midlife, we're bound to be whirlwinds of emotion. Yet few of us make enough time to be just alone with ourselves. "We think that self-development is just going to happen without us necessarily paying attention," says DiNatale. "It's often at the midlife point where we realize that if we don't make a conscious choice about something now, it's not going to happen."

Exercise can be a time-out period for spending quality time with our inner thoughts and feelings.

LEAH O'TOOLE: SERIOUS ABOUT HEALTH

People look at me today and just assume that I'm a natural athlete. In fact, it wasn't really until I was 38 that I got serious about exercise for health.

After years of suffering with fibroid tumors, I had a hysterectomy. The recuperation process gave me the impetus to improve my life and health.

I began taking body-sculpting classes twice a week at a health club. They were basically just movement to music. At first, I felt self-conscious. But my body started to change very quickly. I felt and looked better and started to get a lot of compliments.

As my self-image improved and my confidence grew, I got the courage to change jobs. I was tired of working late hours in a restaurant. I applied at a health club as a locker-room attendant. Talk about a Cinderella position! But it got my foot in the door.

There, I read everything I could about bodybuilding. In my spare time, I worked out. Eventually, I was lifting weights for an hour and a half, four times a week. That's when people started coming to me and asking me to teach them how to lift weights—to be their personal trainer.

Working out gave me a sense of control over something very valuable—my body. Then, at age 45, I was hit with another major illness: breast cancer. I had a lumpectomy. What really wiped me out, however, were the chemotherapy and radiation treatments that fol-

"I argue for taking a walk or riding a bike over other kinds of leisure activities," says Judy Mahle Lutter, president of Melpomene Institute for Women's Health Research in St. Paul, Minnesota. "If you take a half-hour during the evening to read a book, your spouse or children will think you're fair game. If you're out the door on a walk or run, you're unavailable. It's truly your time."

lowed. To keep my spirits up, I performed my exercise workouts in my mind.

I'd start by picturing myself getting off the elevator and checking in at the front desk of the health club. In my mind, I'd get dressed, go upstairs and do the treadmill or the bike. Then I'd perform absolutely every weight repetition, taking a full hour and a half.

Throughout my ordeal with breast cancer, "working out" was the high point of my day.

About six to eight weeks after surgery, I was able to go back to the gym for real. At first, it took all my strength to get there, and I'd have to push myself to walk on the treadmill for just five or six minutes.

To make matters worse, during the surgery, lymph nodes were removed under my arm, and this impeded my mobility. I had numbness in that arm and tightness around the incision. I knew that if I didn't push myself, I'd never regain my full range of motion.

Fortunately, my years of physical training had given me tremendous self-confidence to accept physical challenge. But this was the biggest challenge of all. In essence, I had to start all over. That was a real psychological hurdle. It took quite a while to get movement back in my left arm. But I did it. In the process, I gained new respect for myself. I didn't know I had that much discipline and courage.

"What happens as we go through life is that we literally get bent out of shape," says Suki Munsell, Ph.D., registered movement therapist and founder of the Dynamic Walking Program in Corte Madera, California. "By reestablishing physiologic balance, exercise gives us a chance at emotional balance."

Think of your life as a wheel, she suggests. "Where on the wheel would you want to be—at the end of a spoke, where you're up and down, up and down with every turn? Or in the center, where it's hardly moving?

"Exercise," she says, "puts us back in our center, where we can survey the world with greater clarity."

34 UPLIFTING MOMENTS

Strength training skims flab and tones bellies—
in no more than 80 minutes a week.

You remember dieting—that torturous activity we all at one time put ourselves through to get flatter tummies, firmer legs and thinner thighs. Like carbon paper, the eight-track tape and the dreaded leisure suit (you remember yours), dieting has become obsolete. It's been replaced by a better, simpler way to achieve results that stay around forever.

That simpler way no doubt involves a healthy eating regimen of low-fat foods—all becoming more and more plentiful in our supermarkets each day. But it also relies on exercise—a remedy-in-motion that not only reduces risk for a variety of illnesses but also skims off flab, tones bellies and sleeks down hips.

Exercise, you say? What else is new? LOTS. Wayne Westcott, Ph.D., national strength consultant for the YMCA, has laid out the exact exercise formula to get the job done. He's used it at his own gym, conducting studies with hundreds of participants—with dramatic results.

Dramatic results—but by simple means. The time put in each week by Dr. Westcott's subjects amounted to no more than the time it takes to watch a made-for-TV movie. In roughly 80 minutes per week for eight weeks, the folks in this program saw results dieting alone could never offer. Read on for the whys and hows.

THE KEY ISN'T JUST MOTION— IT'S MUSCLE, TOO

Aside from being a miserable activity, dieting is also mean-spirited. It steals away the very material you need to excuse yourself from ever having to diet again. We call that stuff muscle, the weight your body can't afford to lose.

"The scale tells you how much less you weigh without telling you what you really lost, which is fat and muscle," says Dr. Westcott. "Muscle is so important in so many things we do throughout the day—you can't afford to lose it." Plus, because muscle devours calories more hungrily than fat tissue can, the more of it you have, the less likely your body needs to diet.

Now, you don't need to be on a diet to lose muscle—just being inactive can sap the hard stuff from your body. The typical sedentary American loses an average of 5 pounds of the hard stuff each decade—while gaining 15 pounds of fat at the same time. "On a bathroom scale, that would indicate a 10-pound weight-gain problem (15 fat pounds minus 5 muscle pounds)," says Dr. Westcott. "But the reality is that it's actually a 20-pound problem—15 pounds more fat plus 5 pounds less muscle."

This situation sends you on a bullet train to Blobville, as increasing muscle loss slows your metabolic rate, or your body's calorie-burning engine. This makes it even more difficult to maintain a healthy weight, as your sluggish furnace allows more body fat to gather. "Overall body composition, not just body weight, should be stressed," says Dr. Westcott. Manipulating body composition means not just watching fatty foods and taking brisk walks, but also upping your muscle activity.

THE 20–20 SOLUTION

Dr. Westcott proved this point in a recent eight-week study. He took a group of average Joes and Josephines and put them through a program using both resistance and aerobic exercise, showing how easy it can be to rework your body composition for the better.

During the program, 282 adults performed 20 minutes of muscle strengthening, along with 20 minutes of aerobic exercise, two or three days a week. That's all. Sure, some may have added extra walking on the weekend. The bottom line: The folks who worked out for just 80 minutes a week over eight weeks saw great results.

The average fat loss was 8½ pounds (a little over a pound a week—a healthy pace, say most experts), with an accompanying burst of a 3-pound muscle gain. That translates into a mean body composition improvement of 11½ pounds (8½ plus 3), in just eight weeks!

Now, if you were simply out to lose weight, you'd be pretty miffed. After all, if you weren't hitting the weights, you'd be three pounds lighter. But you'd also be weaker, less toned, less fit and, all in all, not as healthy without that extra muscle. It's the stuff needed to maintain basic daily functions as you grow older. A street gang of age-related degenerative processes arrives largely because of muscle loss and its impact on function.

"Your muscle is like an engine, and losing it is like going from a six- to a four- to a two-cylinder car," says Dr. Westcott. "Soon you can't go up even small hills anymore when you used to be able to go up mountains!" With that in mind, it's no wonder each increase in muscle expands your boundaries of daily activity.

Not only that, but more muscle means a firmer, shapelier body, as well. Of course, improving function and metabolism is nice, but looking good isn't so bad either.

RESULTS GO INTERIOR

Dr. Westcott's research also supports previous strength-training studies, suggesting that the benefits of this program aren't strictly limited to slimmer waistlines and better function. "We are also seeing significant blood pressure reductions in some of the older folks," says Dr. Westcott. In fact, the workouts have done such a number on high blood pressure in a few people that they actually decreased or eliminated their use of medications.

"We also have reports of participants with adult-onset diabetes responding quite favorably as they increase muscle mass," says Dr. Westcott. No surprise—increased muscle mass and activity help out by burning more glucose, which is running wild because the insulin isn't taking effect. "With that in mind, strong muscles should prove a major aspect of preventive medicine and rehabilitation," says Dr. Westcott.

Other, more immediate benefits also occurred for the older people who entered the study at ground zero in terms of fitness. Some folks coming in with canes or walkers finished the program without them. "Many of the participants are able to do things on their own that they couldn't do before," says Dr. Westcott. This is especially true in seniors where quadriceps (front thigh muscle) strength is critical in getting up and out of chairs and cars and going up stairs. The leg exercises used in this program help combat that weakness.

THE BODY-SHAPING RECIPE

The complete program boils down to two to three aerobic sessions and two to three strength-training sessions, each lasting approximately 20 minutes. It's up to you how you'd like to spread it out over the week. For example, you may want to work out three times a week, with the strength and aerobic components done together—or you may want to have one workout each day for a six-day cycle. Keep in mind, however, that you don't want to strength-train the same muscles two days in a row, because those muscles need time to regroup and repair to get stronger. Here are the two elements you need.

Go aerobic. In Dr. Westcott's plan, participants choose from treadmill walking, bench stepping and stationary cycling. Basically, though, any sustained aerobic activity you enjoy will do fine. And if you're going to do your aerobics and strength training on the same day, it really doesn't matter which one you do first.

"We have found that improvements are the same no matter what you do first," says Dr. Westcott. Of course, it always helps to include a warm-up session before and a cooldown after exercise—just a few minutes of walking or easy jogging should be enough. Once you do get going into your 20-minute session, aim for an exertion level that gets you sweating but still allows you to talk without feeling winded.

Muscle up. Dr. Westcott chose the following strength exercises for two reasons: (1) They're highly efficient—hitting all the major muscle groups—and (2) they come as close as possi-
(continued on page 282)

Dr. Westcott's Body-Shaper Program

• *Bench press:* Lie on an exercise bench with your knees bent so your feet are flat on the floor. Grasp dumbbells or a barbell with your hands slightly more than just shoulder-width apart. Slowly lower them to your chest. Press the weight up until arms are fully extended, with elbows almost locked. Repeat.

• *Leg press:* Sit in a leg-press machine, place your feet on the foot pads and press out until your legs are straight. Let the weights return to the original starting point. Repeat.

• *Seated pulley row:* Sit on the machine with your knees slightly flexed. Your feet should be up against an object to maintain stability. Keep upper torso erect and your lower back flexed. Grab hold of the handle and pull it slowly and smoothly to your chest just below your chest muscles. Try not to use your torso to pull the weight. Return to the starting position, with the weights going back down. Repeat.

• *Seated quadriceps extension:* Sit with feet under pads. Straighten your knees, then lower your feet. If your knees hurt, or it's too difficult to go to the full extension, just do a partial repetition, shortening the path. (Use ankle weights if you don't have an extension machine.)

• *Hamstring curl:* Lie facedown, with heels under pads, holding on to the front of the leg-curl machine. Curl your legs up until your calves touch the upper part of your thighs. Return to the down position and repeat. If you don't have a leg-curl machine, a partner can help provide some resistance against your legs.

• *Overhead press:* Raise the weight to shoulder height. Sit with your feet firmly on the floor. Keeping your back straight, press the bar to arm's length overhead, pause, then lower. Repeat. This can be done with free weights or on a machine.

• *Biceps curl:* Hold a barbell with both hands, palms facing up. Stand with your back straight, with the bar at arm's length against your upper thighs. Curl the bar up in a semicircular motion until your forearms touch your biceps. Keep your upper arms close to the sides of your body. Lower the bar slowly to starting position using the same path. Repeat.

• *Triceps extension:* While sitting with your feet firmly on the floor, hold a dumbbell, with both hands overhead at arm's length. Lower the weight behind your head in a semicircular motion until your forearms touch your biceps. Return using the same path. Repeat.

• *Lower back:* Position the front of your upper body over the end of a waist-high bench and anchor your feet. Bend over with your head down and your hands placed lightly behind your ears. Slowly raise your torso until you're level with the bench. Repeat.

• *Neck exercise:* Sit on a bench with your back straight, head up. Place both hands on your forehead. Push your head back as far as comfortable while resisting with neck muscles. Use only moderate resistance. Do ten repetitions. Then place your hands on the back of your head and repeat movement in reverse.

• *Abdominal curl:* Lie on your back with your knees bent, fingers lightly touching ears. You can place your hands behind your head as long as you don't use them to pull your head forward. Slowly curl your upper torso only until shoulders leave the floor. Hold for a few seconds, go down and repeat, inhaling as you go down. If this is too difficult, keep your arms at your sides.

ble to mimicking your daily activities so you can do those activities more effectively.

"Compound exercises, such as leg presses, bench presses and rows, involve several muscle groups at the same time," says Dr. Westcott. "These are more useful than other exercises in terms of function because they use movements similar to what we do in normal life—that is, all the pushing and pulling."

The workout also includes simpler moves, such as leg extensions, arm curls and trunk curls. "You might want to just start out with the three compound exercises I mentioned earlier. By so doing, you have worked almost all your major muscle groups in a very functional manner," says Dr. Westcott. "Progress from there as you become stronger, working in the other exercises, like the lower back and neck exercises, which really help the vertebral column."

The most astounding thing about the program isn't just the modest amount of time needed, but also the volume of exercise required. Dr. Westcott included 11 weight-training exercises in his program. But the participants performed only one set, doing 8 to 12 repetitions in each, during each workout. For your own muscles, find a weight or resistance level that you feel comfortable doing for your single set at those repetitions. By the last few repetitions, the exercise should feel pretty tough, but still doable. After a few weeks, when the exercise gets easy, kick up the resistance a bit or do more repetitions to make it more challenging.

"It helps to work the large muscle groups first and move down to the smaller ones," says Dr. Westcott. That way you won't tire the small muscles first, hindering the larger exercises.

INDEX

Note: Underscored page numbers indicate boxed text.

Crowders
  Beans in a Flask, 48

D

Dairy products, 22. *See also
    specific foods*
Dandelion greens, beta-carotene
    in, 33
Dander, allergy to, 127–34
Depression
  cholesterol and, 18
  exercise for, 272, 273
  heart disease and, 183
  meditation for, 19
  stress and, 179
Dermabrasion, 256
DEXA, for testing bone density,
    145, 146, 228
DHA, in self-tanning lotions,
    259
Diabetes, 4, 144–45, 202
Diary, for monitoring
  exercise, 93
  food intake, 93
  medical care, 222
Dietary fat
  budget for, 60–61
  calories from, 51, 59–61
  intake of, during illness, 107
Dietary supplements. *See*
    Nutritional supplements
Diet-induced thermogenesis, 5
Dieting, 59–61. *See also* Weight
    loss
Digital rectal exam, 227, 231
Dihydroxyacetone (DHA), in
    self-tanning lotions, 259
Doctors. *See* Physicians
Dogs, allergy to, 127–34
Dolomite, calcium in, 151
Draperies, allergens in, 133
Drinking. *See* Alcoholic bever-
    ages
Dual energy x-ray absorptiome-
    ter (DEXA), for testing
    bone density, 145, 146,
    228
Duodenal ulcers, 122
Dust mites, allergy to, 132. *See
    also* Allergens

E

Eczema, 108–9
Emotions
  exercise and, 269, 272
  heart disease and, 182–83
Endometrial cancer, 153, 157,
    226–27
Endoscopic surgery, 240–49
Estrogen, osteoporosis and, 143.
    See also Hormone re-
    placement therapy
    (HRT)
Exercise(s). *See also specific
    exercises*
  abdominal, 2, 75, 281
  aerobic, 75, 85
  alertness and, 200–201
  compound, 282
  depression and, 272, 273
  diary for monitoring, 93
  enjoying, 88–89
  everyday activities as, 270
  excuses for avoiding, 269
  gender differences and, 80
  growth hormone and, 2
  heart disease and, 9, 10, 267
  high blood pressure and,
    125–26
  illness and, 114
  menstrual cramps and, 158–59
  metabolism and, 62
  modest, 266–71
  osteoarthritis and, 216–17
  osteoporosis and, 146–48
  oxygen uptake during, 7
  sleep and, 17, 205
  time for, 89
  weight loss and, 59, 62
Exercise stress test, 223–24
Exfoliation
  for body, 254–55
  for face, 252–53
  before self-tanning, 260
Eyesight, vitamin A and, 16

F

Fat, body. *See* Body fat
Fat, dietary. *See* Dietary fat
Fava beans
  Beans in a Flask, 48